Minding God

Minding God

Theology and the Cognitive Sciences

Gregory R. Peterson

FORTRESS PRESS
MINNEAPOLIS

MINDING GOD

Theology and the Cognitive Sciences

Cover image: Jan Franz/Getty Images. Used with permission.

Library of Congress Cataloging-in-Publication Data

Peterson, Gregory R.
    Minding God : theology and the cognitive sciences / Gregory R. Peterson.
        p. cm.
    Includes bibliographical references and index.
    ISBN 0-8006-3498-5 (alk. paper)
        1. Cognitive science. I. Title.
    [DNLM: 1. Religion and Psychology.]
    BL53 .P42 2002
    261.5′15—dc21   2002074237

Manufactured in the U.S.A.
07   06   05   04   03   1   2   3   4   5   6   7   8   9   10

In memory of my father
ROY E. PETERSON
who practiced science in the context of faith

Contents

Part Two: Minding Persons

Part Three: Minding Nature

Part Four: Minding God

List of Figures

Preface

In my junior year of high school, a friend introduced me to Douglas Hofstadter's *Gödel, Escher, Bach*, a weighty and entertaining introduction into the then current status and hopes of artificial intelligence. Little did I know at the time that the book was the beginning of a long conversation with what has since become known as the cognitive sciences. Hofstadter's witty dialogues between Achilles, the tortoise, and other sundry characters perplexed, delighted, and annoyed me all at once. At the same time, they also posed profound questions that remained always in the background and increasingly in the foreground of my thought over the next decade. As I progressed in the study of philosophy, theology, and religion, the significance of these questions and their potential for reshaping how we think about some of the most basic issues of life and nature became increasingly clear.

At the same time, I was frustrated to see how little awareness theologians and scholars of religion had concerning cognitive science and the challenges that it posed. The closest thing to a dialogue was that between religion and psychology, and then primarily with the psychoanalytic tradition of Sigmund Freud and Carl Jung, which many cognitive psychologists assign to the prehistory of the current discipline. During the 1970s and 1980s, Paul McClean, Eugene d'Aquili, James Albright, and John Eccles were among the first to explore the connections between religion, theology, and the claims made by the various disciplines that constitute the cognitive sciences. In the past decade scholars have built on this early work, but the full range of implications has yet to be considered in a single volume.

Thus the genesis of this book. I am convinced that the cognitive sciences have the potential to change how we think about a wide range of theologically related questions. Because of this wide range, and because of the unfamiliarity that most theologians and religious thinkers have with the cognitive sciences, I have chosen to emphasize breadth over depth, introducing the relevant topics rather than systematically exploring them. Findings from the cognitive sciences most obviously stand to affect how we think about the human person, from the basis of consciousness to issues of freedom and mystical experience. The cognitive sciences also stand to affect how we think of ourselves in the larger context of the natural world, for my own mind is necessarily connected to many others through culture, through our relation with other animals, and through the evolutionary past. Most surprisingly, cognitive science also stands to affect how we think about God and God's relationship to the world, for often we think of God as a mind or person, and once we do, we ultimately rely on the conceptual categories available to us. Realizing this stands to affect how we think about a range of issues, from arguments about intelligent design to the place of humans in the universe.

Too often, theologians, philosophers, and religion scholars often find themselves stuck in a conversation that belongs primarily in the nineteenth century. One reason for this disconnect remains the powerful notion that religion and science are in conflict or, at best, separate realms. Within the history of at least one cognitive science, psychology, there certainly is some justification for this perception. Both the psychoanalytic tradition and the behaviorist tradition of psychology, which dominated the first half of the twentieth century, had little good to say about religion. While the psychoanalysts did develop a humanistic tradition that could become part of an interesting dialogue, the more psychology stressed its scientific character, the less it had anything positive to say about religion.

This development has been unfortunate, not least because it poisons current perceptions of religion by some cognitive scientists as well as perceptions of cognitive science by scholars of religion. Current trends in cognitive science certainly challenge many presuppositions held by theologians and philosophers of religion. What is little appreciated, however, is the potential cognitive science has to help reformulate traditional religious and theological issues in surprising and satisfying ways. In an age of ecological awareness, cognitive science can help us rethink our relationship to the environment. In an age of materialism, cognitive science can help us rethink our understanding of spirit. In an age of pluralistic dialogue with other religions, cognitive science can even help us rethink our conception of God.

In other words, theology has little to lose and much to gain from a dialogue with cognitive science and, indeed, with all the sciences. For too long, theology has allowed itself to be a cultural cul-de-sac, immune from the travails of culture but, for that very reason, having little prophetic to say to it. I hope that this book in its own modest way will contribute to a new chapter of theological reflection, one that is intellectually confident enough to engage the sciences and, at the same time, to learn from them.

A number of individuals have aided in the completion of this work. I would like to thank Kevin Sharpe and Michael West for expressing interest in the book, despite it lying fallow for over a year. Marshall Johnson and Zan Ceeley of Fortress Press were immensely helpful in the final editing and production of the book. Dennis Bielfeldt (philosophy, South Dakota State University), Marc Bekoff (cognitive ethology, University of Colorado, Boulder), and Michael Spezio (neuroscience, University of California, Davis) each looked over portions of the manuscript and provided helpful comments. The research for chapter 7 and for parts of other chapters was made possible in part by participation in a seminar held at Calvin College, "Biology and Purpose: Altruism, Morality, and Human Nature in Evolutionary Theory," funding for which was provided by the John Templeton Foundation. The members of the seminar provided a lively setting to discuss a wide range of ideas, and I would like particularly to thank the seminar leaders, Philip Clayton (philosophy, University of California, Sonoma) and Jeff Schloss (biology, Westmont College) for their insightful comments and feedback. Both Philip Hefner (theology, Zygon Center for Religion and Science) and Curt Thompson (religion, Thiel College) have each in their own way been immensely supportive of my research work, and for that they deserve special thanks. Finally, thanks must also go to my wife, Kathy, who helped with the glossary, and son, Josh, who endured many a night and weekend with me shut up in my office at the computer.

PART ONE

GOD, MIND, AND COGNITIVE SCIENCE

1

What Does Silicon Valley Have to Do with Jerusalem?

The Game of the Century

It was, we were told, the game of the century. In the spring of 1996, Garry Kasparov, reputed to be one of the greatest chess players in history, lost a chess game for the first time to a computer. The computer in question, named Deep Blue, was not just any machine. Built with the latest technology, Deep Blue could examine millions of chess positions per second, achieving through brute power what it lacked in elegance and finesse. Kasparov went on to win the match, but clearly the writing was on the wall and, indeed, in the following year he would lose. The press milked the match for all that it was worth. Chess, that most rational of games, had long been touted as the pinnacle of human intellectual skill, the symbol of the thinking mind over and against the thoughtless machine. Garry Kasparov was playing not simply for the $600,000 purse but for humankind. He was a modern-day John Henry, defending the dignity of our species.

Of course, the experts knew better. Deep Blue was at best an idiot savant. It could do only one thing: play chess. Critics pointed out that even that statement might be too much. After all, it could not see the chessboard, study its opponent, or move the pieces itself. It certainly could not stretch, read a good book, or order food at a restaurant. If anything, Deep Blue established what many already knew: chess is not a very interesting indicator of what makes us human, and computers are exceptionally good at narrowly defined problems that are relatively easy to calculate. Computers, unlike humans, do not have *minds*.

Many persons consoled themselves with just this observation. That Kasparov had lost to what was in effect a glorified calculator should be neither surprising nor alarming. Comfort could be taken in the fact that the computer had not actually *thought* about its moves but worked largely by searching ahead over billions of possibilities. If a computer had to be able to examine millions of positions a second to beat a human being, then the human mind must be pretty special indeed.

Ironically, these observations and responses, as accurate as many of them are, testify nevertheless to the fragility of the human ego and to the importance that we place on our mental abilities. Over the centuries, humankind has often claimed a special place in the scheme of things. We are, the argument goes, unique among all creatures on Earth, and unique in a way that sets us above all. Wings make birds different, but they do not make birds special. It is our minds that make humans special. We can think, reason, and argue in ways not possible for any other creature on Earth. We can speak, reflect upon ourselves, and act morally. We laugh. We sin.

Enter the sciences. On one account, the story of science is the story of the ever-shrinking significance of humankind in the universe. First, Nicolas Copernicus told us that the Earth—and therefore humanity—were not at the center of the universe. Then Charles Darwin told us that we are not specially created but an apparently unintended happenstance of natural selection. Finally, computers like Deep Blue represent the culmination of humankind's dethronement. First we lose our place, then we lose our bodies, and finally we lose our minds. We are not, it turns out, deeply spiritual beings but merely sophisticated and somewhat clunky calculators. On this reading, not only are we not significant but nothing is. Life is simply a complex concatenation of atoms and molecules colliding in space. The end.

There is, however, another story, a more interesting and persuasive one. It also involves the sciences but yields a radically different conclusion. Here our significance is not lost but redefined. Reduction is complemented by emergence. We are more than clunky calculators; we are rich, social beings, more than the sum of our parts. In this story, the cognitive sciences, the sciences of the mind, play a prominent role. Although the physical sciences are frequently seen to be the enemy of culture, reducing richness to blandness and mystery to a chemical soup, they are not always so. While cognitive science often shares the methodological reduction of the physical sciences, it also reveals the interconnectedness and irreducible quality of the mind. As such, cognitive science can also be a tool for understanding greater realities.

These greater realities, I argue, include theology. On the face of it, the link between cognitive science and theology might not be obvious. Cognitive science, drawing from such disciplines as neuroscience, cognitive psychology, and artificial intelligence, talks about things such as neurons, visual perception, and brain modules. Theology talks about God, redemption, and social justice. While much of theology is God-talk, however, theology is also centrally concerned with broadly anthropological questions. Claims about human nature, human proclivities, and human potential are central to a theological understanding of the world. Cognitive science has much to say about all three. Traditionally and consistently, religious literature has described God in personal—or at least personlike—terms. Indeed, at least a part of the theological tradition has seen the relationship of God and the world as explicitly analogous to the relationship of mind and body. If our view of the latter changes, will the former as well?

Research in the cognitive sciences has revolutionized the way we think about mind, human nature, and our relationship to the world. Although this revolution has sometimes carried unfortunate philosophical baggage, it has dramatically improved our knowledge and understanding. Some of the findings and perspectives of cognitive science have the potential to revolutionize theology or at least subtly provide new insights into traditional areas of inquiry. To this end, cognitive science can provide a lens for doing theology. While a lens can distort, its ultimate purpose is to clarify. Although cognitive science can at times challenge traditional theological claims, it can also provide models and metaphors for clarifying theological understandings of God, the world, and human nature. We stand to gain a richer understanding of ourselves.

Silicon Valley

"Quid ergo Athenis et Hierosolymis?" " What," Tertullian rhetorically asked, "has Athens to do with Jerusalem?"[1] Theologians from time to time since Tertullian have felt as he did, that theology has little to learn and nothing to gain from dialogue with philosophy or, in the modern period, its science-minded offspring. Theology, it is said, is autonomous and relies solely on the revealed word of God. To subsume theology under philosophy is to reduce the significance and distinctiveness of the

Christian message. Likewise, to acknowledge the significance of the sciences for theological reflection is, on some accounts, to misunderstand the domain and even the meaning of the terms "theology" and "science." Theology deals with the spiritual realm, science with the material.

While noble in their intent, such declarations tend to be misguided and even disingenuous in their execution. Tertullian himself could not completely avoid philosophical categories and modes of thought. Modern theologians like Karl Barth built their systems under the influence of such philosophical thinkers as Søren Kierkegaard and Martin Heidegger. Indeed, at the same time that such theologians distanced themselves from philosophical discourse they inevitably used characterizations of theology, philosophy, and science that themselves required sophisticated philosophical analysis. The real question, it turns out, is not whether to engage philosophy but how.

Similar statements might be made about the natural sciences. It might even be said that the real question of the twentieth century was not whether and how theology should engage philosophy but whether and how theology should engage the natural sciences. Much of the dynamics of twentieth-century theology and religion can be seen precisely as a response to the encroachment and shaping influences of the sciences. Neoorthodox and existentialist theologies could establish the distinctiveness of theology only by largely confining themselves to the human subject, which alone seemed impervious to scientific investigation. Religious conservatives and fundamentalists, at least in the United States, have frequently taken a different approach, acknowledging the significance of the sciences but engaging in head-on conflict. Process theologians and those engaged in the ongoing and growing dialogue of religion and science have prominently opposed this trend, arguing instead that theology and science can and should avoid conflict and embrace dialogue or even outright synthesis under a broader metaphysical rubric.[2]

If Tertullian were alive today, he might not contrast Jerusalem with Athens as much as, say, with Los Alamos or Fermilabs. If we were to speak of the cognitive sciences, however, we would have to select another locale. In the early twenty-first century, many might rephrase Tertullian's question: What does Silicon Valley have to do with Jerusalem?

Why Silicon Valley? As home to the computer and software industry in the United States, Silicon Valley has little directly to do with cognitive science. Although Silicon Valley programmers freely use expert systems originally designed by researchers in artificial (computer) intelligence who were interested in modeling the human brain, their interests tend to be commercial in character and to have little concern for the broader research and philosophical questions posed by artificial intelligence specifically or cognitive science generally.

The common desktop computer has in the past half-century become the primary metaphor for understanding the human mind, however inadequate we now realize that metaphor to be. To speak of the brain as "hard-wired" and to speak of mental activities as analogous to software is commonplace. Conversely, computer scientists have often co-opted the language of biology. We may speak of the computer chip as the "brains" of the computer. Computers catch "viruses" that can be transmitted from other computers. More than this, however, Silicon Valley also reminds us of the continual advance of computer technology, an advance that, according to some, will eventually surpass that of the human mind itself. The giant mainframe computers of the 1950s and 1960s are now dwarfed in computing power by personal digital assistants that fit in the palm of one's hand. Moore's law, which predicts that computing power will double every eighteen months, has become a staple of the industry. In this sense, Silicon Valley represents the modern incarnation of scientific progress, an incarnation that threatens eventually to overtake the human subject itself.

This image of Silicon Valley and the computer industry is even promoted as utopian. Futurists such as Ray Kurzweil and Hans Moravec foresee a future when human beings as biological organisms are replaced by artificial life-forms, enabling our very consciousness to be "downloaded" onto a vast computer network and allowing us to achieve a kind of immortality.[3] Implicit in this image is the claim that such technological advances will lead to a complete understanding of the human mind and spirit. It is a short step from here to the claim that human beings are "nothing but" sophisticated computers and that human nature can be understood properly only within a naturalistic, technological context. With religious frameworks marginalized, Silicon Valley seems to leave little room indeed for Jerusalem.

Modern cognitive science, however, roots itself deeper than Silicon Valley, in the grand philosophical tradition from Plato to René Descartes. At its most basic, cognitive science is the science of *thinking*.

The study of language, reasoning ability, memory, and perception—all topics traditionally associated with the notion of thinking—have consequently been key areas of investigation for cognitive science, and much of its early successes and influential theories dealt with these subjects. More recently, as the role of the emotions, the body, and the environment have increasingly come under the scrutiny of the cognitive sciences, the notion of what counts as thinking has changed significantly. Silicon Valley is a mere cipher for what cognitive science engages. Thinking, we are often led to believe, is what Deep Blue and desktop computers do. Presumably we pale by comparison. Yet the cognitive sciences are in many ways showing us something different—something stranger and more beautiful at the same time.

The image of Silicon Valley also fails to convey the breadth and interdisciplinary character of cognitive science. In fact, cognitive science does not represent a single discipline as much as an array of disciplines united by a common perspective and research agenda. One may speak metaphorically of the vertically and horizontally interdisciplinary character of the cognitive sciences. Vertically, modern cognitive science includes such fields as neuroscience, cognitive psychology, linguistics, and anthropology, each analyzing a different layer (so to speak) of the human person. Horizontally, cognitive science is not devoted to the human subject alone but includes the study of artificial (e.g., computers and robots), animal, and (speculatively) extraterrestrial intelligence as well. In fact, one of the strongest implications of the interdisciplinary character of cognitive science is that, whatever we may prefer to believe, it is clear that we are not alone in the universe when it comes to activities of the mind. Without a doubt, we are different, but in a way that intimately connects us with other organisms and with the rest of the physical world.

So no one Athens, no one place or image can adequately symbolize all that cognitive science now encompasses. Yet many places embody its aspects and ideals, such as the Artificial Intelligence lab at MIT, the Yerkes Primatology lab in Atlanta, or the Center for Brain and Cognition in San Diego. Collectively, they form a sort of Athens that is shaping the way that we think about ourselves and our place in the world. Like physics, chemistry, and biology, the cognitive sciences are not some passing trend but are here to stay. It remains to divine what this new Athens is.

Jerusalem

Today's Tertullians may concede that theology and philosophy are inevitably intertwined, but they often draw a line at the sciences. There is a certain intuitiveness to this. After all, theology is focused on the study of God. The sciences, by contrast, not only do not speak of God; they rather purposefully exclude any God-talk or appeal to divine activity altogether. Theology and science are too much like oil and water; they simply do not mix.

Serious study, however, quickly reveals that while we may reasonably conclude that theology is an autonomous discipline with its own norms and subject matter, absolute separation of theology and science relies on a concept of theology that is severely restricted in its claims and scope. Theology ultimately makes claims about the world; indeed it has traditionally been concerned primarily about God's relationship to the world. Doing theology inevitably entails some kind of encounter with the sciences, even if only at the minimal level of radically relativizing either theological or scientific claims in order to make coexistence possible.

As we shall see, the encounter of theology and science is particularly unavoidable in the case of the cognitive sciences. True enough, cognitive science does not study God. Or, to put it bluntly, God is not the kind of intelligence that cognitive science investigates. Despite this, theology is tremendously interested in issues pertaining to human nature, a subject about which the cognitive sciences have much to say. Officially, theology is concerned with the nature and action of God. In practice, however, much of theology is anthropological in character and dedicated to providing an understanding of the human person and the human situation. Theology speaks of God because, in no small part, God is important to human beings. According to Christian tradition, we are made in the image of God and yet suffer from a fallen state that involves separation from God. This sense of alienation is overcome only by the sacrifice of Christ, who offers a transformed life and reveals a future hope. God is important precisely because belief in God profoundly affects how we think of ourselves.

Historically, theological anthropologies have two broad concerns. First, the discipline is often metaphysical in character, providing an explanation of human nature, its ultimate origins, current propensities, and ultimate fate. As a consequence, theology has traditionally attempted to explain what is meant by the image of God, in what ways we are or are not free, and what we mean by such terms as "soul" and "spirit." Theology also explains our place in the world, often through the doctrine of the image of God, as well as our expected purpose and behavior. Second, and perhaps more important, theology is soteriological in character. Theology develops such concepts as sin, conversion, and sanctification because they provide the framework within which human purpose and happiness is understood. Soteriology and metaphysics are inevitably connected. Metaphysics helps us to understand our current predicament; soteriology informs us how to transform it.

Cognitive science affects both metaphysical and soteriological accounts of human nature. Metaphysically, cognitive science profoundly affects how we think of issues of human origins, mind and body, the unity of the human person, and the potential for human freedom. Soteriologically, cognitive science affects how we think of mental health and thus human well-being, our relationship to other organisms, and the nature of human cooperation. Certainly this "soteriological streak" is present among popularizers of psychology and specific branches of cognitive science. We can legitimately view the popular psychology and self-help market as in some ways a competing, secular soteriology whose promoters at least tacitly intend to replace the religious soteriologies that many find no longer compelling. One need only consider the success of Daniel Goleman's *Emotional Intelligence* and Howard Gardner's several books and spin-offs on multiple intelligences to see the influence of cognitive science on the popular psychology market.[4] This soteriological character is even more evident in the futurist writings of Hans Moravec and Ray Kurzweil, both of whom envision a kind of future technological paradise brought about by the union of human intelligence and computer/robot technology.

The theologian may look upon this soteriological streak as illegitimate, an unacknowledged sleight of hand that moves from science to religion. Such works suffer from the mistake of scientism, conflating scientific findings with religious and philosophical claims and generalizations. While these observations are pertinent, they risk missing the larger point: while metaphysics and soteriology are separate and distinct from the cognitive sciences, they no longer should be addressed in isolation from the cognitive sciences, which have a significant potential to affect how we think about these issues. Any claim of human uniqueness (to be addressed in chapter 6, below) needs to take into account at some level the now extensive research on animal (especially primate) intelligence and social behavior. Any soteriology that makes claims about human transformation needs to take stock of the account of the integrated mind/brain/body that the cognitive sciences reveal as well as the increasingly close ties being discovered between cognition, emotion, and concepts of mental health. Such findings may not determine which metaphysical or soteriological move to make, but they have the potential to strongly influence and even limit the discussion.

One of the traditional strategies for declaring the independence of science and religion—and therefore the independence of science *for* religion—becomes particularly problematic when the cognitive sciences are taken into account. This strategy involves the idea that true religion deals with and arises out of human subjectivity. How this occurs has been expounded in various ways. Immanuel Kant began this shift with his account of the transcendental subject and, through it, of moral discourse. Shortly after him, Friedrich Schleiermacher famously tied religion to a particular kind of experience, the feeling of absolute dependence. While Schleiermacher had multiple motivations for moving in this direction, one of the desired effects was to provide an account of religion that was compatible with the Newtonian science of the day. Because the science of the day could say nothing significant about human subjectivity, the identification of subjectivity as the source of religion had great appeal and success. This success is evident in such diverse thinkers as Søren Kierkegaard, Rudolf Otto, Mircea Eliade, and several modern theologians. Although Karl Barth distanced himself from the tradition of liberal theology inaugurated by Schleiermacher, he nevertheless retained its emphasis on the subject. The existentialist theology of such thinkers as Rudolf Bultmann also emphasizes the primacy of the subject, relativizing the claims of religion in a way that avoids statements about the physical world while concentrating on the human subject distant from and even untouchable by the physical sciences.

While a theological analysis of the human subject can contribute something unique and distinctive, it is increasingly clear that such claims can no longer be made as if the sciences have nothing to contribute. A completely transcendent subject no longer seems conceivable, because much of what all subjects do clearly arises out of and is made possible by the processes of the brain. We may reason about morality as cogently as Kant did and feel as deeply as Schleiermacher did, but it is clearly our biology that makes this possible.

What is needed, therefore, is not a kind of theological isolationism but rather interdisciplinary engagement. Theology has been engaged with physics and biology for some time, as can be seen most clearly in the works of John Polkinghorne and Arthur Peacocke.[5] While individuals such as Donald MacKay and James Ashbrook provided early models of dialogue and engagement between religion and neuroscience, it is only within the past decade that a serious body of literature has been built up.[6] Despite this, there is a great deal of work yet to do, and the full implications of the cognitive sciences for theology have yet to be fully addressed.

Jerusalem Engaging Athens

The following chapters contain two arguments, one explicit and one implicit. Explicitly, I argue that serious consideration of the cognitive sciences stands to affect nearly every facet of Christian theological thinking. In arguing so, I engage the classic themes and doctrines that have defined the Catholic and Protestant traditions of Western Christian thought. Consequently, issues of human nature, the nature of God, and the relation of humankind to the world will be major subjects of exploration. Implicitly, cognitive science has implications not simply for conventional, denominationally orthodox modes of theology but for all modes of theological thinking. In the late twentieth and early twenty-first centuries, theology as a discipline has been characterized more than anything else by radical methodological pluralism. While some methodologies such as process thought incline toward dialogue with the sciences, others, such as some versions of postmodern, pragmatist, and deconstructionist theology, have either rejected dialogue altogether or approached the sciences as one "social text" among others, granting them no special authority or importance. While the current work cannot hope to engage this diversity comprehensively, I suggest that all forms of theology stand to be affected by a serious dialogue with the cognitive sciences. Insofar as methodology and content are connected, the content of the cognitive sciences can affect the way we go about *doing* theology.

Moreover, a theology that engages the cognitive sciences must be aware of two other contexts. First, any theology that engages the cognitive sciences does so in the context of a larger science and theology (and science and religion) dialogue. In a real sense there has never been a period when science and theology have not been in dialogue. The reflections of such significant figures as Augustine and Aquinas were as much influenced by the "science" of their day as were later thinkers by the natural theologies of the eighteenth century and the empirical and process theologies of the twentieth. In recent decades, this science and theology dialogue has taken on definite shape, spurred most significantly by the work of Ian Barbour but influenced and shaped by a number of scholars in the United States and Europe.[7] The result is that science and religion (including science and theology) now represents a rather distinct subfield, characterized increasingly by a number of its own specializations. Any current work on science and theology must now be interpreted in relation to this broader dialogue.

At the same time, any dialogue between theology and cognitive science should be cognizant not only of theological pluralism but of religious pluralism as well. As with theological pluralism, religious pluralism is only an implicit concern in the pages that follow. Nevertheless, it is increasingly the case that Christians are not the only ones taking the claims of the sciences (including the cognitive sciences) seriously. There is potential for a rich "trialogue" among religious traditions on the matters of science, as each works through issues of borders, compatibility, and interpretation. Likewise, awareness of this pluralism should make us wary of any attempt to swiftly "baptize" science with the imprimatur of one's own tradition.

Acknowledging these two contexts, one relatively narrow and the other quite broad, is one way to foster the kind of theology and theological dialogue that are most appropriate. For practical purposes, I assume a rather broad understanding of the nature and task of theology while sometimes engaging in quite specific doctrines and issues, such as original sin and the personhood of God. The specificity serves a dual purpose, showing not only how the cognitive sciences require us to rethink particular doctrines but also how thinking theologically about the cognitive sciences should proceed. Arguments about such doctrines as the image of God, therefore, are both substantive and illustrative, pointing to the possibilities for yet further kinds of discussions in different arenas.

Broadly conceived, then, I take theology to be that field of inquiry whose primary purpose is to discern the meaning and purpose of life. Theology, more than any other discipline, is concerned with the task of providing orientation and direction for the individual. Theology attempts to answer those questions asked on clear, starry nights and in the deepest, darkest moments: Who am I? Why am I here? What is my purpose? How should I act? How can I be fulfilled? Historically, these have all been theological questions, and it has been primarily the task of theologians and religious traditions to answer them. Such questions certainly require some philosophical acumen as well but, as philosophy has attempted to answer them, it has become increasingly religious in character. This can be most clearly seen in the philosophies of the Hellenistic and Roman periods, such as Neoplatonism and Stoicism, but the work and followers of Karl Marx and Friedrich Nietzsche provide modern counterparts. The adoption of the term "theology" by Buddhists and Hindus indicates the extent to which this broad understanding of theology now exists, even though to speak of Buddhist theology in a literal sense can be a contradiction in terms.

What has historically given theology much of its character is its effort to answer such questions in terms of a worldview. Any attempt to provide such an orienting worldview is, in effect, a theology. Ironically, the reason why various naturalist philosophies often have so many negative things to say about religion is precisely their theological character. In the "evolution wars," especially in the United States, the importance of natural selection for both naturalists and theists in the debate has, arguably, little to do with the scientific merits of the theory and much to do with the implications the theory is said to have for important theological questions of meaning and purpose. The argument is partially about science but very much about theology.

Christian theology, then, represents only one mode of doing theology. Like most theologies, Christian theology provides a worldview that orients believers in their interior lives and outward behavior. For Christians, this worldview has preeminently spoken of the ultimate role and nature of God, whose actions create, sustain, and redeem the world. Such a worldview is quite specific in many of its claims and consequently quite successful in its attempts to orient and answer the basic questions of meaning and purpose. At the same time, Christian theology has traditionally relied on concepts and claims that are not accessible by empirical observation alone but only through revelation. The category of faith has historically played an important role up to today. To borrow a phrase from the philosophy of science, human experience underdetermines the Christian (and almost any) worldview. As with every theological tradition, Christian theology is a complex mix of considered reasons, deeply held convictions, and—occasionally—best guesses.

Ideally, however, theology is a rational enterprise that finds its place among (some would still say above) other academic disciplines. As such, any given theology needs to justify its claims in the relevant public spheres. Theology, however, is not truly public but at least traditionally relies on some authority (the church, the creeds, the Bible) whose veracity and utility rely more on the categories of revelation and faith than of reason. As a result one primary task of theologians has been to explicate how theological claims are rationally defensible. As with any area of inquiry, they must answer the basic question, "Why would anyone believe *that*?"

For theology, a first task is an elucidation of exactly what "that" is. God, the soul, and salvation are all multivalent terms that have historically taken on a range of meanings. God may be understood as Aristotle's unmoved mover or Hegel's world-spirit. The soul has been variously defined as the form of the body (Aquinas, following Aristotle) or as separate, distinct, nonextended thinking thing (Descartes). In the modern period, such questions of definition and ontology, particularly as applied to God, have become strikingly important and widely divergent. God is variously conceived to be a special kind of "actual entity" (process theology), the "ground of being" (Paul Tillich), or as the mysterious and serendipitous creativity of the universe (Gordon Kaufman).[8] Alternatively, the multivalence of theological terms may also be retained in a way that does not opt for a literal or quasi-literal explication but opts instead for the language of symbol and metaphor. Thus, at the same time that Tillich speaks of God as the ground of being, his acknowledgment of the symbolic character of religious language guards against overly literalistic accounts of God that presume more than we know.

This symbolic character of theological discourse has been a partial consequence of the historically holistic nature of theological reflection. Unlike other rational enterprises, theology as a discipline has been much more inclined to draw from the philosophically messy realms of personal experience, literary analysis, and artistic insight. For most practicing scientists, words are descriptive, used to provide as transparent an account of the relevant phenomena as possible. For many forms of theology, however, words are also disclosive, harboring the potential to elicit new experiences and insights on the part of the reader.

As a result, most theologies can be seen to lie along what might be called a poetic-scientific continuum. Theologies that tend toward the poetic eschew the categories of literal, scientific rationality in favor of modes of writing and expression that seek to open up new vistas, not test new theories. Such theologies are not unique to Christian thought but may be found in Jewish, Muslim, and Buddhist contexts as well.

Scientific theologies, by contrast, seek to do precisely the opposite. In this approach, God denotes a particular kind of being or reality in relation to ourselves and to the world. The purpose of theology, then, is to elucidate a system or theory that is explanatory in character. While poetic theologies tend toward the symbolic and metaphorical, scientific theologies tend toward the literal. As a result, definitions, propositional claims, and rational argumentation can and often do play an important role in scientific theologies.

In speaking of "scientific theology," I use the term "scientific" in its broadest sense to denote any mode of rational inquiry. Rational categories are used either to demonstrate the veracity of specific Christian doctrines or to limit the claims of a universal rational discourse, thereby making room for the category of faith. While Aquinas used philosophical categories to demonstrate the existence of God, Kierkegaard used Hegel's dialectical reason to demonstrate its own limitations in the face of genuine religious commitment. Both rational strategies are commonly used, often by the same thinkers. Theologies that engage a lived faith, however, must consistently attempt (one might say risk) the former, positive approach. For theology to be relevant, it must make claims about the world. To make claims about the world, theology must inevitably engage rational modes of thought.

The notion of a "scientific" theology has been put forward several times over the past century, albeit with quite different ideas about what the adjective "scientific" meant. Neoorthodox theologians have used the term, as have representatives of mid-century empirical theology, like Anders Nygren, Thomas Torrance, and Ralph Wendell Burhoe.[9] More recently, a number of theologians have embraced philosophy of science as a means for providing a theological method. In this approach, theology is scientific to the extent that it shares in the same method of intellectual inquiry as other well-established sciences. Wolfhart Pannenberg, for instance, justifies speaking of theology as the science of God by appeal to theology's ability to follow the scientific method as described by Karl Popper and others.[10] Nancey Murphy has gone much further, claiming that while theology may not currently be scientific in character, it can and should be. Building on the thought of philosopher of science Imre Lakatos, Murphy sees theology in terms of competing research programs, consisting of core claims that are elucidated and evaluated in terms of their empirical confirmation and by comparison to the success of other research programs.[11]

While the cognitive sciences may be relevant to the whole spectrum of theological thinking, the more scientifically oriented form of theology is most engaged in the pages ahead. This is partly because it is this form of theology that is most impacted by the claims of the cognitive sciences. Scientifically oriented theologies make the most specific claims and consequently have the most at stake in those areas where science and theology meet. But also, this form of theology is most engaged because, in my estimate, it has a significant impact on how we think and act. A theology that takes a stand, for instance, on human uniqueness takes a position as well as to how we interact with all other subjects and objects in the world. In the end, such theologies often claim too much, which is one reason why history is replete with bygone theological systems. Even from failures, however, there is something to be learned, and it is only through the process of construction and engagement that true theological wisdom can develop.

Doing Theology through the Lens of Cognitive Science

It is one thing to assert that the cognitive sciences are significant for theology and quite something else to say how. Science and theology can engage one another in a variety of ways. Ian Barbour identifies four modes of engagement between science and religion: conflict, independence, dialogue, and synthesis.[12] This typology is often applied to theology as well, although it is not clear that it is wholly suitable in that context. Conflict is certainly quite possible and, sadly, much in evidence in American culture today, even among intellectuals. Independence, the claim that science and theology occupy separate and distinct spheres, clearly has a respectable academic pedigree; paleontologist Stephen Jay Gould was a well-known advocate of this position.[13] Unfortunately, most independence models work by radically limiting the scope of theology. In Gould's analysis, science is about facts, religion (and therefore theology) is about values, and never the twain shall meet. While Barbour's categories of dialogue and synthesis can be useful for theologians, they do not fully capture the range of possibilities when theologians actually engage the sciences. In thinking theologically about the cognitive sciences, it will often be most appropriate to speak of three modes of interaction.

Reduction/Autonomy

Within the social sciences, there is a long tradition of reducing the categories of theology (God, the soul, the afterlife) to those of sociology, psychology, or anthropology. Beginning with Ludwig Feuerbach's *The Essence of Christianity*, the claims of religion have been variously interpreted as a form of projection, wish fulfillment or, in Karl Marx's famous phrase, "the opiate of the masses." With regard to the cognitive sciences, two forms of reductionist arguments have been presented in recent years. The first of these are what may be called hostile reductions. Hostile reductions attempt to explain away the "higher level" phenomenon of religion by describing it in terms of the "lower level" categories of biology, brain, and psychology. Stephen Pinker's speculative explanation of religion in terms of fictive kin relationships (the extension of family terms such as "brother" and "sister" beyond blood relatives) is one such instance of hostile reduction.[14] Richard Dawkins's notion of religion as a cultural virus (meme), articulated recently by Susan Blackmore, might be considered another example. In both cases, the reduction is hostile in the sense that religious belief is discredited simply by virtue of providing the explanation.[15]

Friendly reductions, by contrast, stand at the opposite end of the spectrum. These approaches generally occur in one of two forms. In the first it is claimed that religious beliefs and attitudes are indeed reducible to biology, brain, and psychology, but this functions as a reason to encourage the continued practice of religion as a natural human activity. Nevertheless, God, angels, and the afterlife do not refer to anything "out there" but are the products of human imagination. Merlin

Donald might be one example of this approach, although his work is primarily descriptive rather than normative.[16] In the second form, cognitive science is claimed to be *the* key for understanding theology, although the objective reality of theological claims are not necessarily denied and may indeed be affirmed. This form of friendly reduction, then, is an epistemological reduction (claiming cognitive science as the only source of theological knowledge) but not necessarily an ontological one (claiming that God does not therefore *really* exist). The recent book by John Ashbrook and Carol Albright as well as that by Eugene d'Aquili and Andrew Newburg have variously taken this approach.[17] Indeed, d'Aquili and Newburg have coined the term "neurotheology" to describe their approach.

My own perspective is that reductionist claims on behalf of the cognitive sciences, either of the hostile or of the friendly variety, are on the whole unconvincing; they will therefore not be covered as extensively here as they might be elsewhere. Nevertheless, there are areas where issues of reductionism are of considerable importance, most notably in the research of the biology of mystical experiences (see chapter 5, below) and in accounts of social evolution (aspects of which are discussed in chapter 6, below).

Cognitive Science as Challenge

Issues of reduction and autonomy strike at the core of what theology is about. The two other forms of interaction, by contrast, presume the autonomy of theology, at least in the sense that the sources and norms of theology ultimately lie outside the bounds of the cognitive sciences. The claims of cognitive science are frequently seen as a challenge to theology, calling into question traditional doctrines and formulations. In its strong form, challenge may lead to conflict (Barbour's first category). Theological critics who still maintain a supernatural soul/body dualism are one likely instance of this. More often, challenge serves as a means to reexamine and reconsider the meaning of the doctrine in question. Sometimes this may result in change, sometimes not. The reemphasis on the doctrine of the resurrection of the dead as opposed to the immortality of the soul among Christian theologians (especially among those involved in the science-religion dialogue) may be one area where scientific findings have led theologians along a particular path of rediscovery.[18]

Challenges can also occur at different levels. The human being is the most complex organism in the universe that we are aware of. While we have discovered much, much also remains unknown. Consequently, the cognitive sciences do produce quite specific, testable, and repeatable results, but it must also provide working models and theories that interpret the results in ways that make their significance plain. It is, for instance, one thing to record the responses from split-brain patients (discussed in chapter 3, below) and quite another to explain why they act the way they do. These theories may in turn rely on prior philosophical commitments that may or may not conflict with contrasting theological claims. These different levels are present in any scientific discipline, but they are perhaps more prominent in the cognitive sciences, not only because of its relative youth as a field and its complexity but also because of its primary subject, the human person. Consequently, the stakes are high, and the debate, even among scientists, can become quite heated.

Cognitive Science as Data

The category of challenge often presumes that there is only one theological story. If the cognitive sciences produce conflicting data or a well-established conflicting theory, it is often assumed that theology must beat a hasty retreat. Indeed, this is a prevalent conception of the historical relationship between religion and science. As science closes the gaps in our knowledge, theology is constantly put in the position of either fighting a losing battle or withdrawing into an ever smaller sphere of influence. To the extent that theologians and scientists of religious conviction have made theologically based claims about the natural world that turned out to be false, there is some truth to this perception. But a close evaluation of the history of theology shows a far more dynamic situation. While the religious skepticism of the Enlightenment was corrosive for the Christian churches in many ways, it did serve to inaugurate a period of theological creativity that continues to the present. Combined with the previous 1,500 years of Christian reflection, it is foolish to continue to think of only one theological story. There are many. While the great majority of these stories have much in common (there are very few Christian atheists, for instance), there are important differences as well. Additionally, theologians are still rethinking the story. Amazingly, 2,000 years later, there are still new alternatives to evaluate.

One way of thinking of cognitive science, then, is as data for theology. Cognitive science helps us to think through and choose theological options. Cognitive science may provide insight, inspiring options that had not been previously considered. It is in this sense that cognitive science may serve as a lens for doing theology. A lens helps us to see what we might not have seen otherwise. Ideally, a lens clarifies. In this approach, cognitive science does not dictate the content of theology but it does provide insight for getting the theology right.

The idea of cognitive science as data or lens will play a prominent role in the chapters ahead. Cognitive science does present challenges. In so doing it helps us to think through theological alternatives. While cognitive science is not the only resource for considering theological alternatives, it can provide essential information for coming to the right decision.

Looking Ahead

After an introduction to the scope and character of the cognitive sciences (chapter 2), the book is divided into three further parts. The second section will look at the question of consciousness and the mind-body relation (chapter 3), freedom and the unity of the self (chapter 4), and the biology and psychology of religious experiences (chapter 5). While many of the issues raised in these chapters are philosophical in character (e.g., recent debates about consciousness and supervenience), there are significant theological stakes as well. Christian soteriology is based in part on a theological anthropology that presumes a "self" or "soul" in need of transformation. Many of the traditional attributes of the self, however, are subjects of scientific inquiry, and the results are sometimes startling.

While part two concentrates on human nature, part three concentrates on our relation to others, human and otherwise. The existence and nature of animal minds and, more speculatively, artificial intelligence, presents one kind of challenge, forcing us to consider traditional claims for human uniqueness more carefully (chapter 6). A second kind of challenge has to do with our own biological and social evolution and the behavioral constraints that this evolutionary history is said to imply (chapter 7). While much of this work has traditionally been done under the rubric of sociobiology, the advent of evolutionary psychology has tried to inject a more cognitivist approach to this thinking. Such issues are central to our conception of our place in the world, theologically defined in terms of the image of God. While this doctrine is often used to defend human status and uniqueness, a rereading of this doctrine, already in progress among many thinkers, suggests a vision not only compatible with the sciences but also with a more sustained vision of the human good.

The final section turns a bit more toward theology proper, that is, discourse about God. This may strike some readers as the most speculative material in the book. After all, what could science tell us about the nature of God? Nevertheless, theological thinking is frequently anthropomorphic in character, at least to the extent that God is described as a person with many of the attributes such a description requires. Many voices in the theology and science dialogue have been insistent on the personal or personlike character of God. Once we start speaking of God as a person or even as a mind (frequently used in the popular language of the "mind of God"), we enter a realm where cognitive science has some relevance, for most of our knowledge of persons comes from human persons, a topic about which cognitive science has much to say (chapter 8). The final chapter pulls back toward a broader look at the question of purpose. Why are there intelligent, cognizing beings like us in the first place? Is there a scientific explanation or is it merely chance? In some ways, we remain the universe's biggest mystery.

2

How the Mind Works:
A Cognitive Science Perspective

Cognitive What?

Imagine that you are driving a car. As you navigate your way to your destination, you are involved in many tasks. Memories provide a mental map of where you are in relation to your destination. Hands and feet are coordinated to move the car at a particular speed in a specific direction, both of which are carefully monitored. At the same time, you are aware of traffic laws that must be obeyed and of the behavior of other motorists. If you are like most people, your journey will be accomplished with relatively little effort; you might even have daydreamed or been in conversation during much of the journey only to find yourself surprised that it was over so quickly.

For the great majority of us, driving is as second nature as walking, albeit with (at least for some of us) a longer learning curve. The ease with which we drive cars and engage in similar tasks, from riding a bicycle to playing tennis, can be deceptive. While driving a car is certainly not the apex of human achievement, it is one of the things that makes us unique. Apes and robots do not drive cars—at least not yet. An ape could probably learn the mechanics of driving but would not know where to go and would probably smash many a stop sign along the way. Computerized cars may soon be able to drive themselves, but only by simplifying many operations. Computerized cars need no hand on the gearshift or foot on the accelerator. They certainly do not daydream.

Even the very modest task of driving is made possible by the fact that we as a species have in great quantity what other species, comparatively speaking, lack. We have minds. True, animals have minds too, and computers and robots seem to engage in mindlike activities. But we have been gifted with an excessive surplus of mind, so much so that our mental abilities alone seem to make of us, despite our physical similarity to the great apes, a wholly new species and even genus.

Strictly speaking, cognitive science is the scientific study of mind. In one sense, cognitive science is as old as intellectual inquiry. As early as Plato, men and women have contemplated human nature and especially those qualities that seem most important to the composition of the self. But the terminology and conceptual schemes have been subject to change over the centuries. Plato's soul has largely been replaced by the modern, autonomous self, which in turn is about to disappear before the postmodern return to the whole, embodied person. Many of the concerns, however, have remained the same. The mind-body problem is as old as the Greeks and is still quite alive, even if the categories have changed.

In another, more relevant sense, cognitive science is quite recent and in its mature form dates only from the 1950s. Despite that, cognitive science has made significant strides, so much so that the label of "cognitive science," once controversial in some quarters, is increasingly seen not as a competing agenda or paradigm but as an established field of research with accepted subfields and graduate programs. The result is that, while there are many ways that even the simple task of driving a car still seems like a small miracle, the abilities behind such feats are becoming increasingly comprehensible. Such discoveries are not insignificant, for in the process we are learning not only about how we are able to drive but also about the more complex and ultimately critical abilities that make us moral and spiritual beings.

Cognitive Science: What It Is and What It Isn't

Cognitive science in many ways is distinctive from other, more established fields of science. This distinctiveness comes in part from the complexity of its subject matter. The human brain is currently the most complex known object in the universe. Partly as a result, cognitive science is younger than many other fields, such as physics, chemistry, and biology, although, as indicated above, its roots are deep. Furthermore, cognitive science is complex because it involves the study not only of the physical but also of the mental. The genius of cognitive science is that it has found a way of speaking of the mind that can make it scientifically comprehensible, at least to a degree. Cognitive science has traditionally understood the mind in terms of information processing, and for much of the twentieth century it has understood the mind primarily as analogous to a computer. Because of this, however, its claims have spurred opposition and sometimes scientific and philosophical controversy. In the process it has also changed and grown, to the extent that those who were once its opponents now adopt the vocabulary for their own purposes.

As a consequence, cognitive science can be spoken of in several ways. It can be described *historically*. In many ways, cognitive science is heir to the field now known as the philosophy of mind. Its antecedents stem first from Plato and Aristotle but continue through the likes of René Descartes and John Locke up to the present. Indeed, the thinkers of the Enlightenment have played a particularly important role, inasmuch as the issues they raised have been the primary questions that cognitive scientists, at least in the earliest phases, have attempted to answer. Like Descartes and Locke, cognitive scientists have been centrally concerned with the category of knowledge, along with the components of psychology—abilities such as memory, learning, perception, and language—that make the gaining of knowledge possible. Indeed, the title of one of Noam Chomsky's early texts, *Cartesian Linguistics*, says much about the mood of early cognitive science.[1]

Scientifically, cognitive science arose primarily out of the confluence of two events: the advent of the computer and the maturation of brain science. By the 1930s, Alan Turing and John von Neumann were developing the principles that are now considered the basis of nearly all modern computers. By the end of World War II, the first computers were being built, initially for military use, and what seemed impossible a century earlier was quickly becoming reality. Equally important, the theoretical framework provided by Turing and von Neumann made it possible for the first time to reflect on the content of the mind and the process of thinking in a quite concrete fashion. While many took the language of computation literally (Turing himself predicted a "thinking computer" within fifty years), its primary role was inspirational, for the computer provided a mode of thinking about the mind that was previously inconceivable.[2]

For this reason, it is difficult to overestimate the influence of the computer for early thinking in cognitive science. Nevertheless, the use of the computer as a model for the human was at least indirectly made possible by the concurrent developments in neuroscience, a fact that is sometimes underappreciated. As early as 1791, Luigi Galvani had demonstrated the electrical basis of the nervous system. Developments in neuroscience, however, proceeded at a slow pace, and it was only in the twentieth century that advances in technique allowed the gradual identification of basic brain-cell structures and the central role of neurons in brain activity. Such advances were tragically accelerated by the attention that two world wars brought to various kinds of brain damage. The growing awareness of the neuronal basis of the brain as well as the synaptic connections that linked all neurons together created for the first time a rough model of how the brain worked.

Such antecedents are important, for they say much about the character of the discipline. At the same time they are inadequate, for as cognitive science has grown and changed since its origins in the 1950s, its commitments to its original ideals have changed as well, at least for some. History, it seems, is a necessary but not sufficient means for understanding cognitive science.

More commonly, cognitive science can be spoken of as a *paradigm*. In Thomas Kuhn's usage, a paradigm is a set of commitments, theories, and exemplars that guide research, set criteria, and provide testable hypotheses.[3] Paradigms underlie the practice of science and in their pure form are resistant to change. Yet, persistent anomalies may occur and, when they accumulate, normal science gives way to revolutionary science. The old paradigm is overthrown, replaced by yet another, more adequate competitor.

In its first decades, cognitive science could be best understood as a paradigm, and many within the field self-consciously saw themselves in competition with other research programs of the period. In particular, cognitive science contrasted sharply with the two dominant modes of approaching mental phenomena at the time: behaviorism and psychoanalysis. Despite the popularity of the latter, early cognitive scientists never seemed to take psychoanalysis seriously; one is hard-pressed to find references to it in the literature. While this is significantly due to the divide between experimental and therapeutic psychology (cognitive science being identified with the former, psychoanalysis with the latter), it certainly cannot be the whole explanation. Psychoanalysis did make claims about the mind (e.g., the role of the unconscious, dreaming, child development, and the cultural basis of all neuroses) that are clearly in conflict—sometimes explicitly—with the general mind-set of cognitive science. For most cognitive scientists, psychoanalysis was unscientific and therefore barely worthy of notice.

By contrast, early cognitive science took behaviorism very seriously, and it was largely against the behaviorist backdrop that cognitive science was formed. Behaviorism, epitomized by the work of John B. Watson and B. F. Skinner, denied the relevance of mental content and limited psychology to the study of behavior. For behaviorists it mattered not at all what, if anything, was happening inside the mind; what mattered is what an organism (including people) actually did. Behaviorism achieved a measure of success, due in no small part to the rigorous experimental standards it set. At the same time, its limitations were obvious to many. Cognitive scientists at times sharply distinguished their approach from that of behaviorists. In direct opposition to behaviorism, cognitive science saw mental content as essential to a proper understanding of the human person generally and of the mind specifically. This was clearly evidenced by Noam Chomsky's scathing review of B. F. Skinner's *Verbal Behavior*, which attempted to explain the origin and nature of language in terms of stimulus and response.[4] As Chomsky pointed out, such an approach was absurd for language, where grammatical rules require forethought and consideration of the whole in order for the sentence to make sense.

Against the backdrop of behaviorism cognitive science defined itself as a research program, and in some cases, as in that of cognitive ethology (the study of animal cognitive behavior), skirmishes between advocates of each view persisted for decades. Differences between behaviorists and cognitivists were not simply about data but about the framework within which such data were understood. In short, cognitive science and behaviorism formed competing paradigms, a competition that recent history has judged the behaviorists to have lost.

While understanding cognitive science as a paradigm has distinct advantages—it characterizes especially well the early history of the field—it is in some ways too limiting. In recent decades cognitive science has undergone its own revolutions. The computational paradigm supported by cognitive science drew fire from several quarters for its commitment to a kind of disembodied, symbolic expression that seemed too reductionistic and incapable of explaining important categories of human psychology.[5] George Lakoff and Mark Johnson argue for a distinction between first-generation and second-generation cognitive science.[6] Cognitive science may be seen as a paradigm or as being composed of competing paradigms.

Because of this, it is increasingly appropriate to speak of cognitive science as a *field of research*, much in the way that physics and chemistry denote areas of investigation rather than paradigms. Cognitive science does differ in that it draws from and influences a number of fields. In this sense, it is appropriate to speak not of cognitive science but of the cognitive sciences. Psychology, linguistics, neuroscience, ethology, and artificial intelligence—all contribute to cognitive science as a discipline. While there are some significant differences between these fields in terms of proximate subject matter, they often share not only many of the same perspectives but also many of the same research priorities. Language, perception, and reasoning strategies—among other topics—form basic areas of exploration, and it is frequently the case that developments in one discipline can have a significant impact on related research in others. Somewhat surprisingly, a number of philosophers have also been active in the development of cognitive science, so much so that philosophy is sometimes included as one of the primary disciplines involved.[7]

As a field of research, cognitive science is organized into well-delineated areas of investigation. Research into the human capacity for language stands as a case in point. Such research has been and still is dominated by the thinking of Noam Chomsky, philosopher and linguist at MIT, who in the late 1950s proposed that all languages share a basic grammatical structure and, furthermore, that our language ability is made possible by a special language module in the brain. Chomsky's approach to language not only revolutionized the field of linguistics but connected the discipline to psychology and eventually to neuroscience as well. Chomsky's claims influenced and inspired such diverse research initiatives as the study of childhood language development, simulations of language production by computers, and the investigation of language abilities in apes. While Chomsky's approach is not without its detractors, it has led to patterns of research that will continue whether or not all of his claims are vindicated. That is to say, the study of language within cognitive science has become an established subfield, significantly independent of the paradigm that inspired it.

A field of research is never completely independent of the paradigm that inspired it, and there is often as much continuity as discontinuity, however reluctant the protagonists of competing research programs may be to admit it. While physics is no longer, strictly speaking, Newtonian in character, modern physics still possesses many of the same values and standards of the earlier, Newtonian era, manifested in its commitment to rigorous standards of testing and falsification, emphasis on mathematical models, and concern that experimental results be, where possible, reproducible. Likewise, modern cognitive scientists might differ on a number of important issues but nonetheless share a commitment to experimental procedure and reproducibility as well as many theoretical commitments.

Because of this, it may be best to think of cognitive science—and perhaps every scientific field—as a *trajectory*, characterized by core commitments and theories that have evolved over time but which also retain some continuity. While much of early cognitive science focused on symbolic and rational thought and often used the digital computer as a literal inspiration, modern cognitive science has expanded to include new domains (such as research into emotion) and shifts in thinking. Contemporary cognitive science takes the peculiar architecture of the brain much more seriously than early cognitive scientists did, and further developments have emphasized the importance of body and environment as well. Nevertheless, these developments are in many ways based on research provided by an earlier generation, made possible both by their successes and by their failures.

While each of these understandings of cognitive science has its place, I will engage the cognitive sciences primarily as a trajectory. As a field, cognitive science is characterized both by core commitments and theoretical disagreements. As a science, it elaborates and tests theories much in the way that other sciences do. Yet, also as a science, empirical data can eventually cause the demise of some theories and the development of new ones. The result is that, while cognitive science has made significant strides, there is much that we still do not know and thus much yet to be discovered.

The Grand Tour

Early cognitive scientists thought the brain irrelevant for understanding the mind. For them, the mind was like a computer and so could be understood as the programmed software that runs on the hardware of the mind. Since any individual program could, at least in theory, be run on any number of different computers, the hardware was unimportant, except for the limitations it set on processing speed, memory capacity, and reliability. Such assumptions potently informed both cognitive psychology and artificial intelligence research for decades.

It now appears that such an assumption was profoundly mistaken. Not only is the brain quite different from a serial digital computer, a version of which now sits in almost every office in the developed world, but it turns out that the particular architecture of the brain is quite significant for understanding who we are as persons and why we tend to think and act in the peculiar ways we do. As we shall see, however, the significance of the brain is only part of a more important lesson: it is becoming increasingly clear that a full understanding of the human person requires a radically integrative approach that acknowledges not only that we have minds and brains but that the brain/mind is itself intricately tied to the biology of our bodies as well as to our physical and social environments. We are not simply minds and not simply brains but rather a social/bodied/mind/brain.

Nevertheless, as our knowledge of the brain has grown, neuroscience has increasingly taken center stage in any appropriate understanding of the mind and of ourselves as persons. It is perhaps of little wonder, for the brain, a mere three pounds of gray flesh, is possibly the greatest wonder of the universe. This is a stunning claim, given the sheer size of the cosmos and the existence of such oddities as black holes and curved space. Yet, barring the discovery of more advanced life (whatever that would imply) on some distant planet, the human brain is the single most complex physical object that we know of. This fact is perhaps some small comfort in the context of our apparent insignificance in the great expanses of time and space that physicists have revealed to us. We are perhaps not so insignificant after all.

To begin to appreciate this, however, requires a tour not of the very large but the very small. It is worth observing that while our brains are quite large (both in absolute and relative terms) when compared with those of most of our animal relatives, it is nevertheless of such modest size as to fit into a medium-size mixing bowl. The earliest computers, by contrast, took up whole rooms while being able to perform only basic calculations. More closely related to us, the blue whale's brain is more than three times larger, yet not nearly as sophisticated. Size is not everything.

Truly to appreciate the brain, however, we must go much smaller yet. While a rudimentary awareness of the nervous system had existed since Galen's time (third century, B.C.E.), it was not until the nineteenth century that neurons began to be identified as the basic building blocks of the nerves and the brain. The reason is their size. Neurons are no more than a mere 70 microns (a millionth of a meter or .001 millimeters) in width, although in length some can be as long as the spinal chord (P. M. Churchland 1986). Each neuron is a nucleated cell but is distinctive in its ability to communicate with other neurons, typically sending electrochemical messages out along the axons and receiving them via the dendrites (figure 2.1)

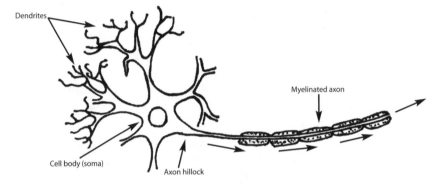

Fig. 2.1. Diagram of a motor neuron

Although there are a number of different kinds of neurons in the brain that play varying roles, it is the communicative ability of neurons that make them so remarkable. The dendrites of one neuron are linked to the axons of another, separated by only a minute gap called the synapse. In a complex electrochemical process, any electrical impulse received by the dendrites from the adjoining axons from neighboring neurons are sent down the neuron and on to its own axons where, if the energy potential is sufficient, they "spike" and send the electrical signal to the next neuron. In the process, the neuron itself is altered, privileging some patterns of firing over others. There is no such thing, then, as a solitary neuron. Neurons exist to communicate, and it is these communications that make up the primary activities of the brain. The familiar brain-wave patterns dramatized in many a television show are a measure of the average firing frequency of large numbers of neurons working together. The magic of modern PET (positron emission tomography) and fMRI (functional magnetic resonance imaging) scans allow us to view, at least indirectly, such neuron activity by measuring the increased blood flow associated with active neurons.

Such dramatic visualization, however, is possible only because so many neurons are at work. It is estimated that there are around 100 billion neurons in the human brain. The typical neuron, in turn, can have anywhere from 3,000 to 10,000 connections, suggesting a likely 100 trillion (10^{14}) synaptic connections. The number is staggering to contemplate. Owen Flanagan observes that if a neuron is capable of 10 different states (a modest estimate), then the number of possible brain states (at least in theory) would be 10 to the power of 10^{14}, or 100,000,000,000,000, far exceeding the estimated number of particles in the universe.[8] On the most basic level, there is little doubt that every one of us is literally unique.

Knowing about neurons, however, is not enough. In order for the neurons to do their jobs they have to be organized in particular ways, the secrets of which current neuroscience is attempting to unravel. The gross anatomy and structure of the brain have been known for centuries. This gross anatomy appears to be largely a result of our particular evolutionary pathway. In the 1970s neuroscientist Paul MacLean spoke suggestively of the triune nature of the brain, noting that we share with reptiles the structures of the lower brain, such as the brain stem, while the developed midbrain (including the cerebellum, hypothalamus, and amygdala) we have in common with other mammals, leaving much of our highly developed cerebrum or neocortex as our truly distinguishing feature.[9] MacLean's anatomical divisions are useful to the extent that they highlight some of the salient features of brain organization. Many of our most basic functions, such as autonomic control of essential life support systems (heartbeat, breathing, temperature regulation) and significant elements of the fight-or-flight response, are clearly controlled by structures in the brain stem that are similar to those found in reptiles, while the elements of the limbic system responsible for emotion, such as the amygdala and hippocampus, can be found among our fellow mammals.

The human neocortex, by contrast, is unusual in its comparative size (approximately three times larger than that of a chimpanzee, our nearest living relative) and in being the primary seat of many of the elements, such as reasoning and language, which are usually considered unique to humankind. The neocortex has two distinguishing physical features. Its surface is unusual (at least when compared to other animals) in its wrinkly appearance. Surprisingly, the folds have a function, for much of the most important activity of the neocortex happens on the surface, and the folds serve to expand the total surface area of the neocortex. The neocortex is also marked by the fact that it is divided into two hemispheres, connected by a structure called the corpus callosum. Both features indicate the extent to which the neocortex has developed in human beings beyond even our nearest biological relatives, the chimpanzees, whose folding and lateralization are much less pronounced.

The notion of a triune brain, while initially useful, is ultimately misleading, for it suggests that everything that is "advanced" is in the neocortex while everything that is "primitive" is in the lower brain, suggesting as well that the later parts of the brain are simply added onto the earlier ones. It would be more accurate to say that, while the brain structures have remained the same, it is the brain as a whole that

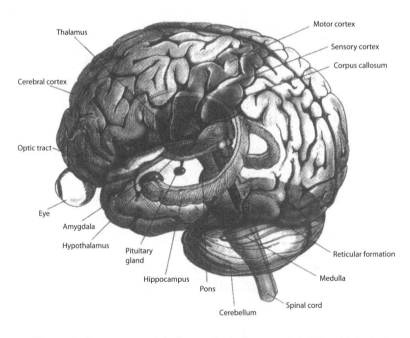

Fig. 2.2. Basic structures of the human brain. [From Brain, Mind, and Behavior by Floyd E. Bloom, Charles A. Nelson, Arlyne Lazerson © 1985, 1988, 2001 by Educational Broadcasting Corporation. Used with the permission of Worth Publishers.]

has evolved and that some of the areas of the lower brain are intimately associated with the proper functioning of the higher brain. While we may share much of our limbic system (the areas of the brain responsible for emotional processing) with other mammals, it is connected in important ways to our unique neocortex.

The gross anatomy of the brain, while important, does not tell us how the brain works. Likewise, neurons by themselves also do not tell us how the brain works. That answer lies somewhere in between these poles, and it has proved very hard to grasp. Neuroscientists who have taken a bottom-up approach have learned that neurons do not act alone but in concert with other neurons. Any individual neuron is itself part of a larger population dedicated to specific functions and activated under specific conditions. Such work can give the kind of precision that scientists dream of, but it has obvious inherent limits. The sheer scale of the human brain makes this sort of detailed analysis at any sufficient level virtually impossible—not to mention the fact that we cannot generally open up people's heads while they are thinking. Scanning technologies do not pick up individual neurons, and it is unlikely they ever will. Work with animals can be more successful, although the closer we get to human beings the more complicated the story becomes. The nervous system of *aplysia californica* (a common sea slug) for instance, has been completely mapped out. Much of our knowledge about the mechanics of vision comes from studies done with cats, but even here the knowledge we have is at a much more general level than that of the individual neuron.

Consequently, most of our knowledge of how the brain works comes from a more top-down approach. Generally speaking, we have learned that certain parts of the brain are associated with certain kinds of functions. One of the first studies that revealed this kind of localization, by Paul Broca in 1863, noted a correlation between a loss of speech production and damage to an area in the left hemisphere of the neocortex (an area now called Broca's area).[10] As modern neuroscience rapidly developed in the mid-1950s, discovery of these sorts of localizations developed at a rapid pace. Wilder Penfield, in a dramatic case, found that he could directly activate memories and sensations of patients undergoing brain surgery by electronically stimulating exposed areas of the brain during exploratory surgery, a technique that led to further mapping of areas associated with language and motor skills.[11] Until recently, most of our knowledge about localization came from patients with brain damage, and it is only with the development of advanced scanning techniques that we can actually observe this sort of localization fairly directly. As a result, large numbers of these correlations are now known, involving everything from emotion to reason to face recognition. Voluntary motor functions, for instance, are clearly mapped out across the middle of the neocortex and even follow in order the actual physical organization of the body (head at top, feet at bottom).

What the localization *implies* is another story. Some cognitive scientists argue that the brain is composed of a large number of distinct and separate modules. Each module serves a particular function and is optimally designed for that function. The mind, claim some, is like a Swiss army knife, replete with all sorts of useful gadgets that help us survive, whether it is on the wild savanna of aeons past or on the streets of New York City. Others argue that the modularist position presupposes an untenable isolation of brain units. Language, once thought to be highly localized, involves not only many regions of the left hemisphere of the neocortex but includes portions of the right as well. While the processing of memories involves specific areas of the brain (damage to which can result in forms of amnesia), the memories themselves seem to be redundantly stored in many areas, with the result that degenerative diseases such as Alzheimer's leads to gradual (albeit eventually debilitating) memory loss. These cognitive scientists argue that the brain functions holistically and that the search for specific modules is misguided. Antonio Damasio's work on the integration of emotion and reason is often taken to typify this approach.[12]

As I will demonstrate below, this debate is part of a larger debate on holism and reductionism that has important ramifications for understanding the mind as well as ripple effects for theological thinking. It reveals both the extent and limitation of our current knowledge about the brain. We know a great deal about what goes on in the brain and where as well as what happens when damage to particular areas occurs. We also know a great deal about how individual neurons behave and, to a lesser extent, how they behave in groups. What we do not know—and in a spectacular way—is exactly how the activity of neurons, when multiplied by millions and billions and even trillions, can ultimately produce things like memories of an autumn day and the exquisiteness of a sonnet. It is as if a laptop computer with a long-lived battery was suddenly dropped on the University of Paris in the Middle Ages. After some experimentation, scholars might well figure out how to operate it and to even use basic application programs. Prying open the computer would reveal circuit boards and, if they had multiple laptops, they could experimentally damage different areas and see the effects of, for instance, disconnecting the soundboard or floppy disk drive. Such knowledge, however, is not sufficient to understand how the computer works, for there is no awareness either of the complex microcircuitry present in each computer chip or of the complex set of instructions contained in the software that makes the computer and its operations run.

Cognitive scientists find themselves in a similar situation. Our minds are not laptop computers, but we lack the crucial information of how "it all comes together," the miracle steps between individual neurons, gross anatomy, and behavior. We may not be as bad off as the medieval scholars, for our ignorance is not as complete as theirs was. But it is significant; therefore, to fill these gaps, cognitive scientists have needed to develop models of the kinds of activities that can connect neurons to sonnets. Since its inception, the dominant model has been the computer. It has been a controversial one as well.

The Mind as an Information Processor

On the one hand, computers seem an unlikely choice for a model of the mind. The earliest computers could perform only the most routine of functions, were rigid in their performance (spawning such phrases as "garbage in, garbage out"), and prone to frequent breakdowns. Computers cannot play, walk, or have fun. After more than fifty years of research and development, many of these limitations are still quite apparent. No one would invite the computer next door over for dinner.

On the other hand, the choice of computers seems almost inevitable. Philosophers of the Enlightenment saw the world as a great machine, and some extended this not only to the human body (as Descartes did) but to the mind as well. Julien Offray de La Mettrie, for instance, was inspired by a mechanical flute player and saw the human mind as an extension of the same principles.[13] Of course, the model of the machine provided absolutely no insight as to how the mind actually works, and it is perhaps to Descartes's credit that he took the principle of mechanism only so far. By the early twentieth century, psychologists such as William James used the metaphor of telephone switchboards.[14] While switchboards perhaps suggested the communicative role of neurons and the "blooming, buzzing" confusion that James understood as the hallmark of consciousness, their potential as a model was obviously limited.

Computers, by contrast, not only suggested strong parallels to the level of neurons but could also perform the very kind of logical tasks that for millennia have been understood as the hallmark of the human species. Computers can do math and even play a good game of checkers. Computers can remember strings of data and then manipulate that data according to preset rules. Theoretical work done by Alan Turing suggested that a serial processor (now called a Turing machine) could perform any conceivable rational task. Additionally, the computer seemed to provide a model for resolving the relationship between mind and body. Historically, the philosophical options have primarily been between dualism, which insisted upon a distinction between mind and body, and materialism, which contended that the mind was no more than a ghost in the machine, as Gilbert Ryle put it.[15] Turing-machine computers, however, were dualist in a way that a materialist could accept, distinguishing between the hardware of the physical computer circuits and the software of the programs, which provided the instructions for what the hardware did. Perhaps the human mind worked in a similar fashion, the brain being merely the hardware (or, more appropriately, "wetware") for the software of the mind.

The model of the computer inspired a number of insights into the human brain that were later confirmed by empirical experiment. An early instance of this line of thinking was George Miller's demonstration of the limitation of short-term memory to seven items. Moreover, Noam Chomsky's argument for a language module in the brain has led to extensive research both in the study of the localization of language in the brain as well as the development of language in children. Work by David Marr and others on visual processing, in turn, has provided insights into the discrete steps required for making sense out of a visual environment.[16]

This computational model, while embraced with considerable enthusiasm, had a number of drawbacks, many of which emerged only gradually as the limitations of computers and the differences between brains and computers became more apparent. Culturally, the notion of computer intelligence spawned collective horror, manifested in any number of science-fiction plots of computers run amok, perhaps the most famous being *2001: A Space Odyssey*. Critics like Hubert Dreyfuss and Joseph Weizenbaum pointed out the obvious limitations of computers compared with human abilities as well as the potentially dehumanizing import of reducing the human person to the categories of information processing.[17] To many of these criticisms, cognitive scientists and especially artificial intelligence (AI) researchers issued promissory notes, sometimes with justification. Those who claimed that computers could never beat a human being at chess have had to beat a steady retreat over the past half century. Alan Turing's promise of a "thinking machine" by the year 2000, however, now appears to have been presumptuously naïve.

The death knell for this early computationalism came from two different sources. The first was the obvious fact that, once one got beyond the surface similarities of logic gates and neurons, the brain did not seem to have much resemblance to the traditional picture of a Turing machine either in its structure or in its operation. There did not seem to be any one central processor in the brain nor an identifiable software or "language of thought," as philosopher Jerry Fodor put it.[18] Neuroscientists were reluctant to employ the computational metaphor with the same zeal as did cognitive scientists, for the simple reason that it was of much more limited use for their own research.

The second problem arose within AI research itself. Known as the "frame problem," it became increasingly apparent that for a computer to perform many of the most basic human actions, such as going to a restaurant and ordering from a menu, requires the writing of programs so complex as to be impossible to put into practice. Too frequently, the computer would come to a situation that the programmer did not (and in many cases could not) anticipate, and it would simply stop running. Something clearly was wrong.

Rather than abandon the computational model, many turned to newly developed connectionist or parallel distributed processing(PDP) models of human cognition. Traditional serial digital computers required a central processor where all the instructions of the program are carried out (figure 2.3). A parallel processor, in contrast, breaks up tasks into smaller units, which are then carried out by a number of processors at the same time ("in parallel").[19]

These smaller units were organized into "neural networks," which required some initial programming but were designed to work on their own (figure 2.4). Each node in the network was assigned a value (often

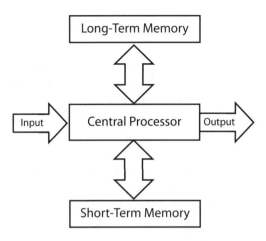

Fig. 2.3. Schematic of a serial computer

called a "weight"), which could change as new information was presented. Such parallel processors and neural networks proved to be vastly superior to traditional serial computers at a variety of tasks, most notably difficult cases of pattern recognition such as human faces. Networks would be programmed with an initial set of parameters and then

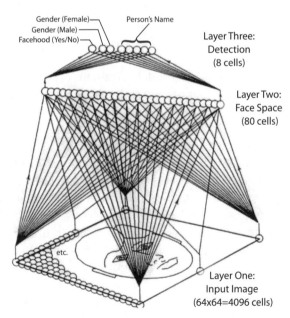

Fig. 2.4. An example of a neural network designed to recognize faces.
[From *The Engine of Reason, the Seat of the Soul* by Paul M. Churchland (1995) by MIT Press. Used with permission from MIT Press.]

trained on a series of example faces, with positive and negative feedback depending on whether the face was identified correctly.

Neural networks were designed with the brain itself as a model but, once successful, have themselves become a model for thinking about how the brain operates. In a neural network, the distinction between hardware and software becomes blurred as the programming takes place in the arrangements and strengths of the individual nodes. The distinction between programmer and program also becomes blurred, inasmuch as it is the computer itself doing the learning and therefore self-programming. Many designers of neural networks will cheerily admit that they have no idea what the exact weights are and therefore what the exact program is. The important thing is that it works astonishingly well at certain kinds of tasks.

Computer neural networks do seem accurately to mimic several of the most important aspects of neural behavior, and it thus does seem legitimate to speak of the brain itself as a vast collection of such networks. But there are differences as well. Current computer neural networks have no analogue to neurotransmitters, which, among other things, play an important role in emotional states. While the evidence for thinking of the brain as a layered collection of such networks is strongly suggestive, it is certainly not the final word. So the question remains: Is the mind/brain a sophisticated computer? If so, what kind of computer is it?

Critics of computational models argue that the computer is precisely the wrong model for understanding it. While some of these criticisms will be discussed below, it is worth mentioning two here. Gerald Edelman, a neuroscientist and Nobel laureate, opposes computational approaches to understanding the brain and advocates instead an approach inspired by Darwin's account of natural selection. Edelman's criticisms, however, seem aimed only at serial-processor Turing-machine models, not the more recent parallel processors and neural networks. Indeed, he endorses these newer approaches and even endorses recent AI research with robots, which can learn to perceive objects and act accordingly. Interestingly, he limits the term "computer" to the traditional serial computer, and coins his own term, "noetics," to describe this more recent research.[20]

Others, such as Roger Penrose, argue that computational models of any stripe simply miss important aspects of the mind, especially consciousness.[21] Such critics claim that there are yet undiscovered principles that underlie the operations of the brain and that what is needed is perhaps a new understanding of physics or even a recognition of the limitations of science and our own understanding. Such concerns have been prompted not least by the extreme literalism with which some cognitive scientists have pursued the computational model. Work in the 1970s and early 1980s on mental imagery, for instance, drew significant criticism because, it was claimed, mental images could not exist because computers do not have them.[22]

The brain is clearly not a Turing machine. Moreover, it is quite possible that the brain is also not simply a PDP processor and that there are basic principles at work that have yet to be discovered and described. But the history of cognitive science has shown that computational models have been enormously fruitful for thinking about the mind and brain and for inspiring research programs and ideas, even though the models themselves are flawed and sometimes misleading. Philosopher Barbara Von Eckardt has argued that, while some have taken and do take computational models literally, such models have been most beneficial as inspirational metaphors.[23] The brain can be understood as an information processor, and to realize that this is a major function of the brain is an important insight. Nevertheless, it is a mistake to limit our understanding of the brain and mind by the still modest computers of our day.

Because of the limitations of modern computers, some would argue that computational models should be abandoned altogether. But, if the recent history of cognitive science shows anything, it is that our notion of what counts as a computer has evolved alongside of our growing knowledge of the mind and brain. As AI moves increasingly into robotics, these models will change again, but such changes will be mutually reflective of developments in other cognitive science related fields until we are able actually to construct a robot with truly human characteristics or until the differences between flesh and blood and silicon and metal become apparent.

The Situated Mind/Brain

Early cognitive science frequently took what may be called a "brain in a vat" approach. Influenced by the model of Turing-machine computers, it was assumed that the mind could be treated in isolation from all other elements. Indeed, since the mind was perceived to be the software of the brain, cognitive scientists saw the mind as something very much akin to Descartes's *res cogitans,* a nonextended thinking thing that depended only incidentally on the limitations and peculiar histories of the physical world. As such, the mind could be studied in isolation from its biological context, which in their view provided merely the scaffolding that allowed the mind to operate.

Discoveries in neuroscience have served at least partially to correct this approach, for one of the indications of neuroscientific research is that the way our minds work is significantly due to the particular construction of the brain and (by extension) to an evolutionary history that has made the kind of skills we possess optimal for survival. To understand the mind requires understanding of the brain and the close link between the two. For this reason, some prefer to speak not just of the mind or of the brain but rather of the mind/brain, indicating that one cannot be fully understood without the other.[24] There is much that is right in this approach, inasmuch it is our brain in particular that marks us as significantly different from other species. But it is becoming increasingly apparent that to isolate the mind/brain is itself too great an abstraction and that to understand the proper functioning of the mind/brain requires also an understanding of biological and environmental contexts.

It is now well understood that genes play an important role in brain development, although precisely how they do so, particularly in the case of the brain, is unclear. The recent discovery that there are only approximately 30,000 active genes in the human genome makes clear that, whatever the case may be, genes do not program the brain synapse by synapse. Yet it is clear that genes do play an important role in brain development. Studies done with identical twins separated at birth provide strong evidence for an important genetic factor for IQ scores, and similar studies show a range of correlations for behavioral profiles, even suggesting some influence on our political proclivities.[25]

Gerald Edelman has argued that brain development is best understood as a kind of Darwinian process.[26] Brain development shortly after birth is characterized by massive die-off of neurons in the brain, the reason for this being that we are apparently born with far more neurons than we need. Rather than simply being born with all our hardware and software preinstalled (as someone from the old Turing-machine approach might argue), our brain learns on the job, with the

effect that during our early years our brain is literally wiring and programming itself. Those neuron groups that end up operating func-
tionally survive; those that do not eventually die off and are disposed
of. As a result, the physical and social environment plays a massively
important role in brain and therefore mental development. One of the
clearest examples of this is language development, much of which
occurs during the crucial first three years of life. In the few tragic cases
where children have been deprived of experiencing spoken language
during these early years, language development can occur but is significantly stunted.[27] There is good reason to believe that emotional development is similarly linked to brain development. Recent evidence
suggests that this development continues throughout adolescence. The
areas of the brain associated with foresight and planning are not fully
developed in teenagers, a finding that will come as little surprise to
most parents.[28]

A significant number of researchers in these areas argue that the relevant conclusion is much more basic than that genes and environment
are important for developing a healthy brain. They argue that to
understand the mind/brain in isolation from biological and environmental contexts is to understand nothing. This research shows that the
mind/brain can be understood only as an embodied mind/brain and
one that is environmentally and socially situated. It is not that we are
minds/brains who happen to have bodies but that we are bodies that
have particular kinds of mind/brains. The fact that we are embodied in
a particular way and in a particular environment is a significant part of
who we are, not only in an abstract sense but in the very physical construction of the brain itself.

Building on this approach, philosopher Andy Clark suggests that
not only are we influenced by our environment but in a real sense we
also become our environment. Clark illustrates this through the example of an Alzheimer's patient who, because of her failing memory, must
organize her apartment in such a way that she does not become a victim of her own forgetfulness. Basic necessities such as the bathroom
and food must be in visible line of sight so that they can be visually
focused on as a constant reminder of her original intent. For this individual, memory is not simply contained in the brain but in the structure of the room itself.[29] Such is an extreme case but, Clark contends,
we all do similar things with our own environments, from the student
who organizes her dorm to provide easy access to her CD collection to

the man who always leaves his keys in a certain drawer so that he can find them in the morning. Not only does the environment influence our thinking, says Clark, but the environment in a real sense *becomes* our thinking.

These observations increasingly lead to an understanding of the human person that emphasizes history, context, and connection. In this context the distinctive capacities play a paramount role, but a brain alone does not produce a mind, let alone a person. To speak of the mind and, even more clearly, to speak of persons is to move beyond the brain alone and into a complex web of relationships. The spinning of a person is less like a printed book and more like a conversation, less like a program and more like a network.

The Cognitive Driver

Once again imagine yourself driving a car. You pull out of the driveway, carefully engaging brake and accelerator pedals, operating the transmission, and visually scanning for obstacles. After navigating several turns, stop signs, and stop lights, you enter the freeway. There you monitor the other traffic and your own speed while making appropriate lane changes and watching for landmarks and road signs that help you know when to exit. After several more similar operations, you arrive at your destination. All of it is done effortlessly. But how?

Cognitive science can tell us much about even this simple process. You know how to drive because of basic cognitive skills that every normal human being possesses. Sophisticated sense perception allows the observation and recording of data that can be stored, retrieved, and analyzed. Our immense memory and linguistic abilities allow for the accumulation of large quantities of data, and our sophisticated reasoning skills enable us to infer and deduce, testing our ideas in the real world or even imagining what would happen if testing is impractical or too dangerous. To drive skillfully requires a large array of background knowledge, gathered through observation and study, then developed through a brief trial and error period during which we develop the requisite motor skills and apply our knowledge or lack thereof to the open road.

For a cognitive scientist, the simple act of making a left turn involves a complex array of activities. In making the left turn, you likely already have a mental map of where you are going. Such a mental map involves both long-term and short-term memory as well as rational skills that allow you to locate yourself within the map and calculate the most viable route to where you are going. As you approach the intersection, you engage in a complex array of motor skills, from operating the brake and accelerator pedals to flicking the turn signal without even looking. These actions are learned so well that they are performed largely below the level of consciousness, which is primarily concerned with the continually updated visual and auditory images provided by a rather sophisticated sensory detection system. If one were inclined, a chart could be made of the processes involved, the arrows indicating the flow of information, the boxes indicating where information is analyzed, processed, and stored. On this analysis, driving a car is a process of receiving, analyzing, and acting on information that is gleaned primarily from the environment.

This, however, is only the beginning of analysis. One chapter cannot give a full sense of the depth and breadth of cognitive science as a field, but I hope at least to have given a taste of its character. More importantly, I hope to have provided a sense of the importance of cognitive science for understanding and ultimately for thinking theologically about the human person. Theologically speaking, we are spiritual beings, but we are quite significantly embodied spiritual beings. Furthermore, our spirit is not simply an abstraction or supernatural substance. If we take the cognitive sciences seriously, what makes us spiritual beings is our very brainy embodiment. Realizing this is the first step in grasping the significance cognitive science might have for the theological enterprise.

PART TWO

MINDING PERSONS

3

Fitting Square Pegs into Round Wholes: The Problem of Consciousness

Of all the mysteries of the mind, the greatest is consciousness. On the face of it, it is not clear why this should be the case. The increase of our knowledge of the brain since the beginning of the twentieth century is astonishing, and the pace of discovery has only accelerated in recent decades. Brain imaging technologies now allow us in ways previously undreamed-of to look at the mind and brain in action in a variety of situations. Consciousness, however, continues to elude us. Brain scans do not show a "consciousness module," and the way that our experiences come together so that the jumble of sounds, sights, and smells form the exquisite experience of blossoming flowers in spring remains, in important ways, a mystery.

Despite this elusiveness, cognitive scientists have shown an increasing interest in the subject of consciousness. Early cognitive science research tended to avoid the subject. Consciousness as a phenomenon was too ill-defined and our knowledge too poor to hazard anything beyond educated guesses. Mid-century philosophers, influenced by logical positivism and its offshoots, also thought little of the topic. There were other pressing matters to deal with, and consciousness, if it was considered even to exist, was left off the list.

As our knowledge has grown, however, the climate has changed. While we are still far from any scientific theory of consciousness, we now know enough at least to think intelligently about the subject in a way that was not possible several decades ago. But many of the old questions still bedevil us. The mind-body question, frequently declared either dead or resolved, has yet to receive any clear consensus. In the interim, there has been much fire and occasionally some light in a debate that includes philosophers as much as it does scientists. One might expect this to be the case, for the question of consciousness strikes at the heart of who we are. At stake are the most basic of questions: Who am I? What am I? Is there such a thing as human nature and, if so, what is it?

Because of this, the question of consciousness is important for theology as well. According to the biblical tradition humans are created in the image of God and yet, because of their sinfulness, are in need of salvation. Theologians have subsequently grappled with the meaning of these primal claims in order to understand our predicament more fully as well as to understand the salvific claim that the gospel makes on us.

What Is Consciousness?

The initial perplexity in the attempt to understand consciousness is the meaning of the term itself. It might seem that consciousness is one term whose meaning should be self-evident. We all share consciousness; it differentiates us from rocks and trees and automobiles. A blow to the head, anesthesia, or simply falling asleep can cause us to lose consciousness. Science fiction and fantasy narratives are replete with examples of creatures—zombies, robots, and golems—who appear to have consciousness but really do not. While sometimes we may be fooled, ultimately they give themselves away, usually by their lack of emotional response and social awareness.

This very intuitiveness, however, makes consciousness difficult to define. Consciousness is not *like* anything else. While we are intimately familiar with our own conscious awareness, we cannot perceive the conscious states of others directly but can only infer them from outward behavior. We can therefore only imagine what it is like to be someone else. The problem becomes more acute when we think of other species because, while we regularly attribute conscious states to dogs, cats, and other animals, we have only a vague notion (if that!) of what it would be like to be a dog or cat.

One result of this has been a strong tendency, on the part of psychologists and philosophers alike, to dismiss the reality of consciousness. One strand of this thought began with the eighteenth-century philosopher David Hume, who argued that in introspection one never finds an "I" that is above and separate from one's own experiences.[1] Following this line of thought, William James was similarly skeptical about being able to identify a unified knower behind cognitive processes. For James, life began as a "blooming, buzzing confusion" that meshed very poorly with traditional metaphysical claims about an immortal soul or transcendent self.[2] Psychological and philosophical behaviorists, who in many ways dominated their respective fields during the mid-twentieth century, only reinforced this skepticism. Gilbert Ryle's famous demotion of the soul or higher-order self to a "ghost in the machine" represented the dominant mind-set of its day.[3] Consciousness could neither be observed directly nor studied scientifically. Therefore it does not exist.

The problem is not so easily solved. The behaviorist position barely needs refuting and ultimately collapsed under its own absurdities. But, while both Hume's argument and James's phenomenology are often taken to be attacks on consciousness, they are really questioning the concept of a unified (often transcendent) knower, a quite separate albeit related question. Those who apply Hume's argument to consciousness have not proved its nonexistence but merely redefined it.

Philosopher David Chalmers has observed that the redefinition of consciousness in order to make it a suitable subject of investigation is a common occurrence, both in philosophy and in cognitive science.[4] Generally speaking, the approach here is to understand consciousness in terms of one of several closely related functions. That function can then be explained by means of biology or computer models and so, the argument goes, the existence and nature of consciousness are satisfactorily explained. Thus, for instance, consciousness is frequently conflated with attention. Attention is clearly an important biological trait, and it is strongly associated with consciousness as well. We are aware of what we are attentive to. To be inattentive, however, is not the same thing as being unconscious, and we are often aware of things that are outside the scope of attention. Noted biologist Francis Crick identifies consciousness with our experience of a visual field and, in providing a hypothesis that could explain how the visual field comes together, Crick claims to have explained consciousness as well.[5] More commonly, consciousness is identified with self-consciousness, where self-consciousness primarily means some sort of self-knowledge or ability to monitor and represent one's self.

Chalmers refers to these endeavors as attempts to solve what he calls the "easy problem of consciousness." By easy, he does not mean that it is simple or simplistic. In most cases it is anything but that! Instead, Chalmers means that these approaches present solutions to phenomena related to consciousness while not truly explaining consciousness itself. Crick could indeed be right about the visual field, but this would not truly be an explanation of consciousness. One can be conscious without a visual field. Although it is a real question whether one could be conscious without any sensory experience, to identify consciousness with sensory processing itself would be a mistake. Likewise, while self-knowledge, at least in humans, is an important component of our awareness, it is not the same thing. Indeed, somewhat paradoxically, it is not clear that consciousness is required for self-consciousness or self-knowledge at all. Our immune system distinguishes self from others. Lobsters, as Daniel Dennett pointed out, have enough self-knowledge to not eat their own limbs, but it is not clear that this means they are conscious.

Chalmers contrasts the "easy question" of consciousness with what he calls the "hard question," namely, the fact of consciousness itself. Why should there be subjective experience at all? Why is not the world populated with zombies who perform exactly as we do but experience nothing? A number of philosophers, skeptical of questions that seem unexplainable, have denied that this is even a legitimate question. For them, consciousness is nothing more than the representations we have of the world.

This viewpoint seems less prevalent than it once was. Many have argued, for instance, that the problem of qualia (the subjective qualities of an object, like the redness of an apple or the sweetness of sugar), brings up the hard question of consciousness in a way that is undeniable. Why does the color red appear just as it does, bright and brilliant, yet indescribable except in relation to other colors? Presumably we perceive objects as being red because light of a certain wavelength bounces off an object and into our eyes. But this is only part of the story, for the color we perceive is actually dictated by a number of factors, such as ambient lighting and adjoining color perceptions. Red is clearly a construct of the mind. Complex neural mechanisms no doubt underlie this experience, but the question still remains: why the *experience* of red at all? Why should some brain processes constitute experience while others do not?

The question of subjective experience is *the* question of consciousness. To solve it from a scientific perspective requires not only finding the physical causes of consciousness but also discovering why those and only those physical causes produce consciousness while others do not. This last point is often never addressed, but it is the most crucial for, unless we have answered both elements of the question, we have not really answered the question at all.

Can Cognitive Science Tell Us Anything about Consciousness?

Cognitive science and neuroscience in particular presumably should be able to tell us a great deal about consciousness. Whatever its ultimate nature, consciousness is closely entangled with the activities of the brain, and there is little reason to believe that consciousness does not in fact arise out of the activities of the brain. Some brain regions cannot be damaged without a loss of consciousness, but it is not always clear whether and in what ways these areas are related to consciousness. What is clear is that there is no one area in the brain responsible for consciousness, either in the easy sense or in the hard sense, and that consciousness results from the interactions of several areas.

Earlier attempts to locate consciousness in the brain have been relatively sparse. René Descartes proposed the pineal gland as a conduit between the physical brain and the immortal soul, a choice inspired more by the necessity to specify *some* locus of interaction rather than on any true knowledge of brain functions. In the 1970s, Julian Jaynes proposed that consciousness arose as a result of the connection of the cerebral hemispheres by the corpus callosum, an evolutionary step he rather improbably placed shortly after the Homeric period.[6] In doing so, Jaynes attempted to link religious experience, schizophrenia, and the omnipresence of the gods in ancient literature. Time has been no more kind to his thesis than to Descartes's.

Increased knowledge of the brain and growing scientific interest in consciousness, however, have begun to produce more interesting proposals. Gerald Edelman and Antonio Damasio have independently put forth models of consciousness that are quite similar in many ways.[7] Edelman argues that we must differentiate between primary consciousness, associated with perception, and higher-order consciousness, which is associated with language and self-consciousness. For Edelman, primary consciousness arises out of the construction of a "scene," a unified experience of our surroundings and state of being. The construction of the scene requires the participation of the thalamus and areas of the cortex. Edelman also suggests, however, that the experience of this scene is also linked to our value systems, and so consciousness must also include the limbic systems, which are associated with emotion. Those areas of the brain, furthermore, have highly integrated "reentrant circuits" that provide rapid feedback, thus enabling the experience of a "movie-in-the brain." By identifying which brain areas are involved, Edelman claims that we can also determine which other animals are conscious as well. Snakes probably are, depending on the temperature, but lobsters are not.[8]

While Damasio uses different language and has different emphases, he makes much the same argument. For Damasio, core (or primary) consciousness arises out of the body's need to map itself in relation to objects. The need for this mapping is continual and central for survival. Like Edelman, Damasio names the brain structures he believes are primarily involved and, like Edelman, concentrates on the thalamus and areas of the cerebral cortex. Like Edelman, Damasio emphasizes the integration of emotions. Consciousness is the *feeling* of what happens.

Edelman and Damasio are respected scientists, and their proposals, built on extensive research, deserve serious consideration. But they are proposals yet to be fully tested and in that sense remain beyond the current science. More importantly, both Edelman and Damasio choose to tackle the easy problem of consciousness. Like Francis Crick, both Edelman and Damasio associate consciousness with the development of a "scene." Having explained the possible neurological basis for the scene, consciousness is said to be explained as well. To be sure, both Edelman and Damasio seem aware of the larger issue of the hard question but, because it is untreatable by current neuroscience, it is ignored. In the meantime, the functional features of consciousness can be explored.

But what would it imply if Edelman and Damasio are on the right track? What would it mean if neuroscience could in fact eventually solve even the hard problem of consciousness? Despite being in its early stages, this endeavor has been the subject of much philosophical interest, and the lines are being drawn.

Consciousness as Function

Cognitive scientists and philosophers who have worked closely with their concerns have generally understood questions of the nature of the mind, including consciousness, in terms of functional processes. That is, contra Descartes, they did not view the mind as a separately existing substance that communicates by some conduit with the brain. Instead, because the mind is like a computer (so they claimed), thought could be understood to be something like a computer program, manipulating information in order to analyze and eventually prescribe appropriate behavioral output.[9] If this were so, it implied that terms like "thinking" and "consciousness" did not refer to a reified soul but to the symbolic operations of mental software run on the hardware of the brain. The mind, including consciousness, is the result of organization. Because the mind is characterized by symbolic processes, and it is the organization and sequence of these symbolic processes that characterize the mind, every activity of the mind can be understood as one or another kind of process. More visually, one can think of the mind as a pattern or sequence of events.

It is this sort of thinking that led to Noam Chomsky's argument for a language module in the brain.[10] In Chomsky's analysis, all individual languages share a common structure or "deep grammar," which follows the basic rules no matter what language you speak. This was possible, he argued, because there is, in effect, a preprogrammed module in the brain that we are all born with, and this module contains all the basic rules of grammar that makes language possible, even though details of vocabulary, word order, and the like vary from culture to culture.

On a functionalist approach, the understanding of consciousness must be quite similar in conception. For a functionalist, if consciousness is going to be said to exist, then it must be understood in terms of a particular kind of information processing. The only thing that needed to be determined was: what kind? Douglas Hofstadter, for instance, identified consciousness with self-consciousness and argued that it could be understood as the result of a recursive process where one level of the mind (one might say the mental program) analyzes and acts on another.[11] Consciousness was a sequence of operations, a pattern of a particular kind, and many were optimistic that its secrets would soon be found out.

As it became increasingly clear that the mind is not like a Turing machine, one might have expected functionalism to have fallen by the wayside as well. The old computational models were shown to be deficient, leaving out the important roles of emotions, the body, and the particular architecture and history of the brain. Arguably, the opposite has occurred. The functionalist approach, at least so far, seems to be integral to the trajectory of cognitive science, even as the field has increasingly moved away from the early Turing-machine model.

For many, the old Turing-machine models of the mind have been replaced by models based on connectionism and parallel distributed processors (PDP; see chapter 2, above). Philosopher Paul Churchland has eloquently developed this position, using computer models that have proved to be highly capable of emulating such basic cognitive tasks as face recognition to suggest that all of the mind/brain in fact operates as a parallel processor on a massive scale. Since there is no strict separation between hardware and software or between programmer and programmed in PDP models, the boundary between mind and brain collapses. But it is still the pattern of information processing that is all-important. It is the configuration of each neural net that, combined, gives rise to any particular behavior. Such configurations are a particular pattern of organization that can be described in terms of a phase

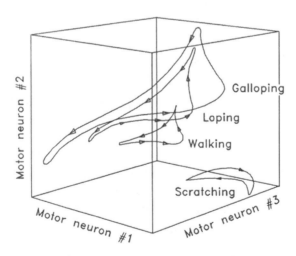

Fig. 3.1. A phase space for three motor neurons, mapping the possible range of interactive states. [From *The Engine of Reason, the Seat of the Soul* by Paul M. Churchland (1995) by MIT Press. Used with permission from MIT Press.]

space (figure 3.1) As with the Turing-machine model, it is this pattern, this organization that is all-important. Consciousness must therefore be a particular kind of pattern, in Churchland's case the result of a neural network that centralizes and manipulates representations.[12]

The approaches of both Damasio and Edelman are biologically oriented and do not rely as heavily on computational models. Edelman in particular argues that he does not rely on such models at all. Both are careful to approach the human mind through the particular biology of the brain as well as the broader contexts of body and evolutionary history. Despite these modifications, which are in some ways significant, both models remain essentially functionalist in character. In Damasio's theory, for instance, consciousness is a complex phenomenon that involves several processes that orient the organism in relation to objects in its environment. Such orientation necessarily involves a concept of self, for the organism must always have a sort of internal gyroscope that monitors bodily positions (head, eyes, arms, torso) in relation to one another as well as in relation to the object or objects. This object-organism relation is represented in the brain and involves the coming together of several complex streams of information, as the information from the senses (sight, sound, smell, etc.) must be coordinated with self-monitoring characteristics of what Damasio calls the proto-self. According to Damasio, this core consciousness of self and organism representation is connected to the more complex processes of the extended self in the human being, most notably language. In the end, the extended self draws on a great number of areas in the brain.

Consciousness, then, is the result of the functional relations of many areas of the brain, in particular those areas that are involved in various kinds of representation, whether it be of the organism itself or of the environment. These charts clearly imply that it is the functional relations and information bearing states that are important for understanding consciousness. Even more unmistakably, these accounts still imply that consciousness is primarily associated with information processing. While the computational language is not nearly as prominent (in Edelman's case it is disowned), the computational metaphor underlies the whole discussion. It seems that the conclusion remains that consciousness consists in a particular kind of information processing, a particular form of organization.

For a variety of reasons, functionalism has been severely criticized by a number of philosophers and some scientists over the decades.

Most criticism stems from the inconceivability of providing a satisfactory account of first-person conscious subjectivity from the seemingly sterile ground of information processing. While a number of these attacks apply most directly to Turing-machine functionalism, most tend to indict functionalism wholesale. Philosopher Thomas Nagel, for instance, has argued that truly to understand consciousness is to understand what it is like to be something.[13] Using the intriguing example of a bat, whose ability to perceive objects via echolocation is totally beyond our experience, Nagel points out that no account we might develop about the bat's brain and neurophysiology will ever be able to tell us what it would be like to be a bat. Although we may in fact even be able to construct our own bat models and determine what the bat would do in any given situation, there would still be that small but nevertheless hugely important gap. Because of this gap, Nagel claims, any functional explanation, based on neurology or otherwise, is doomed. A similar argument has been made by Frank Jackson.[14] In place of bats, Jackson asks us to imagine a completely color-blind neuroscientist named Mary attempting to study color vision. However much Mary studies color vision, down to the exact wiring of the brain and a precise understanding of which neural activities produce exactly which shade of red, she would still learn something more if she could have surgery and actually experience color herself. That there is something to be learned beyond the functional relations of the brain, argues Jackson, shows that functionalism cannot be the whole story.

An equally famous thought experiment proposed by John Searle asks you to imagine yourself locked in a room with a book that provides extensive instructions for translating Chinese sentences into grammatical English.[15] Even though the Chinese use pictograms that are totally unrecognizable to you, you could in theory still translate any Chinese document into English just by using the complex book of instructions. This, Searle argues, is precisely what a computer does. It follow sets of instructions without any higher-order grasp of the situation. Computers, argues Searle, are excellent at producing the appearance of syntax, grammatical arrangements, or more abstract sets of symbols. But computers are incapable of producing meaning or semantics, which is precisely what the human mind does on a regular basis—it assigns meanings to things. The result, says Searle, is that the mind, although undoubtedly based in the brain, cannot be merely a computer.

While these arguments have convinced many that functionalism must be fundamentally flawed, they have also drawn fire from defenders of functionalism. Paul Churchland, for instance, argued that Nagel and Jackson have confused a knowledge claim with a perspectival claim.[16] There is certainly a difference between knowing about something and actually experiencing it firsthand. Mary does not *know* anything more about color vision after having finally experienced it, but she does know about it quite differently, that is, from a first-person rather than a third-person perspective. Likewise, we would not know more about a bat by actually being in a bat's shoes (or wings), but we would know it differently than from a strictly neurological perspective.

Searle's argument has drawn a wide range of criticisms over the years. Interestingly, Searle does not see his argument as applying to connectionist models of the mind, which do not rely on rigid rules and formal programs in the way Turing machines do.[17] Connectionist models still remain essentially functionalist in character, so it is not clear that he is being consistent in this regard. A frequent criticism by his critics (e.g., Daniel Dennett) is that Searle's thought experiment ridiculously simplifies the situation. As anyone who is bilingual can attest, learning a language is not simply a matter of learning word equivalents in a dictionary, nor is it even learning to translate sentences in isolation.[18] Context is all-important to understanding the meaning of a document, as anyone who has used a computer translator on the internet can testify.

Furthermore, there are compelling reasons to suppose that a functionalist account of both the mind and even consciousness must be true. It is incontrovertible that the brain is the organ of the mind, however much we still use metaphors such as the heart to express our emotional center. The brain is the only organ of the body that causes mental impairment when it is damaged. Since the brain is composed primarily of neurons, and since neurons seem to function primarily as dynamic conveyors of information, it seems to follow that we must understand the activities of the mind primarily in terms of information processing. While thought experiments such as those put forward by Nagel, Jackson, and Searle often have an intuitive appeal, it could be that they are simply wrong. If so, it is only a matter of time before neuroscientists unlock the basic underpinnings of consciousness, even if, due to the sheer complexity of the brain, many of the fine-grained details must forever elude us.

Reductionism or Emergence?

If functionalism were true, what would it imply? Opinions on this are divided. For some, one of the benefits of Turing-machine functionalism is that it preserved for the mind a status that is irreducible to physical constituents. Because the "software" of the mind was distinct from the "hardware" of the brain, physicalist explanations were both unnecessary and wrong-headed. Even though Turing-machine functionalism is now widely seen as a failure, the notion that there are nonreducible qualities of the mind persists among many scholars, even though the distinctions are not as clear-cut as in the case of Turing machines.

For others, versions of the functionalist approach imply a strong reductionism. In the mid-1980s, Stephen Stich, Paul Churchland, and Patricia Churchland advocated eliminative materialism, arguing that only a detailed neuroscientific account could ever provide a satisfactory explanation of human cognition and behavior.[19] For them, modern psychology has been held hostage to a "folk psychology," whose accuracy should be understood as being analogous to the folk physics of ordinary people before Isaac Newton. So unsatisfactory is folk psychology's language of beliefs, intentional states, and emotions that it will need to be entirely replaced by a whole new vocabulary derived from the study of neurons and the brain. Taken to its extreme conclusion, the argument is that eventually we will cease to speak of love and speak instead of the chemical/neural complex that is said to underlie the rather vague and (to them) unsatisfying term.

This extreme form of reductionism, in which the category of mind is simply excised in favor of brain talk, has received harsh criticism, and the Churchlands have seemed to back off from some of their earlier, more extreme statements.[20] But reductionism persists in other forms. Francis Crick, for instance, has pursued a harshly reductionist line, arguing that "you, your joys and your sorrows, your memories and your ambitions, your sense of personal identity and free will, are in fact no more than the behavior of a vast assembly of nerve cells and their associated molecules."[21] The import of many versions of this approach is somewhat ambiguous. Thus Daniel Dennett through most of his career has made careful distinctions between (1) a physicalist stance, which understands systems in terms of their individual particles, (2) a design stance, which understands systems in terms of the ends they are intended to achieve, and (3) an intentional stance, which takes seriously the contents of thought as a means of understanding the total behavior of the organism. His commitment to such language, however, is unclear at best. While he claims that intentional states and artifacts constitute real patterns, he also describes them as useful fictions. For Dennett, consciousness itself is such a useful fiction, but it has no underlying reality. Consciousness itself is no mystery but is something of an illusion produced by the brain as it sorts through and continually revises multiple drafts of events while it interacts with the world. The intentional stance may be useful, but ultimately it is a fiction that is best explained by lower levels of physical analysis.

Opposed to these sorts of reductionism are advocates of nonreductive physicalism, who argue that the mind is an emergent phenomenon that is supervenient on brain states. Versions of emergentism have a long history, dating as far back as the 1920s in the work of C. D. Broad and, depending on how one understands the terms in question, even further.[22] In many ways, contemporary emergentists are modern-day advocates of Aristotle's hylomorphic account of the human person, which distinguished between the soul's formal cause and the body's material cause. Similarly, advocates of emergence argue that while understanding the physical constituents of a system is indeed important, such an understanding is not sufficient to explain complex systems. Complex systems feature emergent properties that are not reducible to the physical constituents and that are necessary for any proper understanding of the system in question.[23]

Key to the emergentist claim is the argument that complex systems reveal many different levels of organization and that these levels of organization are of such nature that they cannot be completely reduced, either epistemologically or ontologically, to their physical constituents. In most (but not all) cases, emergentists do not claim that there are any extra lower-level properties in question. In Arthur Peacocke's language, the mind is nothing more than the brain, meaning that there are no hidden materials or supernatural quantities that need to be invoked to explain the mind and consciousness. These emergent levels, rather, are characterized by organizational patterns that give rise to novel forms of behavior that are not predictable or comprehensible from reductive analysis alone.

The idea of emergence as a means of explaining the mind-body relation has been particularly popular among scholars in the science-religion dialogue as a means of providing an account of the human person that is consonant with both scientific and theological perspectives. Arthur Peacocke has argued at length for emergence as a category for understanding the appearance of novelty and increasing complexity in the universe. Peacocke's approach has been more specifically applied to the human person by Nancey Murphy and Philip Clayton. Murphy has argued for a position of nonreductive physicalism, understanding the human person and consciousness primarily in terms of related, interactive levels, with the conscious mind being an emergent property of the brain. For Murphy, the human being is purely a physical creature, albeit one ultimately created by God and capable of religious experience. Clayton also adopts the language of emergence and supervenience, but rejects the label of physicalism as conceding too much to a materialist/reductionist approach. Clayton, too, understands the conscious mind as an emergent property of lower levels, but is reluctant to identify these lower levels with those currently identified by the sciences. Murphy's account thus seems to understand emergence within the context of a closed and completely understood physical system, whereas Clayton seems to take an approach that sees our understanding of physical reality as significantly open and subject to change.

While there is considerable overlap among the different accounts of emergence, most fall into one of these two categories. The first and most analyzed category is that of closed-system emergence. In a closed system, all levels of a system are well understood and open to analysis, yet are resolutely irreducible, because the higher-order levels exhibit patterns and regularities that a lower-level explanation cannot explain. A wide number of examples have been used to illustrate the principles of closed-system emergence, including soldier termite jaws, steam engine regulators, ant colonies, and cellular automata.[24]

An excellent example of a closed emergent system is a computer running a chess program. The lowest level, that of the motion of electrons moving through copper wire and the like, is presumably well understood. A higher level of complexity is the hardware design, which includes logic gates, microchips, circuit boards, and memory storage devices. On an emergentist account, the complexity and significance of this design are not exhausted by the lower-level laws governing the motion of electrons, although such reductive analysis is tremendously important and has a role to play. Likewise, above the level of hardware design is the software design—in this case a chess program. The hardware is an organization of elementary particles. The software is an organization of the hardware (memory configurations and binary logic gates). The software, in turn, produces on the computer screen an image of a chess game. In discussing the emergent pattern of the program, it is not enough to refer to the total physical state of the computer at that time. What is significant about the software is that it contains a set of instructions and obeys rules of logic and does so in a way quite independently of the hardware and the electrons. Indeed, we could run the same pattern on a mechanical computer (like the old-fashioned adding machines) if we were so inclined. The independence of the program from any particular computer, so it is claimed, shows its emergent character.

When applied to the category of the mind—and consciousness in particular—versions of closed-system emergence have been widely adduced as the framework for providing a satisfactory physicalist account that avoids reductionism. Generally speaking, there has been widespread acceptance of the terminology of emergence but considerable controversy among philosophers over how the precise relationship should be characterized and, in particular, at what level causality should be understood. In other words, if the mind is said to supervene on the brain (where "supervenience" is used to denote an emergent relation), does the mind cause the brain to act, or does the brain rule the mind? Many advocates of emergence have argued that the mind exerts a "top-down" action on the activities of the brain. Accounts of such top-down action are widely understood in terms of part-whole relations, with the mind being understood as the whole that exerts a downward influence on the various parts of the brain. These top-down influences are not causes in the literal sense and do not contradict the causal laws of physics but should be understood as a "downward" flow of information or as a "structuring cause" that constrains the behavior of any local event or, in the case of the brain, local groups of neurons.[25]

The problem of top-down causation lies at the heart of closed-system emergence and has been the subject of intense philosophical scrutiny in recent years. For the most part, the claim that there are distinct emergent levels of reality that need to be taken into account has been widely accepted, so much so that even otherwise avid reductionists such as

Daniel Dennett and Richard Dawkins pay at least lip service to the concept.[26] But many argue that it is mistaken to contend that such closed-system emergence leaves room for a causal role for mind and consciousness. Philosopher Jaegwon Kim has argued that supervenient accounts of for top-down causation simply do not work.[27] Rather, all causation in a closed system is necessarily bottom-up, with the mind merely an epiphenomenal by-product of the activities of the brain.

Much of the controversy surrounding supervenience seems to stem from the variant ways the term is used and therefore the different consequences it is said to imply. Philosophers thus distinguish between strong, weak, and global forms of supervenience—to name just a few.[28] Despite these differences and despite criticisms to the contrary, it does seem that closed-system emergence and supervenience allow for at least a modest understanding of the causal role for the mind. A primary problem in many accounts is an excessive distinction between the mental and the physical. In a closed system, however, a mental action is always also a physical action. To revert back to the computer analogy, software is conceptually and logically distinct from software, but every software action is also a hardware action, which ultimately is the action of fundamental physical particles. Thus, to speak of the causal efficacy of the mind is to speak of the causal effects of those physical events, which, due to the logic of their organizational patterns, are also mental in character. Emergence and supervenience too often become a new form of Neoplatonism, with the result that the mental becomes completely separate from the physical and therefore completely abstracted from the science as well.

A more important problem with the literature on closed-system emergence and supervenience is that it is unclear how it explains consciousness itself. Arguments about emergence and supervenience begin by assuming that a nonreductive physicalist approach can explain both the mind and consciousness, but often they do not give specific accounts of exactly how the mind and consciousness arise physically. The obvious reason for this is that no detailed scientific account of consciousness is currently available. As such, closed-system emergence and supervenience do not really give an explanation of consciousness itself but only tell us what a proper account of consciousness should look like, even though the precise details of such an account are currently lacking. As such, closed-system emergence and supervenience not only attempt to underpin a research agenda that tells cognitive scientists what to look for but also provide a satisfactory ontology that can serve as the basis of an account of human nature.

What does seem to be clear is that, if closed-system emergence is true of the mind/brain, then consciousness must be explained in one of two ways. The first and more widespread way explains consciousness as a product of the functional relations of the mind/brain. That is, consciousness emerges as the result of a certain kind of organizational pattern in the brain. Presumably, not any organizational pattern gives rise to consciousness. It emerges only as the result of a particular set of information-processing events. There have been several proposals to this effect over the past decades. Because consciousness is so closely tied to attention and visual perception, a common strategy is to associate consciousness with representation or a special kind of representation. This is why Crick identifies consciousness with the binding of representations, especially visual representations, to make a coherent and organized representation of the world in the brain. As we have seen, Damasio also gives representation a central role, but in his account it is the representation of the body and bodily functions in relation to the external environment that is of prime importance. Bernard Baars, in another variation of this approach, understands consciousness as a sort of global broadcaster in the brain, providing a centralized base for bringing information together and then sending it out so that the brain works as a unified whole.[29] Alongside of representation, many functionalist explanations also emphasize the link between consciousness, self-knowledge, and self-monitoring. The role of self-knowledge is clear already in Damasio's account, where the need for knowledge of the body is the immediate biological source of the emergence of consciousness. In many of the philosophical accounts that emphasize self-knowledge and self-consciousness it is sometimes implied that consciousness is not itself an information state but an emergent level beyond the information states themselves.

Despite the sometimes significant differences among functionalist accounts, functionalism is persuasive in its ability to formulate theories that cohere strongly with ongoing research in the cognitive sciences themselves. At the same time, functionalism raises serious questions that make it philosophically unpalatable in the eyes of many. Functionalism's early identification of the mind solely with a kind of information processing that emphasized logic and disembodied reasoning gave it a Cartesian character that was distasteful to many.

Feminists in particular objected to the devaluation of the body and the emotions in such early accounts. To a certain extent modern functionalist accounts have corrected these deficits, and current sophisticated accounts of consciousness, such as Damasio's, stress the importance of both body and emotions.

More persistent is the question of why we should expect representational or self-knowledge states to give rise to the subjective character of consciousness at all. It is not clear, for instance, why some representational states should give rise to consciousness and others not. The brain is a massively complex organ, and there is good reason to assume that our conscious representations are a highly refined end-product of the activities of the brain and that not all representations reach the level of conscious awareness. An individual who hears a different conversation in each ear, for instance, will typically be able to attend consciously to only one of them. The other will be obliterated from conscious awareness, although the subject will usually be able to make good educated guesses about its content. The representation is present but not conscious. A similar observation may be made about self-representations. Presumably, not all representations and self-representations are conscious. Why some should be and others not, despite the eloquence of particular theories on the matter, remains unclear.

Functionalism also raises significant questions about personal identity. If I am simply an organizational pattern, is any such pattern identical to my own so that it therefore is me? Such questions have spawned a variety of science-fiction scenarios, some of which are taken seriously. Ray Kurzweil, for instance, sees a future where we shall eventually be able to download our consciousness on giant supercomputers and thereby cheat death.[30] Douglas Hofstadter amusingly proposes that, in principle, Einstein's brain could have been recorded in exactly that fashion. One could then make multiple copies of Einstein and even have Einstein engage in a conversation with himself. Which one would be the real Einstein? From a functionalist perspective, there is no answer to such a question. They are both—or all—Einstein.[31]

For these and other reasons, many see functionalism in any of its forms to be a dead end with regard to the question of consciousness. Of these critics, most fall into the category of what may be called open-system emergence. Here it is presumed that we do not know all of the details at every level of analysis, a situation typical of the scientific endeavor. On an open-system approach, higher levels of organization are not reducible to lower levels, because our understanding of the lower levels is significantly incomplete. The reason why psychology is not reducible to biology, biology is not reducible to biochemistry, and biochemistry is not reducible to particle physics is that each of these underlying sciences is itself incomplete and therefore under-determines the character of the higher-order emergent sciences and the emergent phenomenon they study.

On such an open-system account, the reason why we cannot explain consciousness in functionalist terms is that we are simply overlooking important principles or are still missing pieces of the physical puzzle. Once we are able to do so, then and only then will we be able to give a satisfactory account of consciousness. What this missing link may be, however, is the matter of considerable dispute, with speculation ranging from the relatively conservative to the highly improbable. Colin McGinn, for instance, has argued not only that we lack an adequate account of consciousness but that such an account will forever elude us. While consciousness is, he argues, necessarily physical in its origin, it is far too complex ever to be given a satisfactory scientific explanation.[32]

David Chalmers concurs with McGinn in regard to most current explanations of consciousness, but he argues that consciousness should be identified with information itself, which can be understood as being naturally supervenient on the physical. Chalmers's thesis leads to a kind of panpsychism, for it implies that *any* instance of information processing does in fact have a conscious aspect. Our own consciousness differs not in kind from other instances of information processing but only in degree.[33]

Chalmers's version of panpsychism has strong affinities to process philosophy. Alfred North Whitehead argued that reality is composed of actual entities, each of which has an objective and subjective pole of experience. As actual entities become organized, the integration of experiences begins to occur. Thus, atoms and animals can be said to have experiences, but rocks (which are not organized) do not.[34] David Ray Griffin and Ian Barbour have further argued that this basic level of experience is not identical with consciousness, which emerges only as the result of complex organization of such individual experiences into a unified organism.[35] Consciousness can thus be said to be based on but not reducible to the experiential character of all matter.

Such panpsychist approaches solve some problems while opening up others. Claiming that all things do experience appears to make hash of our own experience of consciousness, which seems to disappear when we are asleep or unconscious. If experience and consciousness are separated (as Griffin and Barbour propose), then it remains unclear how panexperientialism explains consciousness, for the biological basis of consciousness is still missing. Add to this the difficulty of confirming the panexperientialist claim in any real sense (Griffin interestingly appeals to paranormal psychology), and panpsychism in any form seems to raise as many questions as it claims to solve.

Yet another influential approach has been to suggest that a proper understanding of consciousness must appeal ultimately to physics itself. Most of these speculations have centered on the unusual features of quantum physics, which connects in counterintuitive ways the observer and the observed. John Wheeler, for instance, has argued from the paradoxes of quantum mechanics for a kind of idealism that makes consciousness the primary reality, and the world of physical appearances secondary.[36] More influentially, Roger Penrose has argued that functionalist accounts of mind are necessarily deficient because they stop short of explaining particular features of human thought.[37] Penrose has argued passionately that consciousness is linked to yet undiscovered principles of matter that underlie the paradoxes of quantum physics. Along with Stuart Hameroff, he has proposed that microtubules found in the neurons in the brain might be where such quantum mechanical effects could occur. Unfortunately, a number of neuroscientists have observed that microtubules are an unlikely candidate for such a basic cognitive function. Furthermore, neural activity takes place on a scale of size as far removed from quantum mechanical effects as our everyday world of experience is from neurons.

Some, however, reject a naturalistic approach to mind altogether and argue that some form of supernatural dualism is not only viable but the best alternative available. With the advent of modern cognitive science, however, supernatural dualist arguments face an uphill battle. The traditional substance dualism of Descartes seems particularly difficult to hold in light of what we now know about the mind and brain. Descartes, like many philosophers before him, reserved for the immortal soul the basic functions of human cognition, most especially reason and language. One of the clearest results of modern cognitive science, however, is that both reason and language emerge as functions of the brain, and that damage to certain areas causes quite specific kinds of reasoning and language deficits. A supernatural dualist might argue that the brain is merely a conduit for such reasoning ability, but this also seems contrary to the evidence. In many forms of linguistic impairment due to brain damage, for instance, it is not simply that individuals lose the ability to hear language or the motor skills associated with language production. They lose instead the ability to think linguistically. Take away those areas of the brain associated with language and reasoning, and those abilities are lost forever.

Nevertheless, modern forms of supernatural dualism can be found. Two prominent neuroscientists of a previous generation, Wilder Penfield and John Eccles, advocated forms of supernatural dualism. Noted philosopher of science Karl Popper also advocated dualism, although his approach had more in common with emergentist approaches than with the more explicit dualism of his coauthor Eccles.[38] Noted philosopher of religion Richard Swinburne has also advocated a form of supernatural dualism that takes evolutionary biology into account.[39] Swinburne's account is not based on biology but on the logical distinction between the mental and the physical. Like most philosophical approaches to dualism, Swinburne's argument rests more on a priori reasoning than on familiarity with the science involved. Arguments such as Swinburne's, however, face numerous difficulties. With the exception of a few individuals such as Penfield and Eccles, most supernatural dualists reveal astonishing little knowledge or concern about the actual state of scientific knowledge about the mind and brain. Such knowledge would render most supernatural dualist accounts unviable. While cognitive science does not necessarily rule out all forms of supernatural dualism, its poor track record and philosophical difficulties have made it for many impossible to support.

If I Die before I Wake: Rethinking the Soul

A popular children's prayer among twentieth-century Protestants went as follows:

Now I lay me down to sleep
I pray the Lord my soul to keep
And if I die before I wake
I pray the Lord my soul to take.

Over the decades this simple prayer has expressed the hopes and fears of many a devout believer. (It scared the willies out of me as a kid. I suspect that it has caused many long, sleepless nights for countless children afraid to close their eyes lest they die before they wake!) A major component of the faith of Christians, Jews, and Muslims alike has been the hope of resurrection and immortal life, free from the sufferings and trials of this world. For many centuries, the belief in an immortal soul—the seat of the rational, reflective self—has been integral especially for Christian understanding. A central question for Christian theology in the modern era has been the viability of such soul language and, more generally, Christian anthropology as a whole.

By and large, philosophers and cognitive scientists do not talk about "souls" anymore. The reason for this has little to do with religious considerations and much to do with the fact that the term as used historically is too broad and vague to be of much use. Theological conceptions of the soul have been heavily indebted to the philosophical frameworks of Plato and Aristotle. While each of these frameworks has its own richness, they have not shown a great value for addressing modern questions of human psychology. As a result, the soul has been replaced by such categories as mind, the self, and consciousness. Does the children's prayer need to be updated? Should we instead pray the Lord "my consciousness to keep"?

To answer such a question is to address the border of theology and cognitive science. As long as cognitive science remains a science, it cannot dictate theological concepts, for the simple reason that its scope and findings are too narrow. At the same time, any serious theological account must take seriously the findings of the cognitive sciences where they are relevant, benefiting from insights as well as making prudent judgments about possible impacts for particular doctrines. With regard to the question of consciousness, theologians have primarily been concerned with two issues.

The first issue is the very nature of the self—what was in traditional language called the soul. Here the nature of consciousness as understood by the cognitive sciences can loom large. In discussions about the relation of mind and body, consciousness has in many ways taken the place of the soul as the prime locus of attention as well as identity. Personhood is defined by many qualities but, without consciousness, all other attributes are moot. Reasoning without consciousness is mere computation; emotion without affect, the "raw feels," is merely a form of behavioral response. If we search for ways to speak of the essence of an individual, consciousness is the prime candidate.

On the precise nature of consciousness, however, cognitive science still offers only a rudimentary guide at best. On purely scientific grounds, some form of functionalist account seems most likely. What we know of the mind/brain relation from neuroscience, cognitive psychology, artificial intelligence, and other disciplines strongly suggests that the primary task of the brain is information processing and that consciousness arises out of the complex operations of the brain. There is to date simply no credible evidence of any other principles at work, whether from quantum mechanics or elsewhere. When neuroscientists such as Damasio and Edelman develop essentially functionalist accounts of the mind, they do so because that is where, in large part, the evidence leads them.

Despite this, the philosophical problems with functionalism are serious and should not be taken lightly. Reservations about functionalism come not only from supernatural dualists committed to the doctrine of an immortal soul but from a wide range of naturalistic philosophers as well. Even so, most of the proffered alternatives to functionalism seem even less likely. As such, the wisest course for those who are outside of scientific research is a prudent agnosticism about the ultimate nature of consciousness. This need not be the defeatism of McGinn, who claims that we can never unlock the secret of consciousness; it is simply an acknowledgment both of the limitations of our current scientific knowledge as well as the intractability of the question itself. Perhaps we will discover the key to consciousness, but we are not there yet.

Such an observation, however, does not mean there is nothing to learn from the current debates about consciousness. Two important trends have emerged that have some impact for theological anthropology. The first is the increasing ability of cognitive science to explain on a naturalistic basis most, if not all, the functions of the mind. The language of Genesis 2, which depicts Adam as being created from the dust of the earth, seems more accurate now than it probably did for much of Jewish and Christian history. It seems most likely that the mind and even consciousness do not descend from above but emerge naturally as the result of biological development. When this first happened in the history of the world and when it first happens in fetal and child development remains unclear, but that it does happen seems nearly incontrovertible.

The second trend is the assumption that, while any satisfactory account of the human person must include consciousness, consciousness in itself does not make the human person; consciousness makes best sense in a framework that emphasizes its embodiment. Conscious experience is always experience of something, and it is by the means of our very embodied brain that we do that experiencing. The quest for consciousness is important, but those who would make consciousness into a surrogate for a self-subsisting soul independent from the body would be making a profound mistake. It seems that there can be no person without consciousness, but consciousness alone does not make a person. Consciousness is bound with reason and emotion, with motor control and sense of bodily position and awareness—all of which are made possible by the multifaceted activities of the brain. In fact, one of the most intriguing aspects of Damasio's proposal for consciousness is his linking of consciousness with the specific form of awareness called proprioception that provides a constant monitoring of the body in relation to its environment. The implication is that we (as well as many other animals) are conscious precisely because of the kind of bodies we have.

Interestingly enough, both of these trends are consistent with what current biblical scholarship has been revealing about theological anthropology in scriptural texts. While much of Christian history has presupposed a dramatic distinction between the human body and soul, such a distinction is not strongly evident in biblical texts themselves. Oscar Cullmann was one of the first modern biblical scholars to show that the biblical texts exhibit belief in the resurrection of the dead rather than the survival of an immortal soul.[40] Hebrew terms like *nephesh* and Greek terms such as *psyche* are not used in the Bible in a way that clearly separates soul from body; they refer instead to the inner self or spirit in the context of a more holistic anthropology.

Biblical anthropology, then, supports the view that human beings, while being made in the image of God, are nevertheless part of the natural order. Our spirits are natural, embodied spirits that grow, flourish, whither, and die. In the process, we foster community, nourish others, and experience both sorrow and joy. For many, that would be the end of the story; indeed, a number of theologians are content to observe this consonance and consider the case closed. After all, the main point is to show that theological truths are consistent with scientific observation and, once having done that, we may move to other issues. The story of human nature, however, is incomplete both scientifically and theologically. At base, we still really do not understand consciousness, and there may indeed be scientific surprises ahead as our knowledge and research progress. At the core of human nature mystery still resides, a mystery acknowledged also in the biblical texts. Joel Green has observed that, although biblical anthropology does not support a supernatural, dualist perspective of the Cartesian variety, it is nevertheless a mistake to try to force biblical anthropology into modern categories.[41] Biblical anthropology is complex and multifaceted, as can be seen by the apostle Paul's attempt to explain the resurrection in 1 Corinthians 15. Paul there struggles to express both the continuity and discontinuity that resurrection implies. For Paul, resurrection is indeed an embodied resurrection, but our physical bodies shall be replaced by "spiritual" bodies.

What are spiritual bodies? Paul is not very clear and in the end must resort to poetry and metaphor to make his point. But his struggle is suggestive of the openness of the theological task itself. Theology's encounter with cognitive science is not simply one of confirmation or disconfirmation of particular doctrines but a process of creative, mutual exploration. Premature closure is the enemy of both disciplines and, to the extent that new discoveries are possible, both theology and cognitive science stand to benefit.

4

Do Split Brains Listen to Prozac?

In the autumn of 1524, Desiderius Erasmus published a treatise on the freedom of the will. Erasmus was concerned with Martin Luther's statements regarding the bondage of the will and the human inability to do good. While Erasmus had been a sympathetic supporter of many of Luther's reforms, Luther's claim that the will was in bondage to sin and incapable of doing good without the grace of Christ seemed incomprehensible to Erasmus. How, Erasmus argued, could we expect God to judge us on our moral actions if we are not truly free to do both good and evil? If we are not free either to accept or to reject the grace of Christ, in what sense is God's damnation of those who reject Christ just?

Luther's now famous and intemperate response not only rejected Erasmus's arguments but insulted his character as well. Luther argued that to admit any human freedom to do good was to admit that the grace of Christ was not necessary. Not only did such a position make the death of Christ on the cross cruelly meaningless but it made those who could not achieve such moral perfection all the more guilty. If some could achieve perfection, then all could. Not only did such a claim run counter to Luther's own experience but it made the hope of salvation impossible for all and undermined the foundation of church, scripture, and sacrament. For Luther, the question of freedom was not simply academic but an intensely personal issue that determined the state of one's own salvation. The vehemence of Luther's reply stunned Erasmus, with the result that their once cordial relationship soured as they went their separate ways theologically and politically.[1]

As the debate between Luther and Erasmus shows, freedom is a profoundly theological category, with significant implications for the way we see ourselves in the world and how we perceive our ultimate goals. Freedom, however, is not an abstract category of intellectual fancy but a lived reality that, for most of us, is experienced or frustrated daily. As such, freedom is not only the property of theology but of psychology and biology as well. It is thus not surprising that, while freedom is not a subject matter per se of cognitive science, research in the cognitive sciences nevertheless touches on our understanding of human freedom. Such insights will not ultimately decide the issue between Luther and Erasmus, but they do show us that the freedom that we have is of a very special kind, profoundly shaped by our biology, but profoundly open as well.

The Theological Subject

Luther's position is now unpopular, not simply because many now resist doctrines of predestination, but because freedom has come to mean so many things that are held in high value. Freedom is the most cherished of values, enshrined in political documents and the basis of many of our cultural convictions. Certainly the value of political freedom laid the ground not only for democracy but also for racial and sexual emancipation. The claim of moral freedom underlies our ethical and legal systems. It even underpins much of the Western approach to education, for to study the *liberal* arts is to engage in a kind of study that makes one free.

Defining freedom, however, is a more complex task. Among other things, freedom implies a unified subject who does the choosing. It also implies the ability for real and substantial transformation. The path of freedom is typically nonlinear, revealing many twists and turns as life progresses. Such freedom implies choice, the ability of the individual subject to select between alternatives without coercion. In many ways, the quest for freedom has been the quest of modern Western society.

In addition to this, freedom has a theological dimension. The task of theology, as indicated in chapter 1, is to provide a framework for understanding the meaning and purpose of life. From such a framework issues a soteriology, a path of salvation or liberation from the chains of sin and evil that bind us. In some ways, freedom is the most important of theological categories, for it denotes that which we ultimately value the most. The question of freedom ultimately addresses the most basic of questions: Who am I? A free person is presumably different from one who is not. Those who can hope for freedom have a purpose in life that orients them in relation to their current situation. To the extent that freedom becomes the basis of such hope, it becomes one of the starting points of theology as well. This has certainly been the case in contemporary theology. As a theological category, freedom has loomed large for neoorthodox, existentialist, process, and liberation theologians alike. While there are significant differences among these theological movements as to how freedom is understood, as a generalization the category of freedom is theologically important in two ways.

First, the category of freedom is important for understanding the human plight. To the extent that theology needs to develop a metaphysic, it requires an anthropology that situates humans in relation to the world. Here the theological question of freedom is in many ways identical to the philosophical one. Are my decisions made by volition or are they controlled by outside forces, whether it be gods or demons, the billiard ball particles of Newtonian physics, or the selfish genes of extreme neo-Darwinism? Freedom is here contrasted with determinism. Such freedom presupposes an autonomous, unified subject capable of making decisions. Without the autonomous subject, the question of freedom in this sense becomes moot. This conception of freedom has been a core issue in theological debates about predestination dating back to Augustine and was at the heart of Erasmus's concern about Luther's position on the bondage of the will.

Second, freedom is important for understanding our ultimate purpose and direction, that is, for soteriology. In Christian theology, freedom is important not only for understanding how we act now but also in defining what we seek ultimately. This conception of freedom is not simply identified with choice but with entering a new state of being. Soteriologically, freedom means freedom from sin and the evils of this world, as well as participation in the spiritual community both in this life and the next. (This soteriological sense of freedom is not unique to Christianity but has its version in many of the other religions of the world as well.) Arguably, the debate between Luther and Erasmus hinged in part in their different usages of the word "freedom." While Erasmus was somewhat concerned with freedom as a soteriological category, the target of his attack were those issues most related to philosophical, metaphysical freedom. Luther, by contrast, was almost exclusively concerned with freedom in the soteriological sense. Ultimately, the two are linked, but the Luther-Erasmus debate shows how the different emphases can lead to profoundly different perceptions about what is so important about freedom.

Cognitive science poses provocative questions and possibilities for thinking theologically about freedom. Metaphysically, cognitive science poses questions about the kind of freedom we have and particularly the extent to which we can consider ourselves a unified autonomous subject. Soteriologically, the study of emotions may prove to be of some importance for thinking about personal transformation, orientation, and well-being. In both cases, we see a glimpse of the complexity of the human person.

One Body, One Mind?

I am. Such a statement seems unproblematic. Generally, we face the world as a unified individual, and we assume the same for others. This unity is the most basic of premises and has often served as the foundation of philosophical systems. Descartes's thinking self was the undoubtable core of his philosophy. Kant's transcendental subject played much the same role in his critical philosophy. The experience of unity is fundamental on a more prosaic level as well. We simply expect there to be one mind to one body—no more and no less. Such expectations allow us to assume considerable continuity among those we interact with. My colleagues in the English department may have their ups and downs, but I can expect them to have the same personality and roughly the same behavioral repertoire not only today and tomorrow but even across years and decades. What a great surprise it is when this is not the case. Of someone who has undergone a radical change in lifestyle and behavior, we might say, "She's not the same person anymore!"

That we are unified subjects is central for traditional understandings of human freedom. Metaphysically, I am free because it is "I" who makes the decisions, not someone else. Some among us do recognize the complexity of our inner lives. In his *Confessions*, Augustine perceptively describes the inner conflicts he suffered on the path to conversion. Ultimately, however, Augustine rejected a radically dualistic understanding of the human person and held that such conflicts occur within the unified individual, who is thus responsible for both the good and ill deeds that he or she performs.[2] Such an understanding of unity underlies our sense of personal responsibility and the legal system. To say that the devil or my genes or my environment made me do it usually does not go far as a legal or personal defense. After all, *you* did it, not someone else.

As the preceding chapters have hinted, however, the easy unity that we experience is not as comprehensible or simple as it appears. While the fact and physical roots of our consciousness may lie forever in mystery, it is nevertheless clear that our consciousness exists very much in context. The old dualist metaphor that the body is like a ship and the soul like a ship's captain seems exceedingly unlikely. Rather, we are conscious, because that is necessary for the kind of complex beings that we are. Our conscious selves play an important and integral role in our day-to-day activities and, for much of the history of our species, in the basic struggle for survival. As such, our conscious life does not exist in the abstract but is intimately tied to the whole of our experience. Philosophers have often differentiated between the fact of consciousness and the more holistically conceived self-conscious person, a distinction increasingly made by neuroscientists as well, who differentiate between core and extended consciousness.[3] A person is not simply a bundle of experiences but an intentional subject who thinks, feels, remembers, and interacts with the surrounding environment. Degenerative diseases that cause the loss of personhood without significantly impairing core consciousness are among the most tragic fates we can face or witness. Anyone who has seen the distressing toll that Alzheimer's disease or severe stroke damage can take is able to testify to the devastation such tragedies inflict.

Loss or diminishment of personhood can occur in other ways as well. Damage to the hippocampus can result in anterograde amnesia, a condition that involves the total inability to establish new, declarative memories. This condition was first made famous by a patient known as H. M., who suffered catastrophic memory loss after removal of brain tissue in the hopes of ending his debilitating epileptic seizures.[4] The seizures ended, but H. M. was left in world that consisted of only those memories he had accumulated before the surgery and an eternal present that could never be recalled. As a result, H. M. could not remember for more than a few moments anything that happened to him since the surgery. Each encounter, each individual, each event was new to him. Quite suddenly he was forever unable to make new relationships or maintain old ones. Each time he inquired about his uncle, he would grieve anew on hearing that he had passed away. As he grew older, he even became unable to recognize his own face in a mirror, so different was it from the memory of his own face as a young man.

Despite the tragedy that had occurred, H. M. still retained conscious functioning, expressed emotions, and showed no diminishment in IQ. For these reasons, most of us would grant H. M. the status of personhood, but it was a significantly diminished personhood. Not only was H. M. essentially cut off from the rest of the world but he was also significantly cut off from himself, unable to grow, mature, or tackle new challenges, which are normal functions of life. There was one exception. While H. M. had indeed lost declarative memory, it was eventually discovered that he retained procedural memory. H. M. could not remember a new name or face but he could learn new skills, such as drawing a circle. It was discovered that, unlike declarative memory, procedural memory does not rely on the hippocampus for proper functioning. Consequently, H. M. could learn new physical tasks even though he could not remember when or how had learned them.

Cases such as H. M.'s were among the first in cognitive neuroscience to demonstrate clearly that the "I" of my extended, reflective consciousness arises out of the complex interactions of a number of brain processes operating in parallel. When specific areas of the brain are damaged, we begin to see how much of the self is a construct of complex interactions. The unity that we experience appears to be the end result of a finely tuned and ongoing process. The self is truly an emergent reality, blossoming out of the interaction of mind, brain, body, and environment.

The realization of this constructedness of the self eventually leads us to question how truly unified our self-conscious awareness is. We see a glimmer of this in H. M.'s case, for if his procedural learning is unconscious, in what sense is it truly *he* that is doing the learning? To put it bluntly, is it H. M. that is learning or is it his body?

Such a question emerges in prosaic form in the familiar case of hypnosis. Usually classified as a parlor trick and tarnished by long association with such pseudoscientific practices as mesmerism and past-life regression, hypnosis is nevertheless a real phenomenon. Individuals in a hypnotic state appear for all practical purposes to lose consciousness. But if it is not the conscious self that is responding to hypnosis, who is answering the hypnotist's questions? The perplexity returns after the subject recovers from the hypnotic state. During the hypnotic state an individual may be given a task to perform after reawakening, such as to open the window immediately after hearing someone cough. Such suggestibility makes hypnotism a fun parlor trick. What is psychologically interesting, however, is not only that the individual has no memory of the suggestion planted by the hypnotist but that, if asked to explain why she opened the window, an alternative explanation ("It's too warm in here!") is readily and unself-consciously given. In such situations, the conscious mind seems quite willing to confabulate (make up) an explanation that is perfectly consistent with the action performed but at odds with what the observer perceives to be the real motivation for the deed.

The impact of such hypnotic behavior has been blunted both by its familiarity and by the frequent suspicion that there should be a simple and straightforward explanation available. Similar kinds of disassociation between conscious intentionality and behavior have emerged in a wide number of contexts One of the most famous of these came from the research of Roger Sperry and Michael Gazzaniga with epileptic patients who had undergone a commissurotomy, a splitting of the cerebral hemispheres. In a normal human brain, the cerebral hemispheres are connected by a dense, neural structure called the corpus callosum. Beginning in the 1940s and 1950s, severing the corpus callosum began to be used as a last resort to treat severe cases of epilepsy. Separating the hemispheres prevented the development of grand mal seizures that affected the whole brain; the procedure proved to be a clinical success.

While patients could by and large function normally after the surgery, later experiments began to suggest that the severing of brain hemispheres resulted not only in a split brain but also, it appeared, a split mind. These experiments capitalized on the fact that each hemisphere is responsible for most bodily functions on the opposite side of the body. Thus, the left hemisphere controls movement and hearing on the right side of the body as well as the right half of the visual field of each eye. The right hemisphere, by contrast, controls movement and hearing on the left, as well as the left half of the visual field.

The experiments developed by Roger Sperry, Michael Gazzaniga, and others capitalized on this separation of function.[5] Requiring the subjects to stare at a central point in front of them, material was shown to the left and right portions of the visual field in such a way that it would not be present to the other half. Since language skills reside largely in the left hemisphere, any verbal response to a question would represent what the left hemisphere (so to speak) saw. If the patient was asked to respond by pointing with the left hand, however, this could be understood as a response from the right hemisphere.

Surprisingly, when the two hemispheres are simultaneously shown different material, their responses are indeed different and appropriate to the information that each hemisphere alone would perceive. In one such series of experiments, researchers flashed composite faces before their subjects, where the left half of the face (for instance) would be that of a man's, the right half a woman's.[6] When subjects replied verbally, they claimed to have seen a woman's face. When asked to point with their left hand (controlled by the right hemisphere), subjects instead pointed to the man's face. Even stranger, verbal responses indicated that the subject had seen the entire woman's face (both left and right halves), even though only the half was presented. Somehow, it seems, processes in the brain fill out the image in a way undetectable to the verbal self.

Another sort of confusion arose in other experiments. If the written command "laugh" was flashed before the left visual field controlled by the right hemisphere, the subject would laugh. If asked to explain the behavior verbally (thus involving the left hemisphere), the subject would respond with a comment along the lines of, "You guys come up and test us every month; what a way to make a living!" Similarly, if the command "walk" was flashed, the patient would often get up and do so, giving an explanation for the behavior that seemed to be at odds with the actual cause. Patients shown frightening scenes became agitated, whereas patients shown calming scenes (such as ocean waves) became serene, all the while invoking, if asked, alternative causes than those of the slides.[7]

This kind of confabulation was present across a range of experiments. But what do these results mean? The most straightforward interpretation would seem to be that after the surgery there are two persons present, one in each hemisphere. Each hemisphere seems to be able to understand the tasks asked of it and respond accordingly. Each hemisphere possesses distinctive functions, the left clearly better at language and the right at spatial abilities. Each hemisphere seems oblivious to the perceptions and motivations of the other. The implications of this conclusion, however, seem a bit bizarre. Am I one person who would become two if my hemispheres were split? Or am I two people all along, simply never having realized that what I thought of as my body is not really my body after all, but *our* body? This last conclusion seems odd both philosophically and scientifically. What biological function could such a duality serve?

Because these experiments touch at the core of human identity, they have attracted considerable philosophical attention and thus a range of explanations. In some ways, functionalist, information-processing accounts seem best able to explain the results of the experiments, despite their weakness in accounting for the problem of consciousness generally. On a functionalist account, the conscious self is a product of the activity of the whole brain. When the brain becomes divided, the self does as well. Where there was one person there are now two, albeit with truncated abilities. Because consciousness and personhood are not any one thing but a property of the overall system, there is no point in wringing one's hands over which self of the split brain is the real one, for it presumes a kind of continuity and identity that does not exist.

Daniel Dennett has put forth one of the more radical solutions to this sort of problem, arguing that the mind is made up of a number of competing modules, each vying to become part of the master narrative that is consciousness. In this model, the mind is characterized more by its plurality than by its unity. In the end, the conscious self is understood largely as an epiphenomenon, a continually modified central narrative that is constantly shifting as lower level modules compete to update and revise the narrative that make up the whole person. As such, it is certainly conceivable for a second center of narrative gravity to emerge under the right conditions.[8] Patricia Churchland similarly argues that such results show the inadequacy of such folk-psychological terms as consciousness, self, and person. Such terms do not denote real entities as such, but are used only because we are so vastly ignorant of how the mind actually works.[9]

Others, however, are not so willing to give up the idea of basic unity. Neuroscientist John Eccles, defending a dualist position, argued that the experiments provide evidence that the conscious self is housed only in the language-rich left hemisphere. While the right hemisphere can occasionally show remarkable ability, there is "nobody there" and, consequently, it may be considered a sort of independent automatom.[10]

Critics also point out that the results of the experiments are more complex than is usually indicated in popular accounts. Only a minority of the patients made any response when information was flashed to the right hemisphere alone; most made no response at all. Moreover, while direct connection between the cerebral hemispheres was severed, the hemispheres retained indirect connections via the brain stem and other areas. These and other complications make it difficult to say whether there are suddenly one or two selves in the brain. What can be said is that in some of these cases a fairly developed and strong level of disassociative behavior is displayed, even though the meaning and implication of such disassociation remain unclear.

This kind of disassociation, where either the unity of the person is called into question or the conscious mind seems prone to fabricate information when it no longer has proper access is not unique to split-brain cases. Blind sight represents a similarly intriguing case. Evidence for blind sight emerged from patients who had suffered significant damage to a portion of their occipital cortex, which is significantly responsible for visual processing. Such damage typically results in a large blind patch in the visual field, with patients suffering damage on the right hemisphere of the cortex unable to see objects on the left, and vice versa. Surprisingly, experiments led by Lawrence Weiskrantz established that even though patients insisted that they could not see objects in their blinded area, they could nevertheless guess fairly accurately what was there. Thus, if patients were asked to guess whether a square or circle was present in the blind spot, they responded at a rate consistently better than chance.[11] How did they know? The implication seems to be that visual processing and information occur at several levels and in different brain locations. Some of these brain locations are responsible for the visual field that we consciously perceive. Others are capable of providing limited information but seem to be only indirectly accessible to consciousness. If I experience blind sight, *who* sees the square in the blinded area? I do, but only in a sense that goes beyond what I regularly think of as my conscious experience.

Even more unusual than blind sight are cases of anosognosia. Anosognosia typically occurs as a result of a stroke that impairs the right parietal lobe. Patients who suffer from this sort of damage are suddenly unable to acknowledge anything that appears on the left side of their visual field. Sufferers of anosognosia will shave only on the right, dress only on the right, and eat only off the right half of a plate.

The left half of the body remains paralyzed and, for the sufferer, is essentially nonexistent. If a sufferer of anosognosia is asked to move his left arm or to get up and walk, he, like the split-brain patients, will confabulate, claiming that he does not feel like moving his arm or going for a walk right now. In some cases, the denial is even stronger, with subjects claiming that the limbs on the left side of their body do not even belong to them. In one highly unusual case reported by Oliver Sacks, a patient kept falling out of bed because, so he claimed, someone had put a corpse in bed with him, and he kept trying to push it off the bed. When he pushed the corpse off, however, he fell too, for it was really his own unrecognized arm that he was trying to push off![12]

What is unusual about anosognosia is not merely the fragmentation of the unified person or the confabulations that patients produce. It is instead the quite specific derangement of rational thought that seems to accompany it. How, after all, could people not know that they are totally unaware of the entire left side of their body and visual field? It is not only the fact that sufferers of anosognosia have lost all representation of what happens on their left side but that they are totally oblivious that such a deficit exists.

V. S. Ramachandran argues that such deficits should not be understood merely as a form of neglect but that they reveal a particular impairment of reasoning. Building on a theory proposed by Marcel Mesulam, Ramachandran proposes that our left and right hemispheres are responsible for different kinds of rational operations.[13] Whereas the left hemisphere is responsible for more focused attention, the right is responsible for detecting global coherence and anomalies. When this area in the right hemisphere is damaged, the left hemisphere is left to its own devices. Unable to detect anomalies such as paralysis on the left side, it constructs a world in which such paralysis does not exist.

Ramachandran's theory needs further elaboration and analysis. What is clear from research on anosognosia, blind sight, and split-brain subjects is how much the *self* is a construction from a number of quite special abilities. The ease with which we perceive and act in the world is the result of many complex, interacting brain systems. More than this, my self is significantly shaped and defined by these interacting systems. When some are impaired, who I am may be radically changed in the process as well.

While brain damage may reveal in dramatic ways our own constructedness, it should not be altogether surprising, for own development from fetus through childhood to adulthood reveals the extent to which we are not born as whole, ready made, but are made up as we go along. Advances in neuroscience and developmental psychology have only accentuated what we on a personal level already know. While earlier generations of psychology have placed great emphasis on the role the environment plays in psychological development, modern research indicates that childhood development is in fact a complex interplay of biology and external stimuli. Throughout much of childhood, the brain itself is a work in progress. Not only are we born with virtually all the neurons we will ever have but we are born with far more than we will ever have again. In the first years of childhood, brain development is characterized by massive neuronal death as the brain essentially wires and programs itself as the child interacts with the world. Far from being a bad thing, such die-offs are a necessary part of brain development. A child's brain can therefore be understood as a massive evolutionary project. Mental development is also predominantly physical development.

Such findings accentuate the question, Who am I? Am I merely the conscious flow of experience? Or does the self include the various sophisticated, unconscious cognitive processes that are often hidden from my conscious ponderings? It is questionable whether we can even make the distinction so clear-cut. What appears to be the case is that the "I," the self, the person, is in fact a kind of ongoing process, developing across time and emerging as a result of a large number of brain and body processes. Rather than a ship and its captain, the relation of self and body more resembles a surfer on the sea. While a surfer can exert control on his or her direction, it must always be done with a sensitive awareness of the actions of the water beneath. But even this metaphor is misleading, for it presumes that the surfing self and the sea of brain and body can be treated as completely separate entities. As cases such as anosognosia indicate, such complete separation is illusory. The "I" is composed of brain processes of which it itself is totally unaware.

Painful Pleasure: The Paradox of Emotion

Although we often feel in control of our thoughts and actions, such confidence frequently melts with respect to our own emotional states. I am occasionally confronted in class with the eager libertarian student who claims to be completely free and in charge of himself or herself. On those occasions, I sometimes command the student, "Be happy!" or "Be mournful!" or "Fall in love!" Of course, it's impossible. It seems paradoxical, but the one thing we have least control over is our own emotional states. I can no more *make* myself happy than I can move a mountain. As a result, we all engage in elaborate behavioral patterns that in one way or another are designed to produce happiness and a sense of well-being while avoiding pain and sorrow. It is going to a dinner and movie with friends and family that makes me happy, not any direct willing of happiness on my own part.

This lack of control also seems paradoxical because, more than anything else, it is our emotional states that are important to us. Human beings will do almost anything to achieve happiness and avoid pain and suffering. Our lives are defined in no small part by the fact that states of well-being are often so difficult to achieve on a regular basis. Early to bed and early to rise may indeed make one healthy, wealthy, and wise, but there is no guarantee that health, wealth, and wisdom, consistently produce happiness. Indeed, the many celebrity biographies in books and on television suggest that, while wealth can indeed make life easier, it does not guarantee happiness. And even though many reply on national surveys that they are content or happy, such sense of well-being stops short of the peak experiences that especially drive us and that tragically lead many to drug use.

Because emotions are so intimately tied to our goals and aspirations, they become theologically important as well. While most agree that it would be a mistake to reduce categories of salvation to emotional states, it would also be a mistake to conclude that emotions are unimportant for our understanding of salvific states. Emotions in no small way define both what we wish to avoid and what we seek. There is much suffering in Dante's vision of hell, whereas eternal bliss awaits those who pass into the heavenly realms. Consequently, emotional states contribute to our freedom in the soteriological sense. Negative emotional states hinder our ability to achieve our desired goals; positive emotional states enable us to achieve such goals and indeed are part of the goals themselves. It is thus not surprising that popular psychology plays such an important role in modern society, for it serves as a kind of secularized soteriology, promising to help us achieve the happiness we so desire but consistently fail to obtain.

Despite its importance, emotion remains one of the least understood features of the human mind. Part of the reason for this is the research perspective of both behaviorism and early cognitive science. Behaviorists limited psychology to the study of behavior. Since emotion seemed to be an internal, mental quality, its study tended either to be excluded from the behaviorist paradigm or understood as a form of behavior. Early cognitive scientists also tended to ignore emotion. Cognitive science was understood to be the study of rational thought-processes, of which emotion seemed to be the opposite. Computers do not emote. This by no means meant that early cognitive scientists denied the reality of human emotion but only that emotion lay outside the scope of their inquiry.

While this lack of research stemmed in no small part from such methodological blinders, it was also due to the fact that emotional states have proved to be extraordinarily problematic to study. A primary problem is simply defining what we mean by emotion. Emotional states can be said to include not only pain and joy but also love and depression, which are a bit more abstract. I can be joyful for a few minutes or hours, but I may be depressed for months and in love for years. More than this, emotional states are tricky to describe. Steven Pinker correctly observes that our experience of emotion is much richer than the language we use to describe them. One result of this is that different languages vary in their ability to capture emotional states. Only Germans have a term for the taking of pleasure at the pain of others (*Schadenfreude*), but upon hearing it explained we instantly recognize what is being conveyed.[14] This primal quality of emotions also seems to render nonsensical those who claim that all experiences can be understood as linguistic constructs. Only a fool would trade the experience of love for a description of it. The rest of us know better.

Despite this lack of concern throughout much of the twentieth century, the importance of emotional life has prevented it from being totally neglected and, as our knowledge of the brain and mind has progressed, it has become increasingly apparent how important emotion is to the proper functioning of the human self. This progress, in turn, has led to the development and discarding of a number of theories of what emotions are and how they work. Many current cognitive scientists trace the beginning of emotion research to William James, who postulated that emotions arise out of bodily states. The reason we feel fear upon seeing a bear, for instance, is that we suddenly undergo significant bodily changes. Our heart starts to race, we begin to breathe quickly and, in most cases, run. James saw emotion arising out of the interplay of mind and body, with the body bearing the causal responsibility.[15]

James's approach eventually came under significant criticism, and exploration of emotions went primarily in two different directions. Cognitive psychologists came to understand emotion primarily in terms of cognitive function. Early theorists proposed that emotion served as a kind of appraisal system that evaluated experiences. The link to the body was kept, but the cognitive role of emotions was emphasized.[16] Steven Pinker, a contemporary example of this functionalist approach, understands emotions primarily in terms of evolutionary function. We have emotions because they help us survive, and they help us survive by urging goals and priorities upon us. The person who stands in front of an angry bear deciding between alternatives will likely perish; the person who runs in absolute terror has at least a chance of surviving.[17] Disgust functions to help us avoid foods that are poisonous, lust makes sure that our genes do not die with us, and our love for our children ensures that they survive into adulthood. In the hands of Pinker and other functionalists, emotions serve as a kind of brain within the brain, orienting our goals and desires relatively independently of our conscious self.

While cognitive psychologists were developing functionalist accounts of emotion, neuroscientists—not surprisingly—were attempting to understand the brain structures involved. Early on, the most influential model was that of Paul MacLean's triune brain (mentioned briefly in chapter 2, above).[18] MacLean understood the brain as a kind of evolutionary layer cake, with different brain structures identified with reptilian, mammalian, and distinctly human stages of development. In MacLean's analysis, the oldest areas of the brain derive from early reptiles. This reptilian brain is responsible for those most basic of emotions tied to survival: fight, flight, food, and sex. Since mammals need to cooperate in large groups and nurture their young, portions of the mammalian brain developed to promote such prosocial behavior. The areas responsible for emotion came to be called the limbic system and involved the amygdala, the hippocampus, and surrounding brain regions. MacLean's claims regarding the existence of a limbic system were partially born out by a number of experiments. Epileptics who suffered seizures in the area of the limbic system, for instance, experienced intense emotional sensations.

Recent work on emotion has begun to integrate psychological and neurological approaches and has revealed a more complex picture than that portrayed by either approach alone. Emotions do appear to be universal rather than culture-specific, although the expression of such emotions depends heavily on cultural circumstances. Paul Ekman has proposed that there are six basic emotions that we all share and which are tied to specific kinds of facial expressions. Regardless of culture, individuals can differentiate between facial expressions of surprise, happiness, anger, fear, disgust, and sadness. Japanese individuals who watch a film will display the same emotional range as Americans, although their display depends on whether other people are present or not.[19]

Our emotional responses, in turn, are mediated by a number of brain structures, some of which occur in the area traditionally denoted as the limbic system. Work by Joseph Ledoux, in particular, has highlighted the role that the amygdala plays in fear responses.[20] Ledoux built on work that indicated that damage to the amygdala and surrounding regions leads to impairment of fear conditioning, and his research revealed the complexities involved in even this most basic of emotional responses. The importance of the amygdala for fear, however, does not extend to other emotions, and Ledoux argues that the limbic system model for emotion is too simplistic. Emotion is more complex and likely involves a number of regions of the brain.

The complexity of emotion and its integration with other cognitive processes has been revealed in the work of Antonio and Hanna Damasio. Their work has focused on the role that emotion plays in reasoning processes, highlighted by what is now the celebrity case of Phineas Gage. Gage, a nineteenth-century railroad foreman, suffered a devastating brain injury when a dynamite blast propelled a iron spike up through his cheekbone, his forebrain, and out through the top of his skull. To the astonishment of all, Gage not only survived but was still able to communicate and, after a short while, was able to move under his own power. Yet it eventually became apparent that something dramatic had indeed happened. Formerly, Gage was one of the best and most trusted workers in the company. After the accident, however, he became unreliable and unpredictable. Once of good character, he now used profanity with such indiscretion that women were advised to stay away from him lest they be offended. No longer able to keep a steady job, he drifted from employer to employer until he finally ended up in a carnival freak show, only to die destitute and unemployed. While Gage's reasoning faculties seemed fully intact, his personality had wholly changed. In the eyes of his friends and acquaintances from before the accident, "Gage was no longer Gage."[21]

Gage's skull and the tamping iron that caused the injury were preserved at the Harvard School of Medicine, and research by the Damasios indicated that the blast caused significant injury to the prefrontal cortex (at the very front of the brain). Modern patients who suffer damage in the same area suffer conditions similar to Gage's. These patients seem perfectly able to reason in a normal fashion, typically retaining average or above average functioning on standard intelligence tests. Experiments also showed that their moral reasoning was sound as well; patients could distinguish between socially accepted norms of right and wrong and, if given a list of alternative scenarios, could identify behavior that was appropriate and explain why it was.

Strangely enough, however, these patients could not consistently apply their perfectly sound reasoning abilities to decisions in their own lives. They typically lost their jobs because of their inability to perform in a dependable and predictable manner. After their injury, spouse and friends found them difficult to get along with, prone to unpredictable bursts and socially inappropriate comments. Strangely enough, Antonio Damasio found that these patients also seemed to suffer from an almost total lack of affect. Except for the occasional outburst of short duration, patients displayed a lack of emotional attachment. One patient even complained that things that once inspired him now no longer did so. Sexual drive was typically lost as well.

Research by Damasio and his colleagues suggests that the two deficits are in fact linked: poor decision-making is in no small part a result of being unable to attach emotional significance to events and proposed alternatives. Effective decision-making requires what Damasio calls "somatic markers." Our reasoning by itself is unable to make us *do* anything. Reasoning processes must also be connected to an emotional evaluation. This was demonstrated in a series of experiments by having normal subjects and subjects with prefrontal cortex damage play a kind of gambling game. Subjects were allowed to select from four different decks of cards. Drawing a card from any given deck resulted in either a monetary (play money) reward or punishment.

Some decks on average gave better rewards than others, although the subjects were not told this beforehand. Over the course of playing the game, normal subjects fairly quickly learned to draw from the decks that rewarded better, and skin conductance responses (used in lie-detection tests and usually a reliable indicator of emotional arousal) indicated that normal patients developed a learned emotional response to drawing from the decks that punished most severely. Although subjects with prefrontal cortex damage did show immediate emotional responses to reward and punishment, they nevertheless failed to demonstrate the kind of learned emotional response that normal subjects did. Consequently, the brain-damaged subjects performed quite poorly and quickly drove themselves into debt.

Damasio's work with these subjects is striking for the way that it integrates emotion and reasoning and, in turn, connects them to bodily states, much as James did more than a century before. Emotion is not simply an add-on component, an epiphenomenon on top of rational processing, but is integral to the proper functioning of the organism as a whole and also to basic rational decision-making. Such research also shows once again the extent to which our personhood is a construct and the extent to which it relies on the integration of body, brain, and mind. The impact of such emotional disconnect is, if anything, even more profound. In some ways it is easier to acknowledge that our reasoning and perceptual abilities emerge from the constructs of the brain. While such abilities are indeed important to us, we do not generally consider them as central as emotional dispositions are for defining selfhood and personality. Emotions touch at the core of who we are. To lose most of our emotional associations, as subjects with prefrontal damage apparently do, seems virtually inconceivable and, to many, hellish.

Brain damage can cause a total change in personality. We prefer to think that our personality, at least to a significant extent, is under our own control. While I may not be able to achieve happiness on command, I can at least determine my own outlook on life and thereby exert control over the type of person I will be. If I have made a mess of my life, and even if I suffered through a horrible childhood and grew up in a negative social environment, the power is within me to turn around. If only Hamlet had resolved to put away his infirmity of character, things might have been different. Shy, emotionally straitjacketed Laura in Tennessee Williams's *Glass Menagerie* draws our pity at the same time as she evokes the thought within us, "I wouldn't put up with that kind of life!"

But is the choice really ours to make? While persons with prefrontal damage indeed suffer a huge loss, their subsequent behavior is not out of the realm of ordinary human experience. We know many who consistently made poor choices and thus wasted their lives. To what extent is this simply a matter of choice and to what extent is it, to put it crudely, a matter of biology? Was Phineas Gage free before the spike blew through his brain, but less so afterwards? In what sense was he responsible for his own decisions after the accident, and to what extent can it be blamed on the brain damage he suffered?

These questions have emerged in a quite different way with regard to our growing knowledge of the role neurotransmitters play in brain functioning and particularly to the emergence of a significant pharmaceutical industry that modifies their production and absorption. When a typical neuron fires, it releases neurotransmitters at the axon; these neurotransmitters then bind to receptor sites on the dendrite of the neighboring neuron. This binding creates an electric potential in the neighboring neuron, causing it to fire in turn. The neurotransmitters are then typically released and taken up again by the originally firing neuron. There are more than forty neurotransmitters in the brain—perhaps many more. Not all neurons respond to all neurotransmitters equally, and some neurotransmitters serve not to transmit as such but to encourage or inhibit transmission. Furthermore, neurotransmitters are produced only at certain sites in the brain, and the supply of neurotransmitters affects the rate and manner in which neurons fire.

The role of neurotransmitters in the brain is highly complex and in some ways one of the strangest features of brain functioning. While the firing of a neuron is often compared to the binary state of a logic gate in a computer, there is no computational analogue for neurotransmitters. This is not only because of the way that neurotransmitters affect the firing of neurons but also because of the way in which neurotransmitters connect the state of individual neurons to the global state of the organism. As is now well known, exercise can result in the release of endorphins. Endorphins affect neuron firing, which in turn can create an elevated mood, sometimes resulting in a "runner's high." Physical, cognitive, and emotional states affect the release of neurotransmitters, which affects the firing of neurons and thus future physical, cognitive, and emotional states.

The connection between these comparatively simple molecules and our emotional states is, on the face of it, perplexing. It is not at all clear why their impact on neuron firing should affect us the way they do. Yet, the fact that such chemicals do affect us in precisely this way has been known, at least on a folk level, since the dawn of recorded history and likely before. Alcohol and drug consumption is hardly a modern phenomenon, and their mood-altering capacity has been used over the millennia for a variety of social and religious purposes. Psychoactive substances typically work by either mimicking neurotransmitters or inhibiting their proper functions in nerve transmission. The fact that such substances can temporarily transform personality hardly needs mentioning.

It is only recently, however, that we have begun to understand the role that natural neurotransmitters play in mental health and self-regulation. This has been brought to public attention particularly by the success of Prozac and similar drugs that work by blocking the re-uptake of the neurotransmitter serotonin, effectively increasing the amount of it in the brain. While originally designed for such conditions as manic-depressive disorder, these drugs have since been widely used to treat clinical depression, sometimes with striking effect. In many cases the drug not only cures the depression, but patients experience a subtle yet significant shift in their personalities. As observed by clinical psychiatrist Peter Kramer in *Listening to Prozac*, such patients sometimes describe themselves as "better than well."[22] Individuals who have struggled all their life with shyness or low self-esteem find themselves for the first time willing to be active in social situations and take risks. Marital and sexual relationships are transformed as individuals marvel at what they had been willing to put up with. Prozac users sometimes found themselves more successful at work as well. In the eyes of some, Prozac and thereby serotonin seemed a kind of cure-all, all the better because it was supposedly nonaddictive and usually did not have any significant side effects.

Such exuberance has sometimes given drugs a bad name. They do not work equally well for everyone or in all contexts. Indeed, they seemed most effective with what Kramer calls "penumbra" patients, those who are borderline cases, not clearly clinically ill. Although such accounts are anecdotal, the effect seems to be real—troublingly so. It seems strange that a single chemical could have such a global effect on personality. Is changing personality really as simple as taking a pill? Are we entering,

Kramer frets, a new era of cosmetic pharmacology, where we can use drugs to change our personality if we do not like the one we have?

Such concerns are, at least so far, a bit overwrought. But, as with the case of Phineas Gage, they do reveal the extent to which the criteria by which we define who we are is affected by the mechanisms of the brain and biology. More than this, however, the ability of fairly simple chemicals to alter our sense of well-being touches on the issue of soteriological freedom discussed at the beginning of this chapter. A significant element of the Christian tradition has been the promise of personal transformation. The fullness of Christ's love is not something simply postponed until the afterlife but something that, at least to a certain extent, is experienced now. In the months leading to his conversion, Augustine experienced considerable pain, confusion, and internal turmoil. Afterward these disappeared. Confident in the promise of God's grace, Augustine seems to have never looked back. Newly assured and transformed, he thereafter led a celibate life and assumed significant leadership in the church.

Would Augustine's spiritual crisis have been better dealt with by taking a pill? Hardly. While serious consideration of our biology may give us pause, brain chemistry alone does not eliminate anguish or set our priorities in life. But Augustine's sense of well-being after his conversion cannot be understood as only a spiritual change but not a physical and biological one, for the simple reason that such neat divisions no longer make sense. Our "spirit," however we may define that, emerges out of the activities of the mind/brain, which in turn are intimately connected to the body. A spiritual transformation, therefore, is in some sense also a biological one. Soteriology must therefore include the whole person. This seems to imply that, while salvation is not limited to brain chemistry, any full concept of salvation must include it.

This seems strange. The sphere of religion is usually understood as separate from and above other considerations. Human biology belongs to medical doctors, psychology belongs to psychologists, and spirit is the province of pastors and theologians. Such a hierarchy presumes that these separate levels are independent of one another. They are not. That this is so has significant implications for soteriology. If theological claims about personal transformation are correct, then this must mean that any account of mental health that relies on psychological categories alone is incomplete, for mental health must ultimately include the whole person, which presumably includes the kind of spiritual orientation that is implied by participation in a life of faith. Likewise, theological claims about soteriology are incomplete unless they take the whole person—body, brain and all—into account. A religious transformation is also a psychological transformation. It is even a biological one.

This may seem a novel and foreign idea, but perhaps it is not. The ministry of Jesus was notable as much for his healings as for his teachings. The coming of the kingdom of God involved not only a spiritual transformation but in many ways a physical one as well. While two millennia and countless technical achievements separate us from the time of the Gospels, it appears that in some cases old insights can still surprise.

Constrained to Be Free

Are we free? The question is deceptively simple, for freedom implies many things. To be free implies that there is someone, a subject, who can act on that freedom. Cognitive science does not deny such a subject, but it does show that the kind of freedom we have is dependent on the complexities of our mind/brain. These are startlingly revealed by extreme forms of brain damage, but they are revealed also in our still limited understanding of our emotional lives. Such complexity suggests that the kind of freedom we have is itself complex. It is not simply a matter of whether we can do anything or nothing but what we are enabled to do.

For some, this may not seem to answer the question directly. Freedom, in the metaphysical sense, is opposed to determinism. In asking whether we are free, the metaphysical theologian wants to know whether my actions are fully determined by my environment or whether they in some sense originate from inside myself. If a person turns to a life of crime, is it as a result of personal choice, environment, or neural chemistry?

Freedom in this sense can take us beyond the cognitive sciences and indeed beyond the realms of the sciences altogether. The sciences by themselves cannot tell us whether the world is fully deterministic. Dominant interpretations of quantum physics suggest, in fact, that it is not. Instead, the world has some indeterminism built in, even though in most physical processes this indeterminism largely disappears at the level of living organisms. But even here there is always the gap between empirical evidence and ultimate claim. One can interpret the physics differently, as unlikely as that now seems to many.

One might do better to draw a contrast between ourselves and our immediate environment. Environmental determinism seems quite difficult to sustain, and our current understanding of cognitive science does little to support it. Behaviorist psychology presupposed such environmental determinism and foundered precisely because it provided no straightforward way to account for complex human behavior. Our environmental conditions certainly constrain us, more so than we probably realize. But the sheer complexity of the human mind and the logic of its internal workings render meaningless any environmentally deterministic position. For any given environmental input there are typically many behavioral outputs, because the actions we take depend crucially on our own history and personality.

One might go further and observe that our behavior is significantly constrained by our genes and by the particular wiring and architecture of our brain. Indeed, many of the experiments cited above are sometimes taken to support just this point. But such observations work only if we assume that these features of my biology are separate from the "me" that decides. This line of thought falls into the trap of assuming that "I" am separate from my body and brain in such a way that I can say that it is my brain doing the action, not I. But it is precisely my body and brain that are integral to my normal functioning. It is as if a follower of Descartes said that I am not free, because all my actions are fully determined by the proper functioning of my soul. Such an argument makes the mistake of assuming that, in a Cartesian dualist framework, the soul and "I" are distinct and separate things.

Owen Flanagan observes that this kind of mistake is frequently made in interpreting a famous experiment conducted by Benjamin Libet.[23] In the experiment, Libet had individuals watch a clock as they flexed a finger. The subjects were asked to occasionally flex their fingers spontaneously and to observe on the clock the precise moment at which they decided to do this. At the same time, Libet had the individuals hooked up to an electroencephelograph that measured brainwave patterns and, in particular, a pattern that Libet designated the "readiness potential" that indicated the onset of an action. What Libet found was that the conscious intent to flex the finger took place approximately 200 milliseconds before the actual flexing, but the readiness potential registered at about 350 milliseconds prior to the conscious willing. The implication seemed to be that the conscious willing is the result of a prior unconscious process, making the conscious intent causally inert.

While the experimental setup does allow differences of interpretation, Flanagan notes that the conscious mind can be considered causally inert only if one presumes no prior history to the experimental set-up. In order for the experiment to proceed, however, subjects previously had to agree to do the experiment and, presumably consciously, listen to and understand the instructions given to make the experiment work. The mistake is to separate consciousness from the rest of the person and its history; when this is taken into account, the simple claim for determinism and the irrelevance of consciousness become harder to claim.

In many ways it is the very determinate structure of our brain and biology that enables the kind of freedom we have. This may not get us fully to a metaphysical freedom, but it is at least empirically consistent with it, which is the most we can ask from the sciences on such an issue. It also suggests that our freedom is developed out of specific kinds of constraints. Human beings are, for instance, quite good at recognizing and remembering faces, and certain kinds of brain damage can result in prosopagnosia, the inability to recognize individual faces while otherwise being visually unimpaired. We do not remember names as well, however, and most of us are familiar with recognizing the face but forgetting the name—only rarely is it the reverse! Our ability to recognize and remember faces provides a degree of freedom and is important in social communication and relationships. Language provides another degree of freedom. The ability to empathize and to think about your thoughts (an ability that individuals suffering from some forms of autism may lack) provides another.[24]

We are, then, both bound and free, and it is because of the particular form of our bondage that we have the kind of freedom that we do. Such an observation by itself does not resolve the Luther-Erasmus debate, in part because their understandings of freedom were so profoundly different. But it might provide a starting point for considering the issue afresh. Metaphysically, one can at least affirm our own empirical freedom, a freedom that means that the self is not simply a product of its environment but is formed by its own decisions and choices. At the same time, our freedom is enabled by the particular, embodied constructive character of our mind/brain/body. Almost paradoxically, we are empowered by our limitations. Out of this comes the need for soteriology. Luther argued that our nature is so bound that we are unable on our own truly to will the good. Consequently, for Luther, true freedom meant a transformation brought about by Christ, which could be achieved only through God's action. Here theological claims transcend what can be ascertained by cognitive science, but the border between the two can be significant. Cognitive science cannot speak of the true freedom that Luther and so many of us seek, but it can at least remind us that such freedom is not merely a freedom of the mind but of the whole person. Recognizing this can correct what has sometimes been an escapist trajectory in the Christian tradition as well as provide new insights into the kinds of freedom worth having.

5

Mysterium Tremendum

In the fall of 1997, neuroscientist V. S. Ramachandran presented a research paper in which he claimed that certain kinds of religious experience originate in the temporal lobe of the brain. While Ramachandran's observations were careful and tentative, the claim that there existed a "God spot" in the brain was quickly picked up by the press and circulated nationally. The implications seemed profound but could be taken in opposite ways. For some, a God-spot suggested that religious experience is integral to human nature. Humans, it would appear, are made to communicate with God, and scientists had finally stumbled onto a clue as to how such communication worked. For others, however, the existence of a God-spot demonstrated the exact opposite. Religious experiences could now be explained as neurological phenomena. People who claimed to speak to God or see visions of the Virgin Mary were in fact doing no such thing; their brains were merely short-circuiting.

Such varied reactions reveal the profound ambivalence that research into religious experience generates. Because science and scientists hold such high status in our modern technological society, any scientific validation of religious claims is highly desirable. But science characteristically explains things by reducing higher-order phenomena to the operations of lower-order objects. If religious experience is real and if we are physical beings, we might assume that it would leave some telltale trace in its wake. But if the sciences can completely explain why and how religious experiences occur, some would argue that such experiences cease to be genuinely religious, arising not from the actions of God but from the activities of neurons.

Is this the case? Probably not. The question of religious experience is often perceived to be in the borderlands of science. Good research on the subject is sparse and interpretations are rarely clean-cut. As a result, research into the biological basis of religious experience is not determinative but suggestive and worthy of consideration, providing a small window into how we might think of the most important of life's events.

On the Road to Damascus

Is research into religious experience really an issue for Christian thinkers? After all, the church historically has had a significantly ambivalent relationship with claims by individuals regarding direct revelations from God or inspiration of one sort or another. Jewish and Christian traditions have been significantly shaped by individuals who had profound religious experiences. Isaiah had a vision of God's throne, and Paul had a vision of the risen Jesus on the road to Damascus. At the same time, individuals who claim to have direct inspiration from God can cause divisiveness and fanaticism. The late Pastoral Epistles of the New Testament thus warn against false prophets, and the early second-century bishop Ignatius of Antioch insisted on the authority of the bishop over those who might claim direct communication with God. Although medieval Catholicism allowed the growth of mysticism, it was with a wary eye. While the Reformation emphasized the category of faith, the dominant Protestant churches quickly intellectualized faith into a more controllable form, only to experience an upswell of experiential emphasis in the Pietist and Wesleyan revivals of the eighteenth and nineteenth centuries. It is safe to say that, generally speaking, Christianity as an institution has encouraged some religious experience, but not too much.

Despite the ambivalence of official doctrine, religious experience of one form or another has been centrally important to many believers throughout the centuries, whether in approved or unapproved forms. The testimonies of such significant figures as Augustine, Catherine of Sienna, and Søren Kierkegaard only touch the surface of those who have emphasized this point in various ways. Religious experience is important also as the basis of scripture itself. The Bible is widely considered to be inspired, and many think that the significance of the biblical message depends on the prophets and apostles authentically speaking God's word, not merely voicing their own opinions. Indeed, the central claim of the Christian faith focuses on the incarnation of God in Jesus, presumably a category of experience apart from what we can fathom.

Religious experience is manifested also in the historical trajectories of specific denominational traditions. While many—although obviously not all—persons get deep spiritual fulfillment out of traditional worship, some traditions are distinctive in the way they characterize and foster certain kinds of religious experience. Catholicism has maintained a high value on rich and pluriform religious experience in both popular and official practice. Such movements as the Quakers and Pentecostalism have embraced particular kinds of religious experience that are in many ways at odds with other mainstream Protestant denominations.

Religious experience serves both to unify and to divide Christianity. At the same time, religious experiences are not confined to Christians, raising issues about the absoluteness of the Christian tradition. Surveys, for instance, indicate that from approximately 40 percent to 70 percent of individuals interviewed in the United States and Great Britain claim to have had some kind of religious experience in their life, the higher percentages greater than than church attendance in these countries.[1] These numbers, however, mask a complex situation. Religious experience is itself a vague term, and different kinds of people are apt to include in the term different kinds of experiences. More than this, even a casual perusal of the quite varied testimonies given by individuals of their religious experiences quickly indicates that not all religious experiences fit into a single framework. Whatever perspective we take, we must finally decide that some experiences are either falsely reported—the result of intentional deception—or the result of self-deception or psychological states that have other, purely naturalistic explanations. This means that religious experience plays a complex role in religious and theological apologetic.

Realizing the diversity of religious experiences makes the theological task more difficult, for interpreting the reality and significance of religious experiences implies interaction not only with psychology and neuroscience but with a diversity of religious traditions as well. One of the great selling points of religious traditions that emphasize meditative practices, such as Zen Buddhism and forms of Hinduism, is that they can claim a sort of empirical confirmation. One need not rely on faith or dogma; one can verify religious truths directly through the experience of enlightenment or higher states of consciousness. Potentially, research on religious experience gives theology an empirical content that it is not normally perceived to have. That religious experiences may confirm or disconfirm particular religious truth claims has not been lost on scholars and laypersons. Indeed, this point has been made by a number of contemporary theologians, although they are careful to point out that theological claims do not rely solely on such experiences.[2] The danger is that religious experience can be used to defend narrowly polemical agendas. The promise, however, is that religious experiences might be able to provide the basis for a kind of genuine dialogue and insight that are sometimes lacking from interreligious discourse.

Are They Real?

When first confronted with someone else's claims to religious experience, our first reaction tends to be disbelief. There are many kinds of incredible, first-person reports, from ghost stories to UFO abduction accounts that, however sincerely delivered, seem impossible to believe. Likewise, more religiously oriented claims such as past-life regression, visions of the Virgin Mary, glossolalia, and demon possession seem equally dubious to many, both because they do not fit very well into a scientifically informed view of the world and because the sheer variety of such experiences (and the truths and values they are taken to imply) are difficult to account for theologically. Indeed, the more extravagant the experience, the more likely we are to associate it with psychological pathology of one form or another than to take it seriously.

On the other end of the spectrum, it is not always clear when an experience should be designated as religious in character. Religious experiences can range from the extraordinary out-of-body experience to the relatively ordinary though no less significant experience of awe or sense of overpowering joy. While a sense of overpowering joy may indeed have religious significance, it can be difficult to define what is distinctively religious about it. At least in some cases it seems that a religious experience is as much defined by its context as by the quality of the experience itself. Both the Grand Canyon and intense prayer may provoke a sense of awe and wonder, but we are more likely to classify the latter as religious than the former.

Because of this ambiguity, scholars such as Wayne Proudfoot and Stephen Katz have argued that religious experiences do not form any separate category of experience.[3] Religious experiences are products of culture, which is why Buddhist monks do not have visions of the Virgin Mary and Catholic nuns do not go on vision quests. When mystics claim that their experiences cannot be put into words but nevertheless insist that such experiences provide significant insight and information as to the nature of things, Katz and Proudfoot argue that the reason such experiences cannot be verbalized is that they lack any content other than what is provided by the cultural expectations of the community of which the experiencer is a part. The implication of this is that religious experiences are not real in the sense that their agency stems from God or a higher plane of reality but are reducible to forms of cultural expression. Any claim to the contrary is simply mistaken.

There is some merit to this view, inasmuch as cultural conditioning can play a significant role in the formation and interpretation of experiences generally and religious experiences specifically. In a well-known experiment by Stanley Schacter and Jerome Singer, subjects injected with adrenaline reacted differently to the sudden agitation of their body according to social cues of other subjects planted in the room by the experimenters. When the planted subjects acted angry, they acted angry; when the planted subjects acted euphoric, they acted euphoric as well.[4] As indicated below, there is clear evidence that cultural conditioning can play a significant role in the formation and interpretation of religious experiences. It would be surprising if this were not the case, for one of the hallmarks of many religious traditions is the elaborate preparations that are made precisely for the purpose of provoking such responses, whether it be the ecstatic dancing of dervishes or the asceticism of medieval monks.

To reduce all religious experiences to the category of culture, however, is a profound mistake. This mistake partly rests upon the philosophical claim influenced by the later writings of Ludwig Wittgenstein, among others, that all experiences are mediated by language and, more strongly, that all experiences, including religious experiences, are reducible to modes of linguistic and cultural expression. Just as the experience of pain is not separable from its verbal expression, so religious experience is inseparable from its description.

Such a view, while once influential, is highly problematic for several reasons. Language certainly plays a dramatically important role in our cognitive processes; virtually all of our conscious thinking is linguistically mediated. But it would be a mistake to say that experience cannot be separated from language and culture or that experiences have no meaning in and of themselves. For one thing, this implies that all those who do not have language—animals, infants, and some stroke victims—do not have experiences or, by implication, thoughts! There are some first-hand accounts of stroke and epilepsy victims who have temporarily lost linguistic comprehension. While they suffered significant hardship and confusion, they were far from incapable during such difficult episodes.[5] More generally, reducing experience to language shears away the significance of a great deal of our everyday experience, much of which is simply not reducible to words. The colors I experience are not limited to my relatively impoverished color vocabulary. No amount of reading about parental love can be equated with and prepare one for the emotional experience itself.

A broader problem with such cultural approaches is the extent to which they seem neatly to separate culture from biology and consequently mind from body. Not only do these approaches imply that culture and mind are completely separate from biology and body but also that culture is active while the mind passive. Yet, as Damasio's research on the role of emotion in cognition (see above, chapter 4) helps to show, the situation is much more complex. Biology, emotions, and thought are intertwined in a way that prohibits such neat disjunctions. Thus, while experiences are often (and in some cases always) culturally conditioned, they are not culturally determined.

It is at this point that the cognitive sciences begin to become important. Because cultural realities are not completely separable from cognitive and biological ones, any understanding of religious experience must include cognitive and biological factors. Consequently, while the causes of religious experiences may be beyond the grasp of science, the physical correlates of religious experience certainly are not. Realizing this has provided a suggestive ground for research, and the result has been the development of a quite varied set of studies. The results, while intriguing, do not by themselves tell a single story. They are nevertheless provocative in their potential for thinking through the issue of the reality of religious experiences and how they are to be interpreted.

Religion on the Brain

Strangely enough, a primary obstacle to the study of religious experience by psychologists and cognitive scientists has been acknowledging its existence. For much of the twentieth century, religious experiences were relegated to the category of pathology. William James, an early exception to this rule, criticized the medical materialists of his day who attributed Paul's conversion experience to epilepsy and who reduced religious experience to the "perverted action of various glands which physiology will yet discover."[6] Psychoanalysts, following Freud, tended to be equally dismissive, and in many psychology texts and manuals, including the widely used *Diagnostic and Statistical Manual of Mental Disorders*, religion was rarely mentioned except as a means to illustrate various mental illnesses.[7] Early speculation on the neurological roots of religious experience proved to be equally unpromising. In his 1976 *The Origin of Consciousness in the Breakdown of the Bicameral Mind*, Julian Jaynes argued that ancient religious experiences and therefore the origin of religion as well stemmed from an early stage of brain evolution when the two hemispheres of the cerebral cortex were not fully connected, resulting in the conscious left hemisphere hearing voices from the right hemisphere. These voices were interpreted by the ancients as the voices of gods, giving rise both to the mythological worldview of the *Iliad* and the *Odyssey* and also to the Hebrew prophets. It was only after that ancient period that the hemispheres fully united, with the result that such religious experiences now occur only among the mentally ill in states associated with schizophrenia.

Strangely enough, despite the lack of any genuine evidence and despite some significant leaps in reasoning, many people took this thesis seriously. Jaynes's ability to synthesize a wide range of material into a single thesis was impressive and, as we shall see, his association of religious experience with the functioning of the right hemisphere might have some merit. His claim that such a major change in brain function and organization occurred as recently as the Homeric age, however, not only lacks any supporting paleoanthropological and genetic evidence (how did such changes get to Australia?) but does a serious disservice to the complexity of ancient literatures from across the world. If anything, its initial success suggests the lengths some scholars will go to categorize religious experience as pathology. To treat religious experience seriously is to give credibility to something that seems, to a reductive modern mind-set, too much like voodoo.

Interestingly, early empirical research into religious experience by psychologists that went beyond simple surveys was conducted as part of broader research into altered states. Experimentation with drugs and Zen Buddhism—and sometimes both—in the 1960s and 70s provided a venue for exploring religious experience that was amenable to experimental control. A number of these studies seemed to support the thesis that religious experience is defined more by cultural context than by the experience itself, at least in the case of artificially controlled situations when ambiguous stimuli are introduced.

Research by Masters and Houston into the potential of psychedelic drugs for triggering religious experiences, for instance, revealed that the use of such drugs as LSD often did produce religious imagery, although such hallucinations were not perceived by the users to be religious experiences as such. A study by Timothy Leary indicated that the likelihood of a drug experience being described as a religious experience correlated with the religious context of drug use.[8] Studies of drug use in this form eventually became illegal and were followed by a quite different approach to exploring altered states, one that used sensory-deprivation tanks. A subject was placed in a tank, essentially a closed coffin filled with a neutral buoyancy liquid at body temperature that allowed a subject to float with virtually no physical sensation. Deprived of any sensory stimulation, it was not unusual to experience the appearance of spontaneous images. In a study conducted by Hood and Morris, it was found that individuals with strong religious commitments were more likely to experience religious imagery, especially if subjects were cued for it.[9]

Such experiments do not tell us much. Plants with hallucinogenic effects have been used in a variety of religious contexts across history and are still used by some Native American groups today. These experiments also reveal something about the importance of cultural context, although even this is fairly minimal, since in neither case do we have a full theory for why or how the religious experiences are generated in the first place—or even whether these cases should be regarded as genuine religious experiences.

More definite results have been obtained from experiments monitoring brain waves in the EEG (electroencephalogram) of individuals practicing meditation. Brain waves are a measure of the aggregate activity of large groups of neurons within areas of the brain, allowing researchers to detect broad patterns of brain activity during specific kinds of activities. In an array of early experiments that measured the brain-wave patterns of meditators, it was regularly found that meditational states corresponded with distinct brain-wave pattern activity and even that transitions into more advanced stages of meditation could be correlated with further brain-wave changes.[10] To give one specific example, Kasamatsu and Hirai studied twenty-three Zen disciples during meditation. They found that a meditator goes through a series of four stages during each meditation session, beginning with the alpha waves (typical of both inward-focused attention and deep relaxation) and ending for advanced practitioners with theta waves, which are usually associated with drowsiness and hypnotic states. Only those who had meditated for more than twenty years showed theta-wave activity. More interestingly, the Zen master responsible for the disciples' development could clearly and accurately distinguish between those disciples who were at different meditational stages without recourse to the brain-wave data. Barring some kind of extrasensory perception on the part of the Zen master, the achievements made during meditation had clear outward effects discernible by someone trained to observe them.[11]

It would be a mistake to assume that such results either prove Buddhist claims about enlightenment or, conversely, that enlightenment is reducible to brain states. What they do suggest is that embarking on a path of meditational practice can lead to a kind of experience that is, to a degree, quantifiable. In the case of Zen Buddhism, prolonged meditation leads to distinctive patterns of brain activity, and these distinctive patterns presumably correlate with certain kinds of experiences. While such evidence does not fully disprove the position of Katz and Proudfoot that religious experience is merely a product of cultural conditioning, it makes the position more tenuous and, it seems, puts the burden of proof on their position. If religious experiences are purely a cultural construct, the sort of physiological states (including brain states) that we see develop during prolonged meditation should not matter. What appears to be the case, however, is that cultural context over time produces new physiological states, which in turn lead to new cultural possibilities. Levels of human experience turn out to be integrated, not separate.

Despite this, brain-wave patterns are limited in their potential for telling us what is going on in the brain during a religious experience and fall well short of providing a full theory of the kind that Jaynes ambitiously attempted. Brain-wave measurements provide little help in identifying specific regions of the brain that correlate to specific forms of religious experience. For this, neuroscientists turn to two other methods that provide more specific data. The first involves patients with existing, localized brain damage who consequently seem to experience new or increased religious experiences. The second relies on brain scans of individuals shortly after activity that correlates with religious experience. Such research is still quite fragmentary, but these approaches have captured significant attention in recent years.

Correlations between brain damage and religious experience have been explored in different ways by Michael Persinger and V. S. Ramachandran, both of whom have drawn inspiration from studies of temporal lobe epilepsy.[12] Described by Hippocrates as the "sacred disease," epilepsy has long had an association with religious inspiration, likely due in no small part to the dramatic seizures that epileptics suffer and that suggest the control of the individual by outside forces. Some epileptics, however, do experience a kind of euphoria prior to the onset of seizure that is sometimes described in religious terms. The Russian writer Dostoyevsky is perhaps the most famous sufferer of this malady, and the religious quality of his seizures was conveyed in his novels.

Ramachandran's experience with patients suffering from temporal lobe epilepsy led him to speculate that there may be an area of the brain significantly responsible for religious experience. Temporal lobe epileptics in his care seemed to show an interest in religion that overwhelmed everything else. Could it be that such people simply found tremendous significance in everything they saw? One of the functions of the temporal lobe is to process the emotional significance of visual images. Perhaps this "temporal lobe salience detector," as Ramachandran called it, becomes overactive in temporal lobe epileptics, resulting indirectly in their preoccupation with religion. If so, this would imply that there is a distinctive area in the brain responsible for religious belief.

To test this, Ramachandran used three groups of subjects. The first had temporal lobe epilepsy that was accompanied by extreme preoccupation with religion. Those in the second group had no brain abnormality but were determined by a questionnaire to be highly religious. Those in the third group had no brain abnormality and were not religious. Ramachandran displayed a variety of words and images on a computer screen to these subjects while measuring galvanic skin responses (GSR, the basis of lie-detector tests) that reflect a person's emotional arousal. The pictures shown to the subjects were quite varied, including such ordinary items as shoes and tables but also emotionally provocative images involving sex, extreme violence, or horror. Included in the presentations were religious words and images. Surprisingly, the response of the temporal lobe epileptics to all emotionally charged imagery was lower than one would expect for normal subjects but significantly higher to the religious words and images. These results led Ramachandran tentatively to speculate that there exists in the temporal lobe an area responsible for religious experience (it was this speculation, and particularly the use of the term "God-module," that led to short-lived but significant media interest). Ramachandran even briefly speculates about a "Godectomy" caused by removing this crucial area of the temporal lobe.

While perhaps excusable in a popular work, such speculations are more whimsical than useful and, at least to date, have not constituted a serious research project. The vast majority of individuals are not temporal lobe epileptics, and it is far from clear that all religious experiences are of the same nature as those experienced by such individuals. Such conditions are not even universal among temporal lobe epileptics. Further, the group of normal individuals who were classified as very religious showed no significant increase in GSR to religious stimuli, suggesting that the increase seen in the epileptic subjects was a symptom of pathology and not an index of religious experience or devotion per se. So it is problematic to associate the temporal lobe with religious experiences or practices in people without brain damage. The rather small sample size (two) and the lack of peer review are also complicating features. The result has been a cautious evaluation of such cases of temporal lobe epilepsy for thinking about religious experience generally.[13] Nevertheless, Ramachandran's findings are significant to the extent that they indicate the general approach that neuroscience takes toward religious experiences. If people do have religious experiences (of which there seems to be little doubt), then such experiences must in some way be an activity of the brain. By locating this brain activity we may not find the ultimate source of such experience (about which Ramachandran is agnostic), but we could at least understand why religious experience takes the form that it does.

Such a broader project has been the focus of the late Eugene d'Aquili and Andrew Newberg.[14] Coining the term neurotheology to describe their work, d'Aquili and Newberg have sought to explain the neural basis of all religious experience. In their approach, the brain works by means of seven cognitive operators (table 5.1) which, somewhat analogous to Immanuel Kant's categories, act on the information that the brain continually receives. The causal operator, for instance, is responsible for seeking out causal relationships, a task obviously important for the physical sciences as well as many tasks in ordinary life. The reductionist operator analyzes an object or idea in terms of its parts, while the contrasting holistic operator tries to perceive parts as part of a larger whole, much as a gestalt. Generally speaking, these operators are understood to be located in specific areas of the brain according to our current knowledge of neuroanatomy and function, although the evidence for some of the operators, such as the emotional operator identified with the limbic system, is better than others, such as the binary operator, which is not assigned any location in the brain.

The Holistic Operator
The Reductionist Operator
The Causal Operator
The Abstractive Operator
The Binary Operator
The Quantitative Operator
The Emotional Value Operator

Table 5.1. The Seven Cognitive Operators
[From d'Aquili and Newberg (1999). Used with permission.]

Since these operators are understood to give an essentially complete account of the brain's cognitive operations, d'Aquili and Newberg claim that they can be used to understand all forms of religious expression and experience. Building on the work of anthropologist Claude Lévi-Strauss, who emphasized an understanding of myth in terms of the resolution of opposites, d'Aquili and Newberg claim that mythic narratives are a construct of the binary operator.[15] Ritual, in turn, is a physical attempt at resolving these polarities. This resolution of polarities, whether in myth, ritual, or meditation, is seen to be at the core of religious experience, understood by d'Aquili and Newberg as a state of Absolute Unitary Being (AUB), which occurs cross-culturally.

The most important element and the one that has attracted the most attention in d'Aquili and Newberg's account of religious experience deals with how AUB arises in the brain. Activities such as ritual and meditation work toward achieving various levels of AUB by causing a cascade of events that stimulate emotional pathways at the same time that areas in the parietal lobe of the cerebral cortex associated with spatial orientation are cut off in a process called "deafferentation." Since the parietal lobes are involved in spatial awareness and self-other distinctions, cutting off these areas would (it is claimed) result in the emergence of a mystical state. Deafferentation is said to occur as a result of the overstimulation of the sympathetic and parasympathetic systems of the brain, described by d'Aquili and Newberg as being responsible for states of arousal and quiescence, respectively. While these two systems usually compete with another (the sympathetic system is active when the parasympathetic system is passive, and vice versa), it is claimed that specifically religious activities such as repetitive ritual dancing and focused meditation often result in a kind of spillover effect that activates both systems. Deafferentation is said to be the result, creating the conscious state of AUB.

In a test of this hypothesis, an experiment was conducted with eight Tibetan Buddhists who were experienced at meditation.[16] In each case, when a meditator had achieved an advanced meditational state, he was injected with a radioactive compound that labeled brain areas according to the amount of blood flow in each area at the time of injection. More blood flow was interpreted as greater brain activity, less blood flow with less activity. Twenty minutes after injection, subjects were given a SPECT (Single Photon Emission Computed Tomography) scan to image the radioactivity bound in the brain. When compared to initial baseline scans, the results were consistent with their hypothesis, showing in particular decreased activity in the left parietal lobe (figure 5.1).

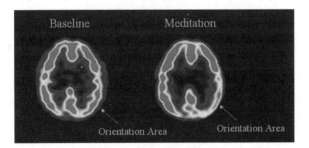

Fig. 5.1. SPECT scan of a Tibetan monk before and shortly after meditation. The view of the brain is as if taken from below, so that the left hemisphere appears on the right, and the right on the left. The parietal lobe shows markedly less activity during meditation. [Photo courtesy of Andrew Newburg.]

What do such results imply? On the one hand, d'Aquili and Newberg are careful to avoid a reductionism that denies the existence and reality of the phenomenal state that the meditators experience. That is, the fact that there are brain states that correlate with the experience of AUB does not mean that AUB does not exist or that the insights that it provides are false. Because all states of consciousness are brain states of one sort or another, d'Aquili and Newberg point out, whatever mode of consciousness we experience will in fact have such correlative brain states. Indeed, they argue, there is no real reason to suppose that normal states of consciousness should be privileged over the forms of consciousness experienced in ritual and meditation, which may indeed provide genuine insights into the nature of reality that are actually cloaked during normal experience. Indeed, because of this they argue that God and religion are integral parts of human experience and that the biological roots of religion explain why—contrary to the expectations of many secular thinkers—religious belief has not only failed to disappear but has even experienced something of a resurgence in the late twentieth century.[17]

On the other hand, it is also clear, although left unsaid, that their work suggests that brain states are to a significant extent the primary causative agent in the formation of such meditational experiences. This point may not be important for some Buddhists, since enlightenment is to a significant extent something that is pursued (somewhat paradoxically) by the individual. For Christians, however, the question of causation is of greater importance, since it has been traditionally assumed that a genuine religious experience will have God as its source. Newberg and associates also performed a similar study on Franciscan nuns during prayer.[18] SPECT scans of the nuns showed deafferentation in the parietal lobe, seeming to confirm that the nuns experience a form of AUB during intense, focused prayer. Assuming that these scans do in fact reveal a component of religious experience associated with prayer, should we suppose that we are seeing the hand of God (so to speak) in the minds of the nuns? Or is the religious experience self-generated by the concentration and verbalization that is a necessary part of prayer? The scans of the nuns' brains show heightened activity in the forebrain and in verbal association areas, but this is what one might expect in any verbal task. Without a control group we cannot tell whether this pattern is distinctive. Additionally, since prayer is not always accompanied by religious experience (a fact that can be testified to by many, both sincere and insincere in their faith), it is not clear how we should interpret this data. Are these states central to the task of prayer, or are they an incidental but positive side effect?

Despite these questions, as Ramachandran's work, d'Aquili and Newberg's research does raise significant questions about how we think about religious experience. Research that shows a biological basis for religious experience seems to be a two-edged sword, for at the same time that it confirms the reality of such experience, it always threatens to undermine the broader religious claims about its nature and cause. As with Ramachandran, d'Aquili and Newberg's work is preliminary and raises as many questions as it claims to solve. For instance, would damage to the left parietal lobe affect a meditator's ability to achieve states of enlightenment? Are such experiences truly cross-cultural, suggesting a potential unifying principle to religions after all? Perhaps more to the point: is that all there is to it?

Messages from Whom?

Research on religious experience remains in its infancy. With only limited data, we are a long way from providing a scientific account that could claim to be both authoritative and comprehensive. Nevertheless, even this early research poses the important conceptual question as to how religious experience should be understood and in what ways we should see religious experience manifested (or not) in the brain. It certainly makes difficult the claim that religious experiences are *merely* derivatives of culture and suggests that there is in such experiences a biological basis, at least in part. At the same time, however, these experiments do not show that there is no cultural element, and it is important to recognize this as well. To achieve such meditational states requires significant preparation that itself is a product of developed religious practice. While d'Aquili and Newberg's theory makes sense of the experiences of unity and bliss that mystics across the world have attested to, it does not support stronger religious claims regarding the origin and significance of these experiences. As far as biology is concerned, there is plenty of room to interpret such states as an experience of nirvana or the love of God culturally. Indeed, if mystics from different traditions could be shown to be having the same brain states despite their different interpretations, would this validate or invalidate their claims? What, after all, are these brain states experiences of?

There appear to be three different interpretations of the evidence obtained so far from brain-wave studies, Ramachandran's work with temporal lobe patients, and d'Aquili and Newberg's work with Tibetan meditators. First, one may argue that the existence of brain states that correlate with religious experiences show that such religious experiences have no basis in reality but are essentially illusory states on par with hallucinogenic and drug-induced states. While this is the interpretation of Michael Persinger, such a move is resisted by Ramachandran and d'Aquili and Newberg, and with good reason. To show that a brain state correlates with a certain kind of experience is not to show that such an experience is false. Because there are correlative brain states for any given experience, such an argument would imply that all our experiences are delusional—a clearly absurd conclusion.

To acknowledge this, however, is not to establish that such experiences have significance but only that it is false simply to assume that they do not. It may well be that such states of the brain are purely natural, having no "supernatural" component, but that they nevertheless provide insight into the nature of reality. Such a position, however, would have to be argued and therefore be part of a larger religious (and in Proudfoot's and Katz's sense, cultural) framework. Such experiences may be significant but are not by themselves self-interpreting. Far from negative, this would suggest a positive, constructive role for a larger religious framework based on multiple considerations, of which such experiences would be one component. Indeed, James Austin's personal narrative in *Zen and the Brain* is a powerful account of how such experiences can have a significant transformative impact within the broader context of Zen Buddhist discipleship, even while acknowledging the purely naturalistic basis of the enlightenment experiences themselves. Recognizing the insight from such experiences may also provide a basis for interreligious dialogue. If such experiences are universal (a long-standing claim of many philosophical students of mystical experience) and if they are taken to give genuine insight, they can at least present one common ground for mutual understanding and exchange of ideas.

A third option is the claim that acknowledging that brain states correlate with religious experiences is not a sufficient basis for understanding the experiences. That is, these experiences have a quality above and beyond what is supported by neuroscience. Such a position would perhaps be necessitated by some forms of Hinduism and Buddhism. According to tradition, for instance, one of the signs of enlightenment was the Buddha's ability to perceive all of his past lives, an ability that clearly goes beyond our current understanding of the brain and natural science. Such claims also take us back to the question of the nature of consciousness (discussed in chapter 3, above) and present significant challenges of coherence.

It is far from clear that either d'Aquili and Newberg's state of AUB or Ramachandran's temporal lobe modules are sufficient to account for all forms of religious experience, and there is good reason to suppose otherwise. Religious experiences are diverse and complex, and it would be surprising if all could be reduced to a single kind of brain activity. It is striking that in all the cases discussed so far, no claim is made that the religious experiences have an external source. Even the difference of Ramachandran's temporal lobe patients lies in their attenuation and even obsession with religious objects and in their experience of unity with God, not in their claims to have (say) received messages of some kind or that their experiences come from an external source.

The claim that God communicates directly or indirectly with human beings in some way has been integral to Jewish and Christian history. The significance of the prophets, for instance, lay not in their personal insight but in their ability to speak the word of God, made explicit in the frequently used introductory phrase, "Thus says the Lord." Furthermore, many Christians (as well as Jews and Muslims) claim to receive some kind of divine communication, whether as a response to prayer or unbidden at times of important transition and crisis. Such divine responses may take the form of broad feelings of love or reassurance or they may be more specific and include visual or verbal components. While the former type is more typical and has generally had wider official support (as reflected in many of the testimonies that William James recounts in his chapters on conversion), the latter have been more controversial, and any prominent acceptance of them is limited either to the distant past or to particular denominations (e.g., visitations of the Virgin Mary in Catholicism or glossolalia and prophecy in Pentecostal traditions).

William Alston, in particular, has articulated a defense of God as the causal source of religious experience.[19] He argues that religious experience can be understood as a form of sensory perception in which the latter is a process of reliable presentation to one's consciousness. Nancey Murphy has built on this approach, incorporating the practice of Christian discernment derived from Quaker practice as a means of confirming or disconfirming the authenticity of such experiences.[20] In both cases, however, the provenance of such experiences is external to the person, quite different from the experience of AUB, which can be understood as something achieved internally, even though the effect is to provide insight into a deeper understanding of reality.

William Austin claims that there need be no separate sensory organ for detecting God's communication. But if one takes the integration of brain and mind seriously, then such communications would presumably have some effect on the brain and would, at least in principle, be detectable in a sufficiently sophisticated brain scan. Recognizing this, Arthur Peacocke has argued that experiences of God can be understood as the imparting of information in a manner that invokes top-down causation (referred to above in chapter 3 in relation to consciousness, supervenience, and emergence).[21] In this view, God would be seen as directly activating the relevant emotional and cognitive areas of the brain responsible for the experience in question. How would we know that such states are from God? Peacocke does not address this, but one might presume that such experiences might have a quality of externality to them, the feeling or sense that the experience is not self-produced but arises from outside of oneself.

While such an account is theoretically possible, it does raise questions. If God's action operates in this fashion, then it is at least theoretically possible to simulate God's voice by stimulating these self-same areas of the brain, either by design or by dint of mental illness. Strangely enough, Michael Persinger has claimed to do precisely this sort of thing. Using transcranial magnetic stimulation (TMS), in which a focused magnetic pulse stimulates neurons in a targeted brain area, Persinger has claimed that he is able to induce religious experiences in subjects and even in himself.[22] While Persinger's claims (which are nothing more than that at the time of this writing) should be treated with some skepticism, they do raise the question of authenticity anew: in what sense can we be sure that such experiences are truly of God?

In truth, we cannot know, and once again we are thrown back onto a larger theological framework in order to interpret such experiences and claims. In addressing the reality of religious experiences, William James argued that we cannot simply take the validity of someone's claims to religious experience at face value. In the end we must judge the authenticity of religious experiences by their effects. Theologically, we are still left in much the same situation. Cognitive neuroscience can provide evidence for the reality of such experiences but ultimately cannot tell us what they mean. While religious experiences are real and have potential for significant personal and communal influence, they are not in the end completely self-interpreting. Rather, they represent one important component in the broader theological endeavor of understanding the most basic questions of life. Who am I? What's out there? Where am I going? Religious experiences give at least some of us profound insight into such questions. At the same time, they are only the beginning of the journey, not the end point, and the wisdom they provide must accompany and cohere with others in the difficult task of living and growing in a varied, complicated world.

PART THREE

MINDING NATURE

6

Alone in the Universe?

On a hot summer day in 1996, a gorilla made national headlines by what seemed to be an act of selfless moral compassion. The gorilla rescued a toddler who had inadvertently tumbled from the viewing area into the gorilla exhibit at the zoo. The child lay unconscious on the ground as panicked adults watched one of the gorillas in the enclosure gently pick up the child and lay him at a door where zookeepers could easily recover the boy and rush him to medical treatment. Named Binti Jui by her human caretakers, the gorilla became an overnight celebrity, thanks in no small part to a bystander who captured the event on videotape.

Was Binti's act one of empathic concern for others or was it a kind of instinctual care for the young, heightened by the fact that she was raising her own child? Pundits on television shows and newspapers weighed in with their opinions. What did Binti's actions say about the nature of gorillas? Equally important, what did Binti's actions say about human nature?

Animal cognition and, in this case, moral sensitivity raise one form of the question of human uniqueness. Our tendency is to think of ourselves as unique, including morally and spiritually. This uniqueness is usually attributed to one of several cognitive attributes. Yet there are challenges to this claim. While no other animal has achieved the cognitive sophistication that we have, a great deal of animal behavior, especially among mammals, seems to rise above mere instinct. It is not only animals that raise this question. Researchers in artificial intelligence have often proclaimed that it is only a matter of time before we create a thinking machine, one that can walk, talk, and perhaps even dream and pray. More speculatively, the possibility of intelligent alien life also raises its own questions about human uniqueness. Are we really unique? If not, what does it portend?

The Presumption of Uniqueness

It has long been a presumption of the Western intellectual tradition that humankind is set apart from the rest of the physical and biological world. We as a species are distinctive in no ordinary way. That birds have wings make them distinctive, but it does not make them "better" than other species. But the qualities that separate us from other creatures, it is argued, make us better than other species. Because of this we have one set of rules for dealing with other human beings and another set for dealing with all other creatures.

While what is said to be the distinguishing feature of humankind has varied over time, the relevant features are usually cognitive ones. This mode of reasoning is found at the very beginning of the philosophical tradition. Aristotle, in particular, argued that human beings are different from plants and animals by virtue of their possession of a rational soul.[1] This emphasis on rationality, reinforced by both Plato and Aristotle, was characteristic of philosophy through the Middle Ages. Since René Descartes, other criteria have included language, consciousness, and self-consciousness.[2] Even when noncognitive criteria are used—such as toolmaking, having an opposable thumb, or bipedality—they tend ultimately to refer to cognitive traits. Walking upright is important because it enables our hands to be free, which allows the use of that opposable thumb to make tools. At least in our species, toolmaking ultimately requires thinking, and so in the end it comes back to cognition.

The emphasis on human uniqueness in relation to animals and nature is found not only in the philosophical tradition but also informs much of the theological tradition. Genesis 1 refers only to humankind as made in "the image of God." The meaning of the phrase has long been pondered by theologians, not least because the text of Genesis itself does not clarify it. Theologians have often adopted philosophical categories of supposed human uniqueness to understand the term, categories that hinge on our cognitive capabilities. Thus the second-century Christian bishop Irenaeus identified the image of God with the human ability to reason, a tradition that continued up through Aquinas.[3] Not all theologians, however, have supported this approach. Martin Luther opposed such identifications, preferring to understand the image of God more in terms of our relationship to God. Whether Luther's definition assumed certain cognitive abilities is an open question, but it is safe to say that neither presumed that animals had the same relationship with God that humans have. The result is that the tendency to identify the image of God with one or another cognitive trait has persisted into the modern period. Schleiermacher, for instance, identified the image of God with the human capacity for self-consciousness. Emil Brunner, in his debate with Karl Barth on the subject, included the criteria of human subjectivity, rationality, and self-consciousness.[4]

Clearly then, the issue of human uniqueness is important, and a little reflection suggests why. The most obvious reason is an essentially ethical one. To be human is to deserve moral consideration. Nonhuman creatures, however, are either due no moral consideration or, at best, consideration unequal to that given to human beings. In the eyes of some, to grant animals rationality or even consciousness forces us to grant them moral status, an issue that has achieved considerable importance in debates about animal rights. Presumably, if a robot ever achieved the kind of cognitive feats that humans are capable of, they too would deserve moral respect and consideration.

The issue of human uniqueness is important also because it raises the very question of what it means to be human. Indeed, one can look at the various debates on animal, artificial, and alien intelligence as a means of working through this question. Together they form a cognitive other that forces us to reflect on our own nature. This sort of reflection has been especially important in the debates over the possibility of artificial intelligence. Since there are no robots even remotely capable of humanlike thought or behavior, the question remains purely theoretical. Because the computer and computational models have had such a powerful impact on how we think of ourselves, however, the question of artificial intelligence has played a major role in the philosophy of mind in reflecting on what makes us human.

On the more purely theological level, these cognitive others raise questions about the nature and scope of redemption, questions that are particularly acute for Christians. The Christian tradition has emphasized the fact that God became human in order to redeem humankind and that God's act of redemption in Christ is a once-for-all event. To acknowledge that there are other morally and spiritually significant creatures renders such a claim problematic. As we shall see, Christians need not tie themselves to such a narrow understanding of redemption but, to many, it creates resistance to any serious consideration of the existence of a cognitive other that has moral and spiritual significance.

Any analysis of the question must take into account actual scientific claims about human uniqueness. Increasingly, it seems the question is not *whether* we are unique but *how*. The continuities are as important as the discontinuities, and any adequate theological account must take both into consideration.

The Locus Humanus

In his witty *The Hitchhiker's Guide to the Galaxy*, Douglas Adams quipped that human beings are not proud of their relatives and never invite them over for dinner. Adams was not speaking of our aunts and uncles, but rather our evolutionary relatives. Most people have generally presupposed a great divide between human beings and other animals. So great is it that we tend to speak of humans and nature, where nature includes everything, living and inanimate, that is not human. Nature, animals included, serves merely as a backdrop to human activity in the eyes of many.

As mentioned, the basis of this difference is often assumed to be one or more cognitive abilities. These form a *locus humanus*, the defining traits that separate humans from all other living creatures on Earth. Our modern criteria stem in no small part from Descartes, who utilized both reason and language as criteria for distinguishing the presence of a soul. Since animals had neither, Descartes argued, they did not have souls.[5] Descartes's psychology was complex, however, and the way that Descartes used his criteria seemed to imply that language and reason were themselves signs of the deeper attributes of consciousness and self-consciousness. In the period following Descartes, all four criteria have been used by a variety of scholars, with self-consciousness frequently emphasized as that attribute that makes us truly unique.[6]

Each criterion taken individually has a certain plausibility. While it is not at all clear that consciousness is unique to humans, it is an important and morally relevant trait. The criterion used by many animal rights advocates to oppose both meat-eating and animal experimentation is whether an organism can experience pain.[7] Since animals have sensory experiences (implying consciousness), we should not inflict pain on them. Plants, however, appear to lack any conscious experience whatsoever, and so one need not have any scruples about being an herbivore. If it turned out, however, that animals do not really experience pain but only seem to (i.e., they are not conscious), one could be a carnivore without guilt. This is, in fact, what some of Descartes's followers argued. Animals are mere automatons, sophisticated machines. As such, they have no conscious experience and can be treated in any manner one wishes.

Reason, language, and self-consciousness have their own plausibility as well. We do seem to be the only species that communicates by language. No other animal is even remotely capable of many of our greatest achievements. Calculus, Shakespeare, and Bach are beyond the comprehension and appreciation of even the great apes.

But the divide is not always as great as it seems. Often we take the pinnacle of human achievement and use that as the standard by which we compare ourselves to other species. Only a minority among us, however, reach such pinnacles. Not all of us grasp calculus, and the beauty of Bach is lost on many. The comparison is further complicated by the fact that we have different levels of capabilities at different stages of development. There is no comparison between the cognitive abilities of a normal adult human and a chimpanzee, but the gap narrows considerably if we compared the chimpanzee to a two-year-old. While the chimpanzee may be more sophisticated than the child in some ways, it is only the latter that is commonly considered human in a morally relevant way.

But perhaps it is merely illusion. Perhaps the chimpanzee or dolphin or dog only *seem* intelligent. Perhaps they are not conscious at all. This was the general stance of ethologists through much of the twentieth century. Heavily influenced by psychological behaviorism, animal behavior was understood solely in terms of stimulus and response.[8] While less prevalent today, versions of this viewpoint still hold sway in some quarters. Philosopher Daniel Dennett, for instance, has argued that consciousness arises only as a result of language. Since only humans have language, only humans are conscious. Any attempt to attribute intentional states to animals, on Dennett's analysis, becomes quickly mired in uncertainty, since animals themselves cannot report their thoughts.[9]

To most, Dennett's claim seems incredible and in some ways counter to human experience. While language profoundly shapes our thoughts and nature, our conscious experience is not limited to linguistic events. We perceive the world around us through visual, aural, and tactile sensations. Indeed, as Antonio Damasio has carefully pointed out, there are several medical conditions that temporarily deprive individuals of language but not consciousness.[10] But denying this helps little in determining whether animals possess consciousness. The animal kingdom seems almost infinite in variety and complexity, ranging from the lowly cockroach to ourselves. It is by no means clear that all animals possess consciousness in any full sense. Indeed, it may be that consciousness is the result of a certain emergent level of activity. We are more willing to grant consciousness to cats than cockroaches.

Presumably, if we could identify the brain structures involved in the emergence of consciousness, we could specify which animals are conscious. Such identification, however, would only beg the question of the cause and nature of consciousness in the first place (see chapter 3, above). Even if consciousness is a property of a particular region of the brain, it is not clear that only that particular type of brain structure can produce conscious experience, an important point in arguments about artificial intelligence and extraterrestrial life.

Not even process philosophy, inspired by the work of Alfred North Whitehead, adequately solves this problem. Process philosophers claim that all physical events (including events involving inanimate objects) have an experiential component. On the process view, experience is a fundamental property of all things, a view often called panpsychism. A number of process thinkers, however, make a distinction between experience and consciousness. In doing so, they reintroduce the problem, for once again we must determine which organisms have experience only and which have genuine consciousness.[11]

A more empirical approach has been developed by Donald Griffin, the individual most responsible for the founding of cognitive ethology as a discipline. Placing the subject of animal consciousness at the center of his program of research, Griffin argues that the fact that we share with other animals the same basic biology, including many of the same basic brain structures and types of neuronal activity, makes it plausible that consciousness is present in other animals as well. Griffin further argues that empirical criteria can also reveal the presence of consciousness in nonhuman animals. The ability to communicate, argues Griffin, implies the presence of thoughts to be communicated. Griffin also sees behavioral novelty and the ability to act in a way that cannot simply be characterized as rigid instinct as an important indicator of consciousness. On Griffin's view, consciousness is not merely passive experience but is associated with the ability to act in ways that are not rigidly programmed into the organism.[12]

Griffin's arguments are far from foolproof. Thoughtless communication certainly seems conceivable. Technically speaking, radio stations communicate information to radios, but there is little reason to suppose that our radios are consciously experiencing the music they are playing. The claim that animals are conscious due to our shared brain structures is more plausible, albeit difficult to prove. There is little a priori reason to suppose that the difference between gorilla brains and human brains is sufficient to deny consciousness to the former. Certainly, human brains are different by virtue of the sheer size of the frontal cortex, but in many ways the similarities are as striking as the dissimilarities. Human beings share all the basic brain structures with other mammals, the difference being primarily one of size and organization As we move further away from our own species, however, the differences grow. Mammal brains, generally speaking, are larger and more sophisticated than those of reptiles, which in turn are larger and more sophisticated than those of insects. At some point there is likely a cut-off line—but where?

Griffin's criterion of novelty might be one such cut-off, although its appeal is more on intuitive grounds than on rigorous argument. We do tend to associate conscious thought with those aspects of our behavior that are flexible and dynamic. Behavior that becomes rote and automatic often slips below the level of consciousness. This is most obvious with motor skills. While a beginning musician or athlete must concentrate mightily on the individual physical motions that create a sonata or a fastball, the professional is nearly oblivious to the actual physical motions. Indeed, the last thing an expert pianist wants to think about is where all her fingers are flying! Such motions take place virtually automatically, leaving the musician able to concentrate on higher-order functions such as the beauty of the music, the overall structure and tempo, and the relation of her performance to other performers that might be present.

On this analysis, animals that display novel behavior should be considered conscious; animals whose behavior is rigid and follows fixed patterns should not. We might expect, then, to find that most mammals possess consciousness but that insects do not. Reptiles and amphibians might represent intermediate situations. The fact that these creatures spend long periods of time completely inert interspersed by periods of activity might suggest that their consciousness becomes active only on an as-needed basis.

The criterion of novel behavior, closely linked as it may be to the traditional criterion of rationality, needs further analysis but at least provides a first step in thinking through the issue. We sometimes use this criterion with regard to human behavior as well—a person under hypnosis being one example. More importantly, a criterion that automatically excludes all nonhuman animals will likely exclude some members of our own species. At least it would seem that the burden of proof is on those who deny any and all consciousness to nonhuman animals. While we are different, it is not at all clear that we are sufficiently different to make such a radical disjunction.

Rational Animals

It is perhaps for this reason that few have used consciousness as a line of demarcation between human beings and nonhuman animals. Reason seems a much more plausible demarcation of the *locus humanus*. Human beings are rational animals, although much of human behavior might lead us to think otherwise. For much of the history of Western thought, nonhuman animals have been considered irrational by nature, driven by base instincts. In common parlance we might say of a person who is ruled by his emotions that he is acting "beastly." A greater divide there could not be.

Or so it seems. As with consciousness, the definition of reason and what counts as rational is difficult to get at. Like the term "intelligence," it seems that we know it when we see it, but it can be difficult to pin down. This might not seem obvious at first glance. After all, there are forms of reasoning that seem readily identifiable and prove tractable for scientific research. We can readily identify instances of learning, for instance, or the ability to follow a set of logical rules. But philosophers observe that rationality involves much more than these comparatively simple traits. Reasoning involves such traits as creativity and insight, and it is these more complex traits that, some argue, define us as a species.

The claim that animals are incapable of any form of rationality in the weak sense is patently false. Animals are quite capable of learning, as any pet owner knows, and one can find modes of learning, at least in terms of stimulus-response conditioning, even in such lowly life forms as slugs. The ability to adopt or follow a pattern is more complex, but well within the ability of rats, who maneuver through mazes with ease. Such animal achievements are not surprising to anyone, but the critic who supports a stronger sense of rationality would counter that these forms of simple behavioral response and conditioning can hardly be counted as genuine instances of reasoning. Such behavior, they would say, is important for the ability to reason but does not count as reason itself.

The behaviors and abilities of a range of animals, however, make absolute distinctions problematic. Mammals in particular are capable of fairly complex tasks of memorization and identification. Generally referred to as cognitive maps, such tasks include the ability to memorize locations of multiple food caches, develop landscape maps important for food and water, and (in the case of social mammals) construct dominance hierarchies. One of the clearest examples of such cognitive mapping is among vervet monkeys, small primates that live in East Africa. Typically living in modest-sized groups of ten to twenty (but sometimes up to fifty), vervets appear to keep meticulous track of status in the dominance hierarchy of the troop. Given that dominance hierarchies change over time and that a monkey's status in a dominance hierarchy can depend on shifts of power and even alliances, this is not as trivial a task as it sounds. Additionally, research by Dorothy Cheney and Richard Seyfarth has shown that vervets communicate with one another by using a set of some ten different calls, each distinct and each serving a different function. Separate alarm calls, for instance, are used for eagles, leopards, and pythons, all of which prey on vervets. Each call elicits a different kind of behavior appropriate to the predator in question. Warning of a leopard, for instance, causes a rush for the trees. Other calls are used to recognize dominants and subordinates, with different grunts being given depending on the relative social status.[13]

Still, it may be argued, such tasks require little cognitive complexity and should not be considered on a par with human reason. It may be argued that human reason is characterized by the ability to do logic, and it is this narrower sort of ability that is distinctive to the human mind. While such a criterion founders in comparison with artificial intelligence (as we shall see), it has an initial plausibility with regard to nonhuman animals. But it does not hold up in any rigorous way. As part of the broader effort to teach apes language in the 1970s, primatologist David Premack tested chimpanzees' abilities to make logical discriminations. Premack's work indicated that chimpanzees are capable of basic logical discriminations of same and different as well as able to discriminate between the logical conjunctions "and" and "or."[14]

Since Premack's work, similar studies have been performed on a number of other species. Of this research, the most striking has been that of Irene Pepperberg with an African Grey parrot named Alex.[15] While most of us are familiar with a parrot's ability to mimic words without understanding (a fact already known to Descartes when he spoke of language being unique to humans), Pepperberg has utilized this ability to teach Alex to recognize verbally more than thirty objects, seven colors, and five shapes, as well as the numbers up to six. Thus, Alex can readily say whether an object is a cork or a key and whether it is green or blue. More impressively, Alex knows what category is being asked for and can respond appropriately. Thus, if asked, "What color?" Alex will say, for example, "Blue," rather than give the shape or name of the object. If given an array of objects, Alex can also respond correctly to the questions, "What's the same?" and "What's different?" Thus, given a red star and a red ball, Alex can discern that it is their redness that is the same, not their shape.

Alex's abilities can hardly fail to impress, particularly given the size of the parrot brain and the fact that birds are not even mammals. And while the work with Alex may be exceptional, it is characteristic of research being carried out with such species as dolphins, elephants, and seals.[16]

For many observers, such experiments and anecdotes would be enough to suggest an element of continuity between nonhuman and human animals. For others, however, what counts as genuine reasoning is yet more sophisticated. Real reason is associated with such traits as creativity and insight and is reflected in the human capacity for language and self-consciousness. These last two criteria in particular thus become a bastion for arguments for human distinctiveness and therefore also human prerogative.

The vast majority of animals in the world obviously do not possess language. As we have seen in the case of vervets, some animals do possess comparatively sophisticated communication abilities. Dolphins are noted for their complex whistling and signaling to one another, lion prides coordinate their attacks with one another, and even lowly honeybees pass on information by the "waggle dance" that gives directions for finding nectar. These abilities nonetheless stop well short of language, which is generally taken to involve symbolic representation and a set of rules (syntax or grammar) that allow the formation of such symbols into a virtually infinite variety of sentence structures. Famed linguist Noam Chomsky and his followers have emphasized grammar as the core of language. So embedded is our understanding of grammatical relations that, as Chomsky noted, such nonsense sentences as "Colorless green ideas sleep furiously" have a sort of rightness to them by virtue of their grammatical correctness.[17] As a result, we might say that Alex the parrot is indeed capable of symbolic representation but falls short of language because of his inability to combine his words into a grammatical sentence.

Whether apes are capable of language has been the focus of some thirty years of controversial research. Unlike parrots, apes are physically incapable of making the sounds necessary for human speech. Early efforts therefore utilized versions of American Sign Language (ASL) as a medium to test ape linguistic abilities. The pioneering work in this area was done by Beatrix and R. Allen Gardner with a chimp named Washoe. According to the Gardners, Washoe came to learn more than two hundred signs and could use them to communicate with her human companions.[18] Research by Roger and Deborah Fouts even suggested that the ability to sign could be transmitted from adult chimpanzees to their young.[19] Francine Patterson made similarly spectacular claims in her work with a gorilla named Koko.[20]

What the apes had succeeded in doing, however, became a matter of academic dispute. Ape-language researchers argued that Washoe, Koko, and others were in fact communicating by the use of symbols and that they even showed evidence of combining words in a regular way that suggested grammar. Critics charged, however, that the ape-language researchers overinterpreted the evidence and fell prey to what in cognitive ethology is known as the "Clever Hans" effect, named after a horse who in the early 1900s earned brief fame for his seeming ability to do arithmetic. In public performance, Clever Hans could regularly give the correct answer to addition problems by stamping out the solution with his hoof. As it turned out, however, skeptics were eventually able to show that the horse was not counting at all, but simply stamping his foot until the audience reacted, reading the cues that might appear on people's faces. In his work with a chimp named (with a fair sense of humor) Nim Chimsky, H. S. Terrace realized that what appeared to be sentence construction on the part of Nim was, when videotape was rolled back, shown to be the result of inadvertent cuing by the trainers. His review of the work of other ape-language projects revealed similar deficits. The apes, Terrace argued, were not producing language but simply mimicking.[21]

Later research by E. Sue Savage-Rumbaugh has attempted to address these difficulties. Instead of using ASL, Savage-Rumbaugh used a keyboard system whose symbols were unambiguous and did not have to rely on gestures that were already a natural part of chimp expression.[22] Savage-Rumbaugh's most spectacular and unexpected success came with a bonobo named Kanzi, who became a subject for experimentation only after spending almost the first two years of his life passively watching his adopted mother, Matata, achieve only modest success in the program. When attention finally turned to Kanzi, the researchers were surprised to learn that not only did Kanzi already understand several of the symbols that were being taught without success to Matata but also he could use them to announce his desires (for example, for particular foods or to play). Kanzi gradually developed a vocabulary of several hundred symbols, the use of which has been carefully tested to exclude the Clever Hans effect. Much more clearly than the case of Washoe and Koko, Kanzi was able to use his symbols to initiate his own actions and express his own desires. Kanzi's pattern of success, beginning with symbol instruction in childhood, has been replicated by other chimps and bonobos in the lab. Equally interesting, Kanzi has shown significant ability to comprehend English sentences and even to comprehend simple grammatical structure.

Kanzi's ability to comprehend the vocabulary and grammar of English sentences was tested in a comparison of him with a child in the early period of language development, one and a half to two years old. Six hundred and sixty sentences were spoken to both subjects, with comprehension being shown by carrying out the commands implied in the sentences. Comprehension of grammar could be determined by how the actions were performed. For instance, the sentence "Make the doggie bite the snake" is different in meaning from the sentence "Make the snake bite the doggie," although the words are the same. Both Kanzi and the child scored well above chance, with Kanzi doing better than the child during the initial months of the experiment.[23]

Such results make it more difficult for the critic to contend that language is unique to human beings. Nevertheless, some researchers might claim maneuvering room. Such examples, they might argue, do not show full-fledged language, because they do not include language production. The ability to comprehend at the level of a child one and a half to two years old is a modest achievement indeed. Any adult who continued to speak at such a level would be considered severely impaired. Furthermore, such abilities are limited (one might say) to the rarefied elite of the animal world. A handful of chimps and bonobos cannot carry the weight of the entire animal kingdom. We should not expect talking dogs or literate moles in the near or even distant future.

While acknowledging these points, it is important to note that the grounds of the argument have shifted, for we are no longer talking about some kind of absolute difference from all other animals but are required instead to make careful distinctions that recognize both similarity and difference. The ability of chimps and bonobos in the experiments seems to exceed by far the behavior that is observed in the natural environment, and one could argue, as Terence Deacon does, that the move to symbolic expression is a radically emergent and new level of experience.[24] But the claim that there is an *absolute* cognitive divide is no longer tenable.

Know Thyself

As a result, self-consciousness becomes one of the last bastions of claims for human uniqueness. Once again, the claim is subject to a number of exceptions and qualifications. Self-consciousness can denote a range of abilities. A lobster is self-conscious enough not to gnaw off its own claw. This form of bodily awareness, however, is usually not what is meant by the term. Self-consciousness is typically taken to imply an ability to think about one's own thoughts or to conceptualize or objectify oneself. Dogs may express their desire, but it takes the capacity of a Hamlet to ponder one's own fate.

As with language, it seems clear that this form of self-consciousness is not available to the majority of animals with which we share the world. Ponder their meal they might; pondering themselves seems impossible. As with language, however, there seem to be exceptions, particularly among the primates. One early set of tests sought to test self-awareness of apes by anesthetizing them and, while they slept, coloring a large dot on their forehead. When they awoke, they were then encouraged to view themselves in a mirror. Both chimpanzees and orangutans were capable of recognizing that their mirror image was an image of themselves.[25] When they looked in the mirror, they did not simply touch the dot on their mirror image but touched the dot on their own forehead. Interestingly, lowland gorillas seem incapable of this sort of self-recognition.

Such tests arguably measure a comparatively low level of self-consciousness or, at least, self-consciousness of a specific kind. To what extent the ability to recognize oneself in a mirror measures other attributes of self-consciousness is unclear. For this and other reasons, cognitive ethologists have increasingly concentrated on the question of whether animals and especially primates possess what is called a theory of mind. A theory of mind, simply put, is the ability to infer the mental states and intentions of another organism. On this analysis, some organisms have only what are called first-order intentional states. First-order intentional states are beliefs and feelings about objects. If John desires an apple, John has a first-order intentional state (desire) about a specific object (an apple). Theories of mind arise with the development of second-order or higher intentional states. A second-order intentional state is a belief or feeling about someone else's beliefs and feelings, for example, "John believes that Mary loves Bill." Humans excel at this sort of thing and can build up to three or four levels of intentionality without too much discomfort. "John knows that Mary thinks that Bill is in love with her" is quite comprehensible. "John believes that Mary thinks that Bill understands Lola's intentions for Robert's future," however, makes even our heads swim. Such second-order and higher intentionality can and often does include self-referential beliefs and feelings. "He thinks I have the goods," is but one of many examples.[26]

Do animals have a theory of mind? There are several anecdotal observations and studies made by cognitive ethologists that suggest that at least some animals do. The first of these studies was performed by David Premack and Guy Woodruff, who tested whether a lab chimp named Sarah (who passed the logical discrimination tasks) could predict a human actor's course of action by being shown a video and a set of photographs that portrayed different outcomes.[27] While the chimp did well on the test, many considered it unclear that she was actually making inferences about the states of the actor.

A range of studies has attempted to determine whether primates and monkeys have a theory of mind. One study by Cheney and Seyfarth involved signal calling among vervet monkeys. They found, for instance, that a distress call from an infant vervet not only elicits a response from its mother but an unexpected result from other vervets. They looked not at the infant but at the mother, implying awareness not only of the relation between the two but some expectation regarding the mother's immediate action. Anecdotal studies of primates in captivity and in the wild have also suggested a high degree of social awareness, with the implication that such social awareness requires a theory of mind to operate. Frans de Waal, for instance, has studied how chimpanzees make and break alliances, which requires knowledge not only of each chimp's social standing in the troop but also anticipation of each chimp's action in a given situation.[28] In some cases, even deception seems to be employed. Richard Byrne has argued that baboons sometimes deceitfully use distress calls to manipulate the behavior of other baboons, a claim made also by Cheney and Seyfarth with regard to vervets.[29] Such deceitful behavior occurs among chimpanzees as well. In one anecdote that all too clearly parallels human behavior patterns, a subordinate male chimpanzee attempts to hide his erect penis after being nearly caught in the act by the dominant chimpanzee in the troop.[30] In another recent study, a subordinate chimpanzee is required to choose between two food sources, one of which is in the line of sight of a dominant chimpanzee, one of which is not. In the majority of cases, the subordinate will pick the food that the dominant cannot see, implying that the subordinate can make inferences about the dominant's mental states.[31]

While the theory of mind research has stirred considerable interest and passion, other researchers choose to focus on sympathy and empathy as categories that reflect some kind of awareness of self and other.[32] They point not only to the many anecdotal reports of fellow feeling by domestic pets but also to such activities as the elephants' communal structure and the visitation and even caressing of old elephant bones.

Play behavior among mammals, including not only primates and monkeys but also social carnivores, also seems to elicit a sense of fellow feeling.

To what extent such traits reflect self-consciousness is debatable. To be able to sympathize or to deceive presumably requires some awareness of the other's states. Knowledge of how others will react to my actions implies some sense of self-awareness, however minute. But determining whether any individual action truly counts as an example of deceit or of sympathy is exceedingly difficult. Daniel Povinelli, for instance, has criticized theory-of-mind arguments for primates and has suggested that other modes of reasoning can explain deceptive behavior.[33] Claims that actions of deception and sympathy are merely instances of instinct and conditioned learning are, strictly speaking, difficult to disprove. But, as evidence mounts, they become increasingly implausible.[34] As so often in science, it is not simply a matter of what is demonstrable but what is plausible, as well as what best explains the range of phenomena. Other animals certainly do not have the kind of self-consciousness that we have. But evidence from cognitive ethology suggests that the mode of discourse should shift away from absolute claims of uniqueness to the *kind* of uniqueness we have as well as to the ways we are similar and dissimilar to other organisms in the world.

Cognitive ethology should also disarm us of the notion that terms such as rationality and self-consciousness have as clear-cut meaning as we usually think. Self-consciousness as we conventionally use the term likely represents a range of abilities. Our capacity to reason is likewise made possible by a number of brain structures working interactively, some of which are shared by other animals and some not. Thus, it is not only the case that chimpanzees are less intelligent or less self-conscious than we are but also that they are differently intelligent, with their own drives, abilities, and emotional repertoire. As a crude analogy, a bonobo such as Kanzi may have the language comprehension of a two-year-old human, the social sophistication of an adolescent, but the passions of an adult.

If this continuity still somehow seems improbable, one need only recount our own evolutionary history and ask, "At what point does it all begin?" Such a question recognizes both our similarities and differences with our own ancestors and, by extension, with other organisms. We are the same and we are different. The difficult part is figuring out the implications of that knowledge.

Feeling Machines?

Ian Barbour once observed, "Since Darwin, human dignity has been threatened by our resemblance to animals. Now human uniqueness seems to be threatened by our resemblance to computers."[35] While Barbour's claim is certainly accurate in terms of popular opinion and even academic discussion, there is a kind of strangeness to the observation. After all, animals are here with us now, and their behavior can be observed and studied. Although computers have grown increasingly sophisticated over the years and can play a good game of chess, they are nevertheless incapable of a host of abilities that are basic to being human. Moreover, the material basis and structure of computers, silicon chips, is significantly different from our web of carbon-based cells. Indeed, when Descartes and his followers argued that animals could best be understood as complex machines, the classification was intended to denote an absolute gap between human and animal.[36]

The clear reason for this popular perception, however, is that the advent of the computer has radically altered what we think machines are capable of. Computers seem capable of doing well precisely that which animals and humans do with great difficulty: reason. Early computers seemed to the researchers of the time to be constructed much as the human mind is. Humans have memory; computers have memory. While we use our brain to reason, computers rely on a central processing unit. Computers seemed to be able of easily performing the very logical and mathematical operations that were seen by some as the apex of human achievement. If even early computers could perform such feats, there could be no telling what the future would hold. After all, as computer pioneer Alan Turing demonstrated, a computer could perform any feat as long as it could be composed into an algorithm—a clear set of instructions. He himself predicted in 1950 that a thinking computer would be possible within fifty years.[37]

Turing's misplaced optimism reflected the near giddy excitement about computers in those early years as well as the impact that the advent of the computer had even for thinking about human beings. The development of computers, computer science, and the field of artificial intelligence was central to the founding of cognitive science as well as to the demise of psychological (and one might even argue philosophical) behaviorism. Computers made it comprehensible to think of the categories of mind and thought that did not invoke, as Gilbert Ryle dubbed it, a ghost in the machine.[38] The computer became for many *the* model of the human mind, and it was only gradually that the complexities and shortcomings of computers and of the field of artificial intelligence have forced a significant reassessment of this simple equation.

Early heralded successes also revealed the limitations of serial computers for producing intelligent behavior. Computers were already developing novel proofs of mathematical theorems in the 1950s, and by the 1960s could play a good game of checkers.[39] In 1972, Terry Winograd published his work with a program named SHRDLU (after a row of letters on old linotype machines). SHRDLU could carry on a conversation in natural English about a virtual world of blocks that could be represented on a computer monitor. Winograd provided the following example of a conversation between SHRDLU and a human operator:

> Person: Pick up a big red block.
> Computer: Ok. (does it)
> Person: Grasp the pyramid.
> Computer: I don't understand which pyramid you mean.
> Person: Find a block which is taller than the one you are holding and put it into the box.
> Computer: By "it," I assume you mean the block which is taller than the one I am holding.
> Computer: Ok. (does it)
> Person: What does the box contain?
> Computer: The blue pyramid and the blue block.
> Person: What is the pyramid supported by?
> Computer: The box.
> Person: How many blocks are not in the box?
> Computer: Four of them.[40]

SHRDLU and programs like it generated considerable excitement because they seemed to be engaging in the kind of intelligent conversation that we ourselves engage in. The central question, however, was whether the computer was actually engaging in a conversation or simply simulating one. SHRDLU's block world was completely imaginary, existing only in the virtual world of its program. Its sole conduit with the real world was via a teletype machine. Thus SHRDLU could talk about its block world, but what did such conversation mean? Certainly, SHRDLU did not understand what it was talking about in any meaningful sense. But, as in the ape-language debate, the computer's ability to produce and mimic human language provoked questions as to the relation of language and intelligence itself.

While SHRDLU was seen at the time as representing a significant leap forward, in retrospect it also revealed the limitations of first generation AI. Early work that relied on variants of what is now the desktop computer proved to be tremendously successful at solving a range of mathematical and logical problems as well as providing information about limited and well-specified knowledge domains like SHRDLU's block world. But they proved to be almost wholly incapable of dealing with many of the simplest tasks that human beings perform daily. A central failure became known as the frame problem, a version of which, surprisingly, turned up in the playing of chess, that most logical of games. The initial approach of programmers to games like chess and checkers was to emphasize the ability to anticipate as many moves as possible and see what the consequences of any given move might be. While this worked relatively well for checkers, for chess it resulted in combinatorial explosion. On any given turn in a chess game, there are potentially up to thirty or more possible moves. Looking five moves ahead therefore entailed something like twenty-four million possible move combinations. While this is eventually what computers such as Deep Blue became capable of, such processing power was unavailable in the 1970s. More importantly, it was patently obvious that expert chess players do not consider twenty-four million moves at each turn. They had learned through experience to concentrate on the few alternatives that were most promising at any given moment.

While the frame problem seems enormous for chess, it is far vaster for the store of human knowledge that is used on a daily basis. When a person moves, we simply expect the person's clothes and hair to move as well. How do we know that a "deck of cards" does not refer to a back porch filled with people who think they are funny? When we pick up a menu, why do we expect to find food listings and prices inside? On conventional AI approaches, the emphasis was on programming into the computer all needed knowledge along with rules of deduction and inference. It quickly became apparent, however, that there was no way for the programmer to be able to determine ahead of time what knowledge was relevant and what was not. What should be done?

In the 1980s, computer scientists increasingly turned to connectionist models to get around the frame problem. Traditional computers relied on a single serial processor that processed each instruction of a computer program step by step. Connectionism relied instead on parallel distributed processing (PDP), which broke problems into several components and then worked on several of these components at the same time. Such processors were often linked together into neural networks, which were claimed to be modeled on how neurons operated in the brain. Neural networks rely on a system of nodes, each of which is assigned a value or weight. A prime advantage of neural networks is that, once the initial parameters are set, they are designed to learn on their own, allowing for greater complexity and responsiveness than any programmer could intentionally prescribe beforehand. Such PDP systems have produced some stunning successes, most notably in pattern and face recognition.[41]

In the 1990s, this move toward neural networks was complemented by a move away from the standard desktop computer toward robotics. AI researchers such as Rodney Brooks emphasized an embodied, evolutionary approach to building intelligent machines. Whereas traditional AI understood intelligence to be separate from any bodily dynamics, Brooks argued that intelligence and other dominant behavioral characteristics of an organism emerge from simple and fairly direct lower-level processing devoted to bodily actions.[42] While early robots emulated insect mobility with great success, the project that has attracted the most attention is a humanoid robot named Cog. Built to emulate the developmental learning patterns of a human being, Cog consists of a torso, arms, and head, complete with binocular vision. Cog's simple hands can grasp objects. As work has proceeded, Cog has demonstrated simple behavioral learning as well as the ability to look human visitors in the face, an ability that unnerves many. It is assumed that the emphasis on embodiment is connected as well to emotional states.[43] While Cog does not have emotions, Cynthia Breazeal has led a team of researchers in developing Kismet, a robot designed to mimic the facial expressions and responses of a young infant. Kismet is designed to act much as a human infant might be expected to act, expressing facial correlates to such emotions as surprise, anger, interest, and disgust. Kismet responds to interaction from human agents, even to the point of becoming upset if overstimulated.

While the achievements of such robots are significant for the field of AI, they may still seem quite modest when compared to human capabilities, not to mention many other members of the animal world. Whatever Kismet may express, no one claims that the robot actually feels any emotions. Yet, both Kismet and Cog might lead us to expect that the development of a truly intelligent robot will eventually happen. As computer chip processing speeds continue to double every

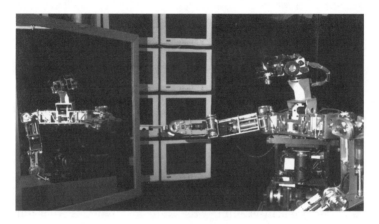

Fig. 6.1. Cog looking at a mirror. [Photo: Donna Coveney/MIT. Used by permission.]

eighteen months and as the knowledge and experience of AI researchers grows, it might seem only a matter of time before we are required to wonder about the rights of a being we ourselves had made.

Many scholars demur, however, arguing that there are reasons to believe that true artificial intelligence is impossible. While computers and robots may help us to model and understand human intelligence (what is known as weak AI), the claim of proponents of strong AI that we will be able eventually to build a robot that has all the intellectual and other relevant qualities of a human being is, according to these critics, simply wrong. Much of the debate surrounding the possibility of genuine artificial intelligence has centered on the Turing test. Developed by Alan Turing in 1950, the Turing test requires a human judge to engage in a conversation with two individuals by teletype or (in its modern form) by a computer network.[44] Based on the conversations that occur, the judge must determine which of the individuals conversed with is actually human and which is computer. If the judge cannot tell, the computer is said to have passed the Turing test and may, therefore, be considered intelligent.

For Turing, the ability to pass the test defines what intelligence (and even human nature) is. As we have seen with regard to animals, Turing uses language and reason as criteria for passing the Turing test. Thus, in an example of a potentially passing conversation, Turing gives the following example:

> Question: Please write me a sonnet on the subject of the Forth Bridge.
> Answer: Count me out on this one. I never could write poetry.
> Q: Add 34957 to 70764.
> A: (Pause about 30 seconds and then gives as answer) 105621.
> Q: Do you play chess?
> A: Yes.
> Q: I have K at my K1, and no other pieces. You have only K at K1 and R at R1. It is your move. What do you play?
> A: (After a pause of 15 seconds) R-R8 mate.[45]

Turing's emphasis on chess and math says much about perceptions about human uniqueness at that time. The broader concern, however, is whether such disembodied conversation really reveals what human nature is about. Philosopher John Searle, in particular, has argued that the Turing test completely misses the point, for it confuses syntactical competence (being able to generate grammatical sentences) with genuine understanding. In a famous thought experiment called "the Chinese Room" (discussed in chapter 3, above) Searle imagines himself locked in a room with a set of instructions for producing grammatical Chinese sentences. Every so often, he is given a string of Chinese characters as input. He then consults his instructions, which guide him in producing a set of Chinese character as output. Searle claims that he could do this, and that the result might be a grammatical and sensible conversation, but that in the end he would still not understand Chinese. Passing the Turing test, according to Searle, does not demonstrate understanding.[46]

While Searle's thought experiment has engendered considerable debate, others have emphasized the disembodied character of the whole discussion. Andy Clark has argued that only an embodied machine that had actual perceptions of and interactions with the world could be considered genuinely intelligent. For Clark, knowledge and meaning arise in our connection to and relationship with the world and do not exist abstractly in a disembodied brain.[47] Like Brooks, Antonio Damasio, and others, Clark emphasizes that we must turn away from a disembodied, Cartesian view of mind and turn to one that understands the mind in the context of a whole, embodied person.

As Clark's comments reveal, however, many of these debates are more about the possible form of artificial intelligence, rather than questions about its sheer possibility. While Searle is exceedingly skeptical of symbol-oriented traditional AI, he is much more open to the development of PDP approaches and embodied AI.[48] Central to this question is the nature of consciousness itself. It is certainly the case that computers and robots are able to do a number of tasks that seem important to cognition and the type of beings that we are. While there are important differences, it also seems to be the case that individual neurons operate much like computer logic gates, and that groups of neurons operate in a way that can be imitated by computer processors. When embodied, we move from computers to robots. Silicon chips still provide the processing power, but they are now connected to devices that provide sight, sound, and touch. For computer scientists such as Hans Moravec, it is primarily a matter of scaling up. As computer processor speeds increase, and as our knowledge of the brain and biology develops, it is only a matter of time—and perhaps not too long at that—before we share the world with a creature of our own design that might qualify as human in terms of basic rights and abilities.[49]

While such a scenario seems plausible and almost inevitable, it assumes that we already know what constitutes the mind and, particularly, consciousness. Proponents of strong AI share the strong functionalist thrust of cognitive science generally that we saw in chapter 3. If the mind and person arise solely out of the functional architecture of the brain, then Moravec and others are certainly correct: it is only a matter of time before we succeed in creating machines that pass the threshold of human uniqueness. Versions of panpsychism developed by process philosophers and recently by David Chalmers (also discussed in chapter 3) would also seem to be compatible with the development of an artificial, personlike intelligence. Chalmers, for instance, identifies consciousness as a property of information, so that any information processing system should be considered conscious. For process philosophers, consciousness emerges as a result of integrated organization. The process account is more complicated, but there seems to be no a priori reason to think that artificial intelligence is impossible or incompatible with the process version of panpsychism.

Artificial intelligence is impossible only if there is some quality of mind and, in particular, consciousness that truly goes beyond information processing and is somehow separate from it. Roger Penrose's claim that consciousness is connected to quantum mechanical events is one such claim, as unlikely as it may seem.[50] Even so, this would once again simply change the grounds of artificial intelligence, not the possibility itself. While there may be practical and moral barriers to ever creating artificial intelligence, it is unclear whether there are any in principle, short of claiming supernatural intervention in the creation of each life. There are both scientific and theological reasons for thinking that the latter is not the case.

Nevertheless, the point stands. There are currently no intelligent robots with whom we can have a nice chat or sip tea. While there will no doubt be significant strides in the future, it is hard to anticipate what they will be and what they will portend. While Moravec and Kurzweil predict that the day of true artificial intelligence is near, the track record of AI prognosticators has been less than encouraging, as even Turing showed. We are thus left with the implications of weak AI. Research in artificial intelligence works best as a model and mirror for understanding ourselves, one that can be both illuminating and misleading. While the claims of weak AI may not always be as startling, they can nevertheless still be quite thought provoking.

As a concluding example, one such area is music, which is associated with some of the highest forms of human creativity. In 1988, composer David Cope created a program called EMI (Experiments in Musical Intelligence) that could so accurately mimic the style of musical geniuses like Bach and Beethoven that even experts were fooled. At one performance at the Eastman School of Music in 1999, the music faculty could not tell the difference between an authentic work by Chopin and one composed by the program. Needless to say, the music faculty were shocked. What does it portend? In some ways, nothing more than SHRDLU. EMI works because it is able to detect structure and patterns in music and then use that knowledge to generate similar works. EMI can neither enjoy composing the pieces nor even listen to them. But it does give pause for how we think about human creativity. Can our creativity be captured in a computer program? There is much that is missing in EMI. An Eroica symphony by a computer does not have the historical context and meaning that Beethoven's has. But it is possible that it reflects in a small way our own creative processes and therefore suggests something about what kind of beings we actually are.

Imaging God

The Gospel of Luke records a dialogue between Jesus and an expert in the law who prompts Jesus with the question, "Who is my neighbor?" Jesus replies by telling the parable of the Good Samaritan, the moral of which has resounded through the ages. Neighborliness, and with it love and obligation, transcend barriers of race, sex, and religious heritage. Rarely, however, has such a value been conceived of transcending the species. Does it? The question is fraught with implications. If animals, plants, and even ecosystems are my neighbors, my relation to them is drastically altered. The possibility of a *Robo sapiens* inspires dread in many, and there are those who would see such a development as incompatible with an orthodox understanding of Christianity. Are animals my neighbors? Could robots eventually become my neighbor? If so, what are we called to do?

The doctrine of the image of God has been used to assert human uniqueness, but theologians have not been greatly concerned with its implications for the status and treatment of other animals. This is largely because the assumption of human uniqueness has been taken for granted, due not only to philosophical and theological prejudices but also to a culture of meat-eating and animal domestication that goes back many millennia. Theological reflection on the status of animals has occasionally taken place. Francis of Assisi is usually cited as one individual who took animals seriously. Vegetarianism has been practiced from time to time in Christian communities as well. These instances, however, tend to be the exception to the rule.

A similar situation obtains with regard to artificial intelligence, for the obvious reason that it is a recent possibility, realistically conceivable only in the past century. Theologians and philosophers have occasionally speculated about the existence of intelligences on other worlds.[51] The possibility of alien civilizations presents many of the same questions regarding human nature and uniqueness as AI does.

While such discussions became of particular interest in the wake of the discoveries by both Galileo and Columbus (who discovered new worlds vertically and horizontally, so to speak), they have nevertheless been considered tangential to the theological tradition, and one is hard pressed to find modern theologians who take the subject seriously.

Ironically, the lack of serious reflection provides an opportunity to reexamine how we should think of human uniqueness, and such reflection has developed along several different lines. The advent of the ecological crisis in the 1960s and early 1970s spurred a number of theologians to reconsider the relationship of humankind to nature as a whole. As early as 1961, Joseph Sittler called for a more ecologically oriented theology, a call that has been most heeded by process theologians like John Cobb and feminist theologians like Sallie McFague.[52] Among these ecologically oriented theologians, some have also been concerned with the more narrowly focused animal rights movement, arguing that animals are indeed worthy of moral consideration and therefore should not be harmed unnecessarily.[53] Feminist theologians and philosophers have also pointed out that arguments for human uniqueness have also been used to assert male privilege and dominance.[54]

A quite different route of theological exploration has focused not so much on animals themselves as on our connection to other creatures by virtue of our common evolutionary heritage. In some ways, the most influential thinker in this regard has been Teilhard de Chardin, who understood all creatures as part of a larger, cosmic process.[55] For Teilhard, evolution is teleological in character, leading to increasingly complex life-forms and culminating in the development of an eschatological "christosphere" that would include all living creatures. Teilhard's thinking about evolution has influenced many theologians.[56] At the same time, such broader evolutionary thinking (discussed further in chapter 9, below) has little to say on the more specific question of the exact status of animals and other creatures.

Receiving far less attention has been the prospect of artificial intelligence. Generally speaking, theologians have been wary of the reductionist tendencies and implications of strong AI. Theologian and computer scientist Anne Foerst has argued that AI and Christianity come out of different and, in some ways, incompatible mind-sets.[57] Nevertheless, she argues that current work with such robots as Cog should be taken seriously. Not only does the embodied approach to Cog reveal much about ourselves but the possibility of AI prompts important theological reflection, not least posing the question of how we understand the image of God.[58] If we create a robot capable of personhood, will it need religion? Would such a creature desire to pray, and would it want to receive the sacrament?

One way of integrating the insights of these theologians is by reevaluating the basic doctrine of the image of God itself. Whereas the doctrine has often been used to emphasize human uniqueness and our difference from all other creatures, it is perhaps time to understand it in a way that acknowledges our similarities as well. One resource for reinterpreting the doctrine of the image of God comes from the apostle Paul. While most theologians have rested their interpretation of the image of God almost entirely on the basis of Genesis 1, Paul uses the term and its several variants in a way that suggests a considerably more dynamic interpretation.[59] For Paul, the image of God is not something that we simply do or do not have but something that we become and grow into. Rather than saying we are in the image of God, we might rather say that we are in the process of imaging God. From there it is not such a great step to say that all creatures are in the process of imaging God. What would this mean? The image of God has traditionally been identified with one of the several traits we have discussed, such as reason, self-consciousness, or the ability to have a relationship with God. One option would be simply to retain these categories and to acknowledge that, while our species is unique in its degree of attainment, such qualities are shared to varying degrees with other creatures in this world and—speculatively—on other worlds as well. A broader option would be to understand all of creation as reflecting the basic character and nature of God. Such a route has been taken, for instance, by theologian Langdon Gilkey, who argued that we should understand all of nature as being in the image of God. In acknowledging this, we acknowledge not only our relation to God but our relation to the rest of creation as well.[60]

The danger of such proclamations is that they can too easily wax poetic without really informing about actual consequences. What would it mean to say that all of creation is in the image of God? Such a claim ultimately implies that all creatures, not just humans, have some kind of intrinsic value by virtue of their relationship with and reflection of God and God's action and intentions in the world. This would not imply, however, that all creatures have the same value or that all creatures should have the status of personhood. What it does suggest is that each creature does have a kind of value inasmuch as it is a reflection of God and that that value should have some ethical import. We should treat organisms devoid of consciousness and therefore incapable of experiencing pain, such as plants and perhaps many animals of lower cognitive complexity, differently from those that do. Those animals that are capable of richer forms of experience, due to increased capacity for social bonding, forms of self-consciousness, and perhaps other criteria such as memory and foresight, should be accorded a yet different status. To a certain extent, such a moral hierarchy is already common wisdom in modern Europe and America, and also to varying degrees elsewhere. We do treat animals as being morally different from plants, and in general we make broad distinctions between animals that appear to have little or no consciousness, such as insects, and more complex animals, especially mammals. While dog and cat owners are often satirized for the moral status they accord their pets, both animals (especially dogs, which are social animals) have a much wider behavioral repertoire than, say, treeshrews, a fact that may be considered morally relevant.

The question of the status of different animals is a thorny one, and the debate among moral philosophers on the topic is ongoing. A similar debate has yet to occur seriously with regard to AI but it might be required in the future. Although a theological perspective cannot determine the final outcome, it can appropriately frame the debate. Hierarchies are always potentially dangerous, since they can often inappropriately exclude whole groups of individuals. That women and ethnic and minority groups have often suffered from being on the wrong side of a moral hierarchy should give pause and remind us to exercise epistemic suspicion about human uniqueness as well.

Dealing with such ethical issues, however, is only half the problem. To acknowledge a broader understanding of the image of God raises soteriological issues as well. Christians have traditionally understood Christ's death and resurrection as proleptic signs of God's intent for all. Traditionally, "all" has meant all humans. But a broader notion of the image of God suggests that humans are not the only object of God's concern. God's plan is one for the entire creation, not for us alone. For many, such a claim is the height of the absurd. What, after all, could salvation mean for a dog? Or a wasp? Worse yet, as a colleague asked me once, is it really heaven if there are cockroaches there?

Such concerns are also linked to questions of theodicy. To acknowledge consciousness and more for many species of animals recognizes the frequent and unnecessary pain suffered through evolutionary time as part of the natural course of things. Such suffering as a necessary component of evolution seems to have driven Charles Darwin increasingly toward agnosticism in his later years. How could a good God create a world with not only such enormous human suffering throughout written history but also the vast expanses of animal sufferings across the millions to billions of years of geologic time?

Answers to such questions are not easy. Perhaps they can never be fully answered by intellectual means alone. It is nonetheless worth observing that, while both scripture and theological tradition have tended to emphasize the human drama of salvation, it has complemented by a broader understanding of *cosmic* redemption. The apostle Paul himself spoke of the groaning of creation (Romans 8:22), and the Gospel of John speaks of Christ's role in creation as a whole. The book of Revelation in its concluding passages rhapsodizes not only of a resurrected humanity but of a new Earth as well. Some modern theologians and philosophers have attempted to give these largely symbolic accounts more definite form. Process philosopher Alfred North Whitehead, for instance, differentiated between objective and subjective immortality. While subjective immortality accords with traditional notions of a prolonged or resurrected conscious self, objective immortality consists of God's memory of all events. While Whitehead rejected the former, it is a move not followed by all process theologians, for example, David Ray Griffin. Even so, the notion of objective immortality may be one way of speaking of a kind of salvation for all creatures.

With regard to theodicy, Holmes Rolston III has argued that we need to take the issue seriously and also understand Christology not simply as salvation from the world but also as God's participation in the world. Rolston argues that nature is cruciform in character, that evil and suffering are necessary aspects of life.[61] Nevertheless, it is through evil and suffering that freedom and goodness emerge, and God's action must be one not simply of triumphalistic victory but of cosuffering in the darkest of hours. Physicist John Polkinghorne, taking a different approach, has argued that freedom is essential to the integrity and goodness of creation. Adopting what he calls a free-process defense, Polkinghorne claims that even the natural evil that animals and humans alike suffer is a consequence of such freedom.

Nevertheless, the evils that do endure will eventually be overcome. We must retain faith and hope in God's final acts.

In the end, however, such answers may not be fully satisfying. The modern era has been unkind to eschatological hopes, and the recognition that we are not alone in the universe seems to make such hopes all the more complicated. At the same time, such hopes give shape and meaning to our understanding of the present, a point that can be too easily overlooked. Our vision of the future ultimately influences our perceptions and actions in the present. A world in which humans are alone in an otherwise silent cosmos is enormously different from one that places us amidst a plethora of intelligent and passionate creatures. It is the latter world that the cognitive sciences are revealing to us. While these developments may be at odds with dominant themes of the theological tradition, they resonate with lesser ones. In the end it is these lesser themes of cosmic creation and a broader understanding of the image of God that may well prove to be the more important.

7

Whence Original Sin?

Reinhold Niebuhr is reputed to have observed that original sin is the only empirically verifiable doctrine of Christian theology. There is certainly more than a grain of truth to the claim. However positively we wish to think of ourselves, the sad reality is that much of human history has been characterized by the grossest of evils, sometimes done in the name of the highest good. One does not need to look so far, however, for we also find our lives full of the petty but nonetheless personal forms of suffering that characterize everyday life. Indeed, since we all fall short of perfection, we need only look at ourselves to see the depth of the problem.

The doctrine of original sin has been a significant, although not universally endorsed element of Christian doctrine. In many ways, original sin captures Christianity's ambiguous evaluation of human nature. On the one hand, we are made in the image of God, thus partaking in the goodness and beauty of the divine. On the other, we are fallen descendants of the first sinners, Adam and Eve, who violated God's will and were consequently expelled from the Garden of Eden. On a traditional view that is still held in many quarters, the entrance of sin and suffering into the world is a historical event from which we draw our understanding of human nature.

For most modern thinkers, however, the historicity of such an account now seems incredible. Our modern understanding of history, archeology, and evolutionary theory has rendered it impossible to believe. Instead, it is argued, we must turn to the sciences to provide a satisfactory understanding of human nature, including even those issues of good and evil that were once the province of religion.

Attempts to provide such an account have not been lacking, particularly in the social sciences. While followers of Karl Marx took an essentially positive view of human nature, Sigmund Freud painted a grimmer picture of the self and culture constantly at war with the individual's baser instincts. Ironically, both thinkers drew on the work of Charles Darwin to bolster the claim, and Darwin's theory of natural selection was utilized for a wide variety of agendas in the late nineteenth and early twentieth centuries. Many such efforts we now recognize as disreputable in the extreme, used as they were to justify racism, sexism, and brutal forms of laissez-faire economics.

Despite this, recent decades have seen a return to evolutionary theory to provide a grounding for scientific theories of human nature, especially in the field of sociobiology. Since the publication of *Sociobiology* by E. O. Wilson in 1975, sociobiologists have made repeated claims that moral behavior can be reduced to biological categories. In sociobiology, original sin becomes naturalized, providing both a story of origins and an account of human behavior.

But is it valid? To its credit, sociobiology has shed light on a number of issues of biological importance that have influenced how we think of our place in the world. But human beings are truly complicated. The findings of sociobiology must ultimately be correlated with a larger story, one that involves minds, persons, and communities. Realizing this, in turn, provides the opportunity for reevaluating our theological options. In some ways the scientific story confirms the theological perspective. Created good, we are nevertheless fallen. In other ways, the scientific story calls for some new wrinkles, ones that may in the end require us to choose between competing theological alternatives.

In the Garden

In its most basic form, the doctrine of the fall is a form of theodicy. How could a good God create a world so full of human suffering? From the very beginning, Christian thinkers have turned to the first chapters of Genesis to explain this seeming conundrum. As testified by the beautiful poetry of Genesis 1, God did indeed create the world good, and the continuing beauty and marvelous complexity of the world serve as a continuing reminder of the basic goodness of God's creation. Human beings, while created good, have nevertheless rejected God, and that rejection is the source of our human suffering. In the narrative of Genesis 2 and 3, the cause of this suffering is understood to be Adam and Eve's violation of God's will by eating from the tree of the knowledge of good and evil. Expelled from the garden, Adam and Eve were sentenced to mortal lives of hard work and suffering. Human suffering is thus not God's fault but our own, and our mixed nature, in the image of God and yet fallen, stems from that pivotal event.

The vast majority of biblical scholars and theologians recognize the mythical (in the positive sense) and even allegorical character of the story in Genesis 2–3. "Adam" in Hebrew means "man," and the name "Eve" likely stems from the root "to live." The symbolic meaning of the tree of the knowledge of good and evil seems clear enough. For this reason theologians have taken the doctrine of the fall seriously, even though they recognize that the Adam and Eve story cannot be understood as history.

What the fall and original sin are taken to imply, however, is open to interpretation, and the history of theology reflects this. In the Western theological tradition, Augustine has had the most significant influence. In Augustine's understanding, we are all infected with original sin, which is transmitted by the sexual act of our parents, who received it from theirs, and so on back to Adam and Eve themselves. According to Augustine, we are born sinful, which is the reason for infant baptism. Not only are we born sinful but we are incapable of any good apart from the grace of God.

This emphasis on human depravity was developed by the reformers John Calvin and especially Martin Luther. Luther saw all our works as tainted with sin and thus deserving of damnation. Taken to its logical extreme, morality in the ordinary sense of the word is not connected to religion at all but merely a means for human beings to get along in this penultimate world. Needless to say, not everyone has followed so pessimistic a line. Anabaptists and Methodists, for example, acknowledge human sinfulness while at the same time holding out hope for the possibility of human perfection.

The Orthodox Christian tradition of the Eastern (Byzantine) Roman Empire and, later on, Russia and Eastern Europe, never accepted Augustine's account of original sin. The Orthodox tradition embraced a position that stems from second-century bishop Irenaeus, who saw the failings of humankind as a result of our creatureliness and consequent immaturity. Made in the image of God, we are nevertheless incomplete and therefore need the act of Christ to make us whole. On Irenaeus's understanding, our *nature* is not corrupted by sin but free, and the choices that we make are consequently our own responsibility. Yet the choices we make are also limited by our own immaturity, and so we are still prone to sinfulness in a way that is difficult to escape, even though this position is not nearly as pessimistic as Augustine's view.

This more optimistic tone is also reflected in the idea of the *felix culpa*, or happy fault. Long a part of Catholic liturgy, the fall of Adam and Eve has sometimes and somewhat paradoxically been regarded as a good thing, since it is the fall that leads to the redemptive action of Christ. While versions of this strike the modern thinker as a bit bizarre, much like picking a fight in order to be able to make up afterwards, the general argument nonetheless is of theological interest. One of the merits of the *felix culpa* is that it suggests that our suffering is not pointless but has value. Indeed, although they are usually portrayed as competing claims, it may be that all three approaches have insightful elements that will need to be taken up in any modern theological approach to human nature in the face of our scientific knowledge.

Saints and Sinners

Understanding the roots of a theological account of human nature, however, may seem only to accentuate the gap between theological and scientific approaches. While the category of sin is often interpreted in simply moral terms (reiterated in popular culture by countless television portrayals of the Catholic confessional, "Forgive me, father, for I have sinned"), for theologians the term has a broader meaning. Sin is not simply the doing of an immoral act; it is rebellion against God. In the original Greek New Testament, sin is *hamartia,* literally "missing the mark." Sin involves a misdirection of the whole being, not simply the error of a single act. Nevertheless, sin does have a moral component. Sin typically involves both thought and action. The struggle of the will in relation to sin has produced some of the most famous passages in Christian thought. In his letter to the Romans, Paul speaks eloquently of doing what he wishes not to do and not doing what he wishes.[1] For Augustine, the problem is precisely the opposite; in his famous recounting of his theft of a pear as a boy he recalls the delight with which he engaged in even such a trivially rebellious act.[2] Moreover, sin may have an objective quality to it. Thus, especially liberation theology speaks of the sinful structures of the world. It is sometimes argued that the natural evil we suffer is also a result of our sinfulness, even if only in an abstract sense. Suffering is simply a part of our lot, due to sinfulness, and it is only by God's redemptive grace that we can ever transcend it.

Similarly, Christian virtue and saintliness are not merely moral qualities in the simple sense of doing good deeds but qualities of character and spirit. Good deeds do not make a good person, although a good person does good deeds. The sayings of Jesus reflect a keen perception of this difference, and warnings against hypocrisy have been a constant if not always well-followed part of the Christian tradition.

On the face of it, it may seem that such accounts of the human person are so distant from anything the sciences would say that any dialogue or overlap is inconceivable. It certainly does suggest that there is an irreducible quality to a theological understanding of the human person that goes beyond what a purely biological or psychological approach can give. But it would be a mistake to say that a theological account of the human person is *completely* independent of the biological and psychological, for this would imply a kind of radical dualism that has already been shown to be untenable. We are not merely theological (or "spiritual") persons but also biological and psychological persons. To the extent that a spiritual transformation involves the whole person, the biological and psychological elements are also included. Consequently, to the extent that biology and the cognitive sciences inform our understanding of human nature, they must be taken into account theologically as well.

Having acknowledged this, however, we run into a second problem. There is not currently a unified approach to understanding the moral element in human nature but, instead, hotly contested and competing alternatives. Much of the research on this subject continues to be dominated by the field of sociobiology and its related disciplines, such as evolutionary psychology. Sociobiologists have generally taken a skeptical and reductionist approach toward issues of morality and religion, which they argue can be reduced to categories of reproductive fitness. As E. O. Wilson and Michael Ruse have infamously put it, "Ethics as we understand it is an illusion fobbed off on us by our genes to get us to cooperate."[3] Sociobiology in its varied forms has encountered significant resistance over the years, with the result that a number of scientists, from Stephen Jay Gould to Lynn Margulis, have put forward a range of proposals and critiques aimed at mitigating the Hobbesian view of nature (human and otherwise) portrayed by dominant interpretations of sociobiology. It would be a mistake, however, to presuppose that these are not ideologically driven as well. Consequently, the first task is to separate the solidly established data and theory from the sometimes frequent armchair speculation, and only then to determine the picture that emerges once we sift the material accordingly.

Born Selfish?

From early on, Charles Darwin's theory of natural selection has been understood in terms of the famous phrase, "the survival of the fittest." Evolution came to be seen as a struggle for survival that involved cutthroat competition between organisms in a cruel do-or-die world. Alfred Lord Tennyson's famous words "red in tooth and claw" from the poem "In Memoriam" (published nine years before Darwin's *Origin of Species*) came to epitomize the basic picture that Darwin's theory provided of the natural world.

Such generalizations, while often exaggerated and frequently misinterpreted when applied to human affairs, nevertheless contained a grain of truth about how Darwin saw the mechanisms of natural selection operating. True, much of nature neither bleeds nor possesses teeth and claws. But Darwin did see competition within and between species as the driving force of evolution. Those animals that survived were those that possessed adaptive traits that gave them an edge over their competitors. In such a competitive atmosphere, those who recklessly waste their resources are doomed to perish. The nastiness of nature that his own theory depicted troubled Darwin greatly and was a major cause of the withering of his faith. How, Darwin asked, could a benevolent God have created such a cruel world? Darwin marveled at such creatures as the digger wasp, which reproduced by laying eggs inside of a paralyzed victim that would remain alive as the larvae consumed it.[4]

Darwin's conviction of the truth of his theory proved to be greater than his faith in God. Despite this, Darwin recognized two weaknesses of his theory of natural selection. The first was that it lacked an adequate account of how adaptive traits could arise and be inherited. Gregor Mendel's work on genetics was not available at the time of the original publication of the *Origin of Species* and would not become widely known until the twentieth century. The second problem had to do with altruism. In biological terms, altruism is defined as the sacrifice of oneself (in terms of reproductive fitness) to give aid to another. Since Darwin's theory emphasized competition, it was difficult to see how such behavior could arise. In a relatively rare abandonment of the principle of individual selection, Darwin sometimes explained cooperative behavior such as that found in social insects in terms of group selectionism.[5] Individuals sacrificed themselves not for the benefit of their own genes but for the good of the group. Nature, it seems, was often red in tooth and claw—but not always.

The solution to the genetic problem came in the 1940s and 50s with the development of the neo-Darwinian synthesis. In particular, the discovery in 1953 of DNA by James Watson and Francis Crick provided a firm foundation for understanding how adaptive traits could be transmitted and even (through mutation) how they might arise. As the impact of the discovery sank in and merged with other disciplines within biology, it came to be seen that the new genetics held the promise for understanding evolution. An increasing number of biologists argued that the gene—not the organism—should be understood as the unit of selection. Since organisms and their behavior could be seen as expressions of their underlying genes, it was the genetic story that was most important. From such a perspective, the question then became one of explaining how behavior arose from an organism's genes and how that behavior enhanced the survival of the genes in question. In the language of Richard Dawkins, we can metaphorically think of genes as selfish, their sole aim being successful reproduction into the next generation.[6]

A new solution to the question of altruism, however, came not from biochemistry but from mathematical models and game theory. W. D. Hamilton developed the first part of the solution in the form of a theory of inclusive fitness, otherwise known as kin selection.[7] Hamilton's solution essentially understood altruistic behavior in terms of genetic relatedness. If heredity is transmitted by genes, then one should expect those behaviors that enhance such transmission to survive. In the case of kin, altruistic behavior makes sense if the net effect is significantly to enhance the survival of an organism's genes into the next generation. The reason parents are willing to sacrifice themselves for their offspring is that many of the parents' genes are also in the offspring. In fact, if the main impulse is the propagation of one's own genes, it need not be limited to one's own offspring. Biologist J. B. S. Haldane is once said to have quipped that he would give his life for two brothers or eight cousins.[8] At least from a purely genetic perspective such a sacrifice would make sense.

Hamilton's theory of inclusive fitness has had an enormous impact on biological research, and its general implications have been verified through a number of empirical studies. The most dramatic of these has been the application of inclusive fitness to social insects such as ants and bees, a form of cooperation that Darwin found most difficult to explain. In an insect colony, however, all individuals are related to the reproducing queen. Indeed, work with social insects has strongly indicated that the level of cooperation is in direct correlation to genetic relatedness, as Hamilton predicted. Instances of kin altruism go well beyond social insects, however, being found in birds and mammals as well. Parental care, characterized as it is by a significant investment of resources of no direct benefit to the parent, is itself an example of biological altruism. In another study, it has been shown that black-tailed prairie dogs are more likely to give predator warning calls if kin are in the social group than if they are not.[9]

Kin selection, however, does not cover all forms of cooperation. While cooperation that has immediate benefits (referred to as symbiosis or mutualism) makes sense in terms of natural selection, altruistic cooperation that does not have such benefits seems more problematic. Robert Trivers developed a model of reciprocal altruism to explain these forms of behavior.[10] This principle is summed up in the aphorism, "If you scratch my back, I'll scratch yours." Because reciprocal altruism is prone to abuse by cheaters (those who get scratched but do not scratch back), organisms that practice reciprocal altruism need to be able to identify individuals and keep track of who is trustworthy and who is not. Political scientist Robert Axelrod later ran a computer tournament that modeled different strategies of cooperation based on the much-studied problem of the prisoner's dilemma. In the original version, the game was a thought experiment to determine when it would be rational for two prisoners arrested for the same crime to cooperate. If they cooperated and told the authorities nothing, both would receive only one year of prison. If both defected and squealed on the other, each would get four years. If, however, one defected and one cooperated, the one who defected would get off with no punishment while the one who cooperated would be stuck with five years (figure 7.1).

Player B

		Co-operate	Defect
Player A	Co-operate	R=Reward=1 year	S=Sucker's payoff =5 years
	Defect	T=Temptation to Defect =0 years	P=Punishment =4 years

Fig. 7.1. The prisoner's dilemma from the perspective of playerA

If one plays the prisoner's dilemma strictly as a game of probability, then on average the best strategy is to defect. In Axelrod's tournament, however, players encountered each other not once but multiple times, simulating a situation in which reciprocal altruism might arise. Contestants (some of whom were prominent scholars) submitted quite different strategies. Those who always cooperated typically lost out quite quickly when defectors were present. Yet, when playing repeatedly with the same individuals, always defecting is also a poor strategy. In a world full of defectors, everyone eventually gets the four-year penalty. Interestingly, one of the more successful strategies was what became known as tit-for-tat, which was to cooperate when others cooperated and defect when others defected. Elegant and simple, tit-for-tat seemed to model perfectly what reciprocal altruism is about, and the computer models seemed to confirm that, at least in proper contexts, reciprocal altruism works.

The world of living organisms, of course, is much more messy than that of computer simulations. Cooperative behavior in the wild cannot be easily quantified in terms of cost and benefits, and the computer models themselves have been subject to revisions and examinations of their limitations.[11] Despite this, some fairly clear-cut examples of reciprocal cooperation exist in the wild, the most famous of which involves vampire bats.[12] Despite (from our perspective) the gruesomeness of their feeding behavior, vampire bats will aid their roost-mates by sharing their meals with one another (via regurgitation) even in absence of kin relation. Such cooperation appears to be based on reciprocal action. Since only a few bats will actually find a meal on any given night, the ability to cooperate in this fashion is of clear benefit. Reciprocity of various kinds is also well attested in primates. Male chimpanzees, for instance, will sometimes form groups to hunt and kill colobus monkeys, which are otherwise difficult to catch and eat. While only one chimpanzee actually makes the kill, the food is shared with all those who participated in the hunt.[13]

Although sociobiologists have emphasized kin- and reciprocal altruism, their opponents have emphasized other approaches that center on cooperation rather than competition. Sociobiologists, for instance, tend to ignore completely the widespread mutualistic (also called symbiotic) forms of cooperation that are found not only within but between species. The work of Lynn Margulis has been particularly important for this line of thinking.[14] Margulis's research showed that the type of cell (known as eukaryotes) from which all multicellular life is composed developed as the result of the cooperation (symbiosis) of two originally independent cells, one of which is now called the mitochondria. Mitochondria were originally independently existing bacteria, but now exist within the eukaryotic cell and functions to convert energy for the cell as a whole. Mitochondria even have their own DNA, distinct from the nucleus and inherited only from the mother. No cooperation with mitochondrial bacteria, no eukaryotes; no eukaryotes, no multicellular life. More importantly, this act of symbiosis is not an exception but the rule. The regular activity of organisms is in fact symbiotic in character. We humans live not only by virtue of our large brains but also by virtue of the lowly bacteria housed in our gut that help make digestion possible. While Margulis is primarily a microbiologist, the general implication of her work is that the conceptual framework of evolution needs to be revised and that we should emphasize and look for accounts of evolution that more strongly incorporate symbiosis into the central narrative. Indeed, the entire planet can be understood as a complex interaction of symbiotic arrangements, represented most strikingly by the composition of the planet's atmosphere, a result due solely to the complex interactions of plants, animals, and microorganisms.

Elliot Sober and biologist David Sloan Wilson emphasize a group-selectionist account as a means of overcoming the excesses of what they call the selfish-gene approach of sociobiology.[15] Their critique is twofold. First, Sober and Wilson call into question the usefulness of the whole metaphoric vocabulary surrounding genes and an approach that emphasizes individualistic competition to the exclusion of all other considerations. Second, they call for a new, sophisticated form of multilevel selection that understands evolution in terms of its action on different levels of groups. The lowest-level group is that of the genes themselves. Rather than emphasizing the selfish behavior of genes, Sober and Wilson note that genes exist only by virtue of being a part of the same genome. This is a kind of "parliament" of genes, where both cooperation and competition take place. The individual organism and groups of organisms, in turn, each represent further, distinct levels that are subject to different selective forces.

Sober and Wilson argue that the effects of group selection are important for understanding the evolution of altruism generally and human beings specifically. Group selection works best when organisms are divided into well-defined, discrete populations that periodically break up and recombine. One example of this is airborne infectious diseases. While such infectious diseases may find initial success in extreme virulence as the result of rapid reproduction, it is usually the less virulent (one might say cooperative) form of the disease that often survives in the long term, for the simple reason that the more virulent forms too often kill their host before a new one can be found. Here the apparently selfish form is actually less successful; cooperation of a sort wins out.

While each independent view is relatively straightforward, the whole picture is more difficult to sort out. Should we regard competition or cooperation as the greater driving force in evolution, and to what extent do such abstract forces relate to the moral and spiritual character of human beings? Sociobiologists emphasize the competitive features of evolution. Indeed, the dominant perspective among sociobiologists has been to treat kin- and reciprocal altruism as forms of selfishness in disguise. Biologically, altruism is defined as giving aid to another organism at the expense of oneself. Sociobiologists, however, argue that what counts as altruism at the level of the organism is actually selfishness at the level of the gene. In the case of kin altruism, it is really not altruism at all, because the kin being helped carry many of the same genes, and the level of help given according to Hamilton's theory is in direct proportion to the degree of relatedness. Likewise, reciprocal altruism survives biologically only because, in the final analysis, it increases the fitness of the organism giving the aid in the first place. As many have pointed out, reciprocal altruism is also not really altruism at all, since aid is given only with the expectation that the favor will be eventually returned.

But, as Sober and Wilson along with many others have cogently argued, this sort of reductionistic view is erroneous, and the metaphorical portrayal of genes as selfish agents can be highly misleading. Because a behavior enhances the reproductive fitness of the organism as a whole and thus the genes that it bears does not mean that the behaviors are themselves selfish; it is simply that certain kinds of behavior enhance fitness in a specific context and others do not. Kin altruism and reciprocal altruism are genuine forms of cooperation at the level of the organism, even though they may not be true instances of altruism if we think of them at the level of the gene.

Despite this, it would be equally mistaken to assume that cooperation is the whole story. Competition remains considerably significant in any evolutionary account. Indeed, the forms of cooperation that are biologically successful are quite specific and limited and in most cases occur in a larger, competitive environment. This does not mean that competition is necessarily the dominant story but only that it is always a complementary story. Symbionts cooperate with one another at the same time as they compete with other organisms. Reciprocal altruism and group selection have similar constraints.

As we shall see, this does not necessarily mean that human beings are limited to these forms of cooperation. But it does suggest some significant biological constraints that need to be dealt with by any organism or group of organisms. With the exception of kin selection, genuine altruism is fleetingly rare in the natural world. That it exists among humans at all is a significant exception, a fact that even sociobiologists have recognized is difficult to explain.

Machiavellian Intelligence?

While evolutionary accounts are important for providing a framework for understanding human thought and action, they are not a full account. If we take evolution seriously, then human physiology and behavior, by adaptation to its original environment, should have developed more successfully than its competitors. If Darwin was right about natural selection, this should be true even if it is cooperative behavior that is adaptive and even if natural selection is not the only force to consider. The kind of cooperative behavior that Sober and Wilson describe is primarily limited to the group to which one belongs. Groups, however, still compete with groups, and there are reasons to believe that the extinction of the Neanderthals occurred precisely because of intergroup competition with our own species, Homo sapiens. Such analysis, however, does not consign us to this kind of tribal warfare. In Sober and Wilson's analysis, there is fluidity in how humans construct their groups, and so it is possible to extend our groups that exclude racism, sexism, and parochial nationalism as long as such groups are adaptively successful.

The question remains, however, as to how this precisely occurs. How do the forces of evolution produce intelligent, moral, and spiritual beings? Here again the neo-Darwinist account seems to intrude. If such traits are in some sense innate, then they must be hereditary. If they are hereditary, then there must be a genetic basis to human behavior.

Evolutionary psychologists, in many ways the successors of sociobiologists, claim that an integration of evolutionary theory and cognitive science is the solution. The program for evolutionary psychology was laid down in an article by John Tooby and Leda Cosmides that has since become a sort of manifesto for the discipline.[16] Tooby and Cosmides argue against what they call the Standard Social Science Model (SSSM), the main characteristic of which is to claim that all human behavior is rooted in culture and that biology has no important role to play. In contrast, they argue that the mind is best understood in analogy to a Swiss army knife, composed of numerous mental modules, each of which is designed for a specific function. These modules significantly shape behavior and do so because in our evolutionary past they were highly adaptive. Since such modules were developed in our distant evolutionary past, they are common to everyone and thus form the basis of a universal human nature. While cultural variations do exist, evolutionary psychologists regard these as rather minor and ultimately dependent on the genetic structures that allow such variation.

For most evolutionary psychologists, the mental module par excellence is the language module first postulated by Noam Chomsky and supported by evidence from a number of studies in developmental psychology.[17] Language clearly sets human beings apart from all other animals and, while chimpanzees and bonobos can learn a rudimentary form of symbolic communication (see chapter 6, above), their abilities pale beside that of human beings. More than this, areas dedicated to language have been fairly precisely mapped out in the brain, and damage to different relevant areas of the brain can result in specific kinds of language deficits.

A language module would presumably have clear evolutionary benefits. Evolutionary psychologists, however, tend to focus on modules that have an impact on behavior. In doing so, they are much influenced by the selfish-gene approach that characterizes sociobiology and that is so strongly opposed by Sober and Wilson and others.

One of the best examples of such research has been conducted by Cosmides and Tooby on the existence of a cheater-detection module.[18] Cosmides and Tooby used a logic test called the Wason Selection Task as a means of determining whether we are uniquely adept at detecting cheaters and better at it than at making logical deductions in other contexts. In the abstract form of the task, subjects are shown four cards and given the rule, "If a card has a D on one side, then it has 3 on the other." Subjects are then asked to determine which cards they should flip in order to ascertain whether the rule is violated (figure 7.2).

Fig. 7.2. Wason Selection Test

As any good logic student knows, the cards that should be turned over are the "D" card, since anything other than a three would violate the rule, and the "7" card, since a "D" on the reverse side of this card would also violate the rule. Somewhat surprisingly, most people get this wrong on the first try, usually being tempted to pick the "3" rather than the "7" card, even though anything could be on the reverse side of the "3" card and not violate the rule. The situation, however, is much different if subjects are instead asked to play the role of bartender and given the rule, "If a person is drinking beer, then the person must be 21 years old." When subjects are presented the four cards in figure 10.3, the majority (about 75 percent) choose the correct cards "drinking beer" and "16 years old."

| drinking beer | drinking cola | 25 years old | 16 years old |

Fig. 7.3. Wason Selection Test, alternate version

After considering a number of alternative scenarios, Cosmides and Tooby conclude that human beings have a cheater's module built into their brains. Such a mental module would have been immensely important in humankind's hunter-gatherer past, when decisions about whom to trust were of prime importance.

By this general method, evolutionary psychologists have attempted to explain a wide range of traits, from nurturing behaviors of mothers even to expertise in landscape aesthetics.[19] Much of the research, however, has focused on behaviors related to reproduction, especially the conflicting reproductive strategies of men and women. From an evolutionary perspective, males tend to maximize their reproductive success by mating with as many females as possible. Since females have a heavier physical investment, their strategy will more likely be long-term, with a preference toward monogamy and keeping the male around to aid in the raising of the young. Evolutionary psychologists have suggested that humans are not immune to these kinds of selective pressures.[20] Citing cross-cultural studies, they argue that evidence shows that, given the alternatives, men will on average choose women who are young, nubile, and chaste, favoring high fertility and avoiding uncertain paternity. Women, by contrast, generally prefer older men who are economically successful. Women rate intelligence in a mate highly, while men consider it only if they are seeking a long-term relationship. Standards of beauty such as facial symmetry or female breast size can be seen as signs of health and fertility. Different patterns of jealousy are also explained on an evolutionary hypothesis. A woman might be less threatened by a husband's one-night fling than by serious emotional infidelity, since the latter is more likely to lead to a break in the relationship. For a man the reverse might be true, since a one-night fling could result in a child that is not his own but whom he will be expected to raise. In one disturbing study, surveys of crime-report data indicated that stepchildren were far more likely to suffer abuse and homicide at the hands of their stepparents than is the case in families in which the parents and children were biologically related.[21]

A central issue in evolutionary psychology is the primary cause of the evolution of intelligence. Many proposals over the years have tried to account for the way natural selection fostered our own inordinate level of intelligence, from tool use to the need to develop complex mental maps in order to find food. Several of the most influential hypotheses link cognitive evolution with the need to live together as a group. One hypothesis, first suggested by Nicholas Humphrey and then developed by Richard Byrne, Andrew Whiten, and others, suggests that it was the social pressures of living in increasingly large groups that required ever-increasing brainpower in order to stay ahead.[22] This "Machiavellian intelligence," as Byrne and Whiten called it, required ever more sophisticated methods of keeping track of individuals, forming alliances, and mind reading. The task of mind reading, or developing a theory of mind (discussed in chapter 6, above), is seen as particularly important due to the great amount of cognitive sophistication it would require. If I know that you know what I know, I can make predictions on how you would act. Furthermore, you may try to deceive me (requiring that you know what I know). This would require new skills on your part, which in turn would prompt the selection of new skills on my part, the very cheater's module that Cosmides and Tooby describe.

The Machiavellian hypothesis can be taken in two ways. On the one hand, social intelligence can occur only within large societies, suggesting that cooperation is important not only for evolution but also specifically for the evolution of intelligent beings. Frans de Waal has argued that research on primate cooperation indicates that strong social bonds are characteristic not only of our species but are found among other primates as well and, as such, should be considered part of our evolutionary heritage.[23] For de Waal, we are moral not in spite of our nature but because of it. Thus, some primates are capable of sympathy for one another, demonstrated by comforting behavior given to those who have lost a conflict or by emotional distress sometimes recorded at the death of kin. Primate societies are made possible by a variety of cooperative behavioral strategies, from the forming of established social hierarchies to behaviors such as grooming, which seem to function as a form of social calming. When conflict does erupt, a new hierarchy is established and peacemaking behavior often follows. Chimpanzees may reconcile with a kiss on the mouth, and bonobos seem to use sex to ease social tension.

On the other hand, the chosen title of the theory suggests that the kind of cooperation engaged in is not very pleasant. The ability to deceive and manipulate others plays a primary role, and it is no accident that experiments on deception and its detection form a major part of the research. The ability to deceive and to detect deception, some argue, is the driving force of the evolution of intelligence. To deceive requires the ability to project intentions other than those you actually have and presumably to recognize how those false intentions will be interpreted by another. To detect deception, on the other hand, requires not only an interpretation of the intentions but a correlation with other behavior and possible motives in order to detect whether the intentions expressed are genuine or false. Even when cooperation does occur, however, a negative side is apparent. One form of cooperation that has received significant attention by de Waal is the capacity for alliance formation by chimpanzees.[24] Like other primates, chimpanzees establish a dominance hierarchy, headed by an alpha male who typically enjoys food and reproductive privileges. While the alpha male in theory holds all the power, the power is dependent on the tacit support of the group. Inevitably, however, challenges arise. Challengers form their own groups, resulting in competing coalitions that may vie with one another over prolonged periods until one side is defeated. Conflict, it seems, is at the heart of cooperation.

Sober and Wilson have also developed a model of cognitive evolution based on social cooperation.[25] On their account, the driving force of cognitive evolution is the formation of groups of altruists who willingly and even sacrificially cooperate with one another. Such groups seek to ban cheaters. Thus cheater detection would be important but not the driving force. The ability to cooperate with the group is what would be selected, because the pressures of group selection in this case would be of prime importance. Groups of altruists that could exclude cheaters would do far better than any other form of group, with the result that group altruism would be selected as a highly favorable trait. But there is a dark side to this hypothesis as well for, although cooperation within the group would be highly advantageous, competition between groups should still be expected. A group that is highly cohesive will clearly separate itself from other groups and may in fact act quite brutally toward those who are not group members. Sober and Wilson see in such behavior the roots of racism and nationalism, both of which are forms of group-versus-group competition. We are, in Sober and

Wilson's analysis, genuinely good-natured, even to the extent of being capable of genuinely altruistic self-sacrifice, but our goodness is limited to the group we identify with. When confronted with members of other groups, the negative side of our nature clearly emerges.

Are We Really That Way?

The claims of evolutionary psychology and cognitive evolution have a certain surface plausibility. It seems obvious that if humans are a product of evolution then we should see it manifested in the specific nature of our being. Once we accept the primacy of competition not only with our environment but also in the group and between the sexes, as many evolutionary psychologists do, then evolutionary theory provides a solid basis for studying human behavior. Yet, such straight-forward reasoning hides a host of hidden premises that make evolutionary accounts of human nature and cognition difficult to establish. For those familiar with the study of human origins, the first major problem is simply identifying what life was like for the earliest members of the human species, approximately two hundred thousand years ago. Too often, an outdated view of "man the hunter" and "woman the nurturer/gatherer" is simply assumed together with the sexist assumptions that such a scenario originally implied. This view is currently under assault among paleontologists. It has been suggested, for instance, that the dramatic hunting of large mammals was not characteristic of everyday life of Pleistocene peoples. If so, this would alter our understanding of male and female roles during the Pleistocene and thereby the roots of our evolutionary psychology.[26] To put the problem more generally, we are using one tentative scientific construction (lifestyle and culture of Pleistocene hunter-gatherers) to develop another (fitness-enhancing mental modules that influence behavior). If we are uncertain in important ways about one, we should not be overly confident about the other. This does not mean that no evolutionary connection should be made or hypothesized but only that we must be appropriately cautious, particularly when we start to home in on issues that are of significant cultural importance, such as sexual morality and gender roles.

This weakness extends to many of the particular studies as well. While the murder and abuse of stepchildren may fit within a selfish-gene framework, the interpretation of data of such incidents is not unproblematic. Stepfamilies, for instance, are often formed from broken families that already have a history of dysfunction, making the probability of violence higher at the outset. Furthermore, many stepfamilies do not experience violence of this sort. Whatever the cause of our violence, we are clearly not like lions, among which a male, prior to mating with the female, regularly kills cubs sired by another male. Such problems bedevil many other studies as well. It has been argued, for instance, that David Buss's survey of 30,000 individuals across a wide number of cultures fails to take into account how effectively Western values have penetrated cultures across the world.[27] More importantly, most such studies do not seriously take into account the major rival hypothesis, that many such behaviors are learned and that cross-cultural instances of such behaviors are not due simply to genes but to the fact that certain cultural universals might arise both out of our nature and our environments. If studies that show that women prefer older and wealthier men are valid, is this the result of genetic programming or from the simple analysis of the alternatives? It would be interesting, for instance, to see whether younger women and older (but capable of child-bearing) women hold such preferences to different degrees, suggesting a significant learned component. Strangely enough, this seems not yet to have been studied. Likewise, do we have a "cheater's module" because we are born with one or because discriminating between cheaters and noncheaters is an important part of growing up?

Hypotheses about the causal factors in cognitive evolution also have their own difficulties. These hypotheses will be addressed in more detail in chapter nine, but here we may observe that, at least to date, most theories of cognitive evolution claim more than is supported by the available evidence. Moreover, other perspectives merit serious consideration. Terence Deacon, for instance, has argued that human evolution is directly tied to the significant enlargement of the frontal lobes, whose primary distinction is in their capacity to facilitate symbolic thought.[28] The extent to which we are able to represent the world, remember into the distant past, and foresee into the distant future are all important and distinctive traits of our species. It is unlikely, however, that the evolution of intelligence should be understood in such a monocausal way. While a single factor such as social competition and cooperation may have provided an initial impetus, once the trend began other benefits surely followed. Tool use, enhanced foraging behavior, and symbolic representation all would have provided powerful feedback that would have accelerated the trend.

Because of these kinds of uncertainties, it is tempting to dismiss such biological accounts altogether. But this too would be a mistake. However we finally construe them, both kin- and reciprocal altruism are clearly part of our heritage. In every culture now known, the family unit has been the inviolable basic unit, and it is not easy to find cultures that do not favor kin over non-kin. With non-kin, the vast majority of our relationships can be understood generally to obey the rules of reciprocal altruism, even though we as a species seem to have considerable leeway in applying them. Broadly speaking, we are loyal to those who are loyal to us and less so to those who are not. While many of these behaviors may have a significant learned component, there is likely a genetic basis for some of this behavior. It is highly unlikely, for instance, that sexual preference is simply a matter of cultural construction, as some would now argue. Indeed, there is some evidence to suggest that prohibitions of incest have biological roots. Unrelated children of the opposite sex who are raised in close proximity typically find one other unattractive as sexual partners, even in contexts where they are expected to be, such as in the Israeli kibbutzim and Chinese child marriages.[29] More generally, we are clearly social animals by our very nature. We seek out social contact and do not develop normally when we lack it. Being social animals requires specific biological characteristics. Indeed, on a broad level, what evolutionary accounts of cooperation reveal is highly consistent with what we might expect from a theological point of view: we are indeed by nature cooperators, but our cooperation tends to be of narrow, specific kinds. Neither angel nor beast, we are nevertheless capable of both the highest good and basest evils. But the question remains: how did we get that way? Is it simply matter of genetic predisposition driven by evolution or is it something more?

Organized to Self-Organize

How do genes produce brains? One of the greatest mysteries of the biological sciences—not to mention life in general—is how the individual fertilized egg transforms into the beautiful complexity of a whole organism. It is now estimated that there are some 30,000 genes that, in the context of their cellular and extracellular environment, are responsible for the development, organization, and, in many ways, the maintenance of the body. The fact that this includes the development of the human brain is all the more remarkable when we recall that the genetic difference between ourselves and chimpanzees is, on average, less than 2 percent.

Genes are clearly important for proper development and the physical character of the body. Are they important for behavior as well? As mentioned earlier in this chapter, evolutionary psychologists such as Cosmides and Tooby have argued that genes program the mental modules that form the Swiss army knife that is the brain. Each module is programmed for a specific, adaptive function that enhances our reproductive fitness. Furthermore, many of these modules operate on an unconscious level, manipulating us in ways that we are not aware of. This emphasis of the unconscious manipulation of such modules gives evolutionary psychology a Freudian cast that is quite different from much of the rest of cognitive science.

The notion of mental modules has some plausibility. As noted in earlier chapters, specific areas of the brain are responsible for specific functions, and damage to these areas causes the loss of these functions. Beyond this, however, it is unclear that the brain is a Swiss army knife in the way that evolutionary psychologists picture it, with mental modules operating independently of one another. As seen in the case of Phineas Gage (discussed in chapter 4, above), our ability to reason effectively turns out to be connected to emotional states and valuation. Human courtship is not simply driven by modules for singling out rich men and beautiful women but, at least in most cases, is ultimately connected to other abilities, such as communicating effectively and showing empathy. To extend the metaphor, many of the blades of the mental army knife might not be completely discrete but in fact linked to one another in complex ways that make difficult the claim that each mental module governs one specific behavioral function.

A more important problem is the question of how such modules are linked to our genes in the first place. Evolutionary psychologists argue that genes directly program specific mental modules, which in turn program our behavior in relatively rigid ways. Evidence from genetics, however, suggests otherwise, although the story is much more complex than usually realized. In the popular press—but much less so among scientists—the relationship between genes and traits is understood in terms of direct correlation. That is, for every gene there is a single, specified trait. On this analysis, we should be able to identify specific genes for specific kinds of behavior. With a few exceptions, such efforts have been strikingly unsuccessful. There have been several claims for the discovery of genes for such traits as alcoholism, risk-taking, and homosexuality, but none has stood up to serious scrutiny. Indeed, it would be surprising if such claims did hold up. The relation between genes and the traits to which they contribute is far more complex than is usually credited, and this is especially true for complex behavioral traits. Genes do not code for behaviors directly but for specific proteins that play important roles in cellular function and development, the organization of which emerges in the behavior of the whole organism. The impact of genes on behavior and development can often occur in tandem with environmental cues and in interaction with other genes as well.

This can be seen in what otherwise appears as a straightforward cor-relation of genes and behavior. In a case that received international attention, a family in the Netherlands was discovered in which four-teen males in the family line were exceptionally prone to aggressive behavior, including attempted arson, rape, and murder. It was found that all of the males lacked a gene on the X chromosome that produces an enzyme, monoamine oxidase, responsible for inactivating a num-ber of neurotransmitters in the brain. While the gene-behavior link is clear in this case, it would be a mistake to claim that scientists had found a gene for aggression. The only reason the absence of the gene appears to increase aggression is the complex interaction of high levels of neurotransmitters, themselves coded in complex ways by other genes. Furthermore, there is no reason to suppose that the presence of the gene and the amino acid it programs is directly related to sup-pressing aggression; indeed, its scope of action appears to be much broader. Even in this case, the aggression seemed to emerge only when the men were highly stressed or stimulated, suggesting the importance of environmental and cultural factors as well.[30]

This does not mean, however, that no links can be made between genes and behavior. The most successful studies in this regard have been of monozygotic (identical) twins who were separated at birth and adopted by different families. Studies have generally shown that iden-tical twins reared together are more similar to one another on any given trait than those who are raised apart, but identical twins raised apart are more similar than dizygotic (fraternal) twins. Such studies have shown important correlations for relationships of genes to intelligence as well as for more specifically behavioral traits. Thus, a study conducted by Lindon Eaves compared monozygotic and dizygotic twins on such items as church attendance, educational attainment, and sexual permissiveness, as well as attitudes on such issues as economics, politics, and the religious right.[31] In all cases, the study found significant correlations with genetic relatedness. For example, the likelihood of female fraternal twins to share political attitudes was about 28 percent; for female identical twins raised apart the percentage jumped to 47. The likelihood of male fraternal twins to have the same attitudes toward the religious right was 31 percent. This likelihood jumped to 51 percent for male identical twins—surely a significant difference!

Do gene-complexes program religious and political values? Not at all. It is more likely that genes program a complex set of physical traits that in turn lead to certain kinds of personality characteristics, which in turn lead to propensities for certain kinds of positions and attitudes within a broader cultural context. The cultural context is certainly not insignificant. If it is indeed the case that there is a genetic component to the development of a kind of personality that, statistically speaking, would find political conservatism more appealing, what counts as politically conservative would vary considerably if one lived in the contemporary United States as opposed to post–Soviet Russia or revolutionary France.

The matter is probably even more complicated than this. While there about 30,000 genes, there are on the order of 100 billion neurons in the brain. Not only is it impossible for so few genes to program instructions for every neuron but it is unlikely that genes program the brain in the narrowly specific way that is sometimes suggested by evolutionary psychologists. Indeed, it seems increasingly likely that what genes in no small way do is to organize the brain to organize itself. We are born with far more neurons than we end up with, the reason being that during the first years of life the brain experiences a massive die-off of neurons. Why? There is good reason to suppose that during this focal period the mind/brain is essentially programming itself on the fly. Gerald Edelman in particular has developed the hypothesis that brain development is itself a Darwinian process.[32] Once exposed to the appropriate stimuli, neurons go through a process of selection and self-organization. Those that self-organize appropriately survive, and those that do not are weeded out. The means that the proper environment is important not only for development but also for the actions of the child. Contrary to the impression that one might get from evolutionary psychology, a child's learning process is dynamic. A child learns not simply by listening and seeing but especially by doing.

This suggests that any genetic programming is a complex interaction of genes, body, environment, and self that is difficult to disentangle. In the case of learning language, for instance, we may argue that there is a strong genetic component. All normal humans learn to speak, but this seems almost completely inaccessible to other species. Moreover, language learning occurs at specific developmental stages. Children who suffer significantly delayed language learning because of a deprived environment will have permanent impairments, as is the case with vision and personality traits as well.

Other traits, however, may not be as directly inherited as what might be called cognitively forced. Cosmides and Tooby fail to seriously consider that cheater detection might a learned behavior of the forced-move kind; that is, dealing with cheaters is frequent enough and significant enough in life that we learn to become quite good at it. It would be interesting if Cosmides and Tooby extended their research to children and combined their work with brain-scan and brain-lesion studies. Would these show a neurological basis of cheater detection, and would they show it developing at certain stages in life? More importantly, can the failure to detect cheaters be associated with the lack of a certain gene? I would be surprised if we could in any straightforward sense show this. Cheater detection must ultimately have *some* genetic basis, inasmuch as it is limited to humans and perhaps some primates. But the full story of cheater detection likely involves much more—the complex historical interaction of genes-body-mind-self-environment. Because this part of the story is similar enough for everyone, virtually all of us are good at cheater detection, but the independent pathways through which we arrive at such a development may be quite different.

Because of complexities of this sort, Francisco Ayala has argued that morality is an indirect result of our more general abilities for intelligence and self-consciousness.[33] On Ayala's account, we are not moral because of certain genes that program for morality, but we are moral because we are intelligent, self-conscious beings that need to develop moral systems in order to survive and get along. While there is much that is right in this view, I suggest that it is too weak. Our human nature is complex and multifaceted, influenced by a number of important elements. The genes we have are due to our evolutionary history, a history in which natural selection has played an important role. Our genes encode basic physical traits, although such encoding may be significantly sensitive to environmental cues. With the brain, genes set the pattern but do not determine development. Acknowledging this, we may say that genes contribute significantly to behavioral traits, but the genetic story is not the only story. Self-culture-environment interactions play an important role. Any satisfactory account of human nature must inevitably include all these levels of analysis.

Realizing this, however, quickly leads to the conclusion that a strictly biological account of human nature must necessarily be incomplete. Human nature is not simply a matter of genes, and human morality is not simply a matter of cooperation and competition. It would be more accurate to say that evolutionary biology is the context out of which human nature and human morality emerge. Indeed, it is because of the startlingly excessive character of human intelligence and the extreme plasticity of human behavior that the development of moral codes and, more generally, a moral worldview is even necessary. We are likely the only creatures on Earth who not only can foresee our own death but see beyond it as well. Out of such a context comes both tragedy and hope.

Falling Up?

How then are we to think of ourselves? Theologically, we are said to be made in the image of God, yet in some sense fallen or incomplete. A scientifically informed perspective suggests that our nature is in no small part a legacy of our evolutionary heritage and our own particular biology. But it suggests also that evolution and genes are only part of the story, that our very nature as cognitive, thinking beings makes us subtle, complex, and free in a way that other organisms are not—so much so, in fact, that we appear capable of overriding what would in other species be inviolable biological drives. We can fast, abstain from sex, and even sacrifice ourselves for others. Such freedom from biological constraints is not always for the good. While rare, parents who kill or abuse their own children are as difficult to explain biologically as the saint who sacrifices all.

Does the scientific account of human nature influence the theological one? On a number of levels, what the biological and cognitive sciences tell us coheres strongly with theological perspectives on human nature. At the same time, however, they may also require subtle shifts on how we think about this most basic of questions.

The greatest shift involves our relation to the rest of creation. On most traditional accounts, humankind is distinctive both in being created in the image of God and in being able to turn away from God. On many of these accounts, nature remains unfallen and either serves merely as a backdrop to the drama of human redemption or as a source of inspiration in the intricacy of nature's design. This absolute divide between humanity and the rest of creation now seems barely tenable, however, not only for the reasons recounted in chapter 6 (above) but also because our moral behavior is in no small part biologically rooted. As a species, we have far greater behavioral plasticity than any other organism, yet we are bound by the same issues of competition and cooperation that many other creatures face. This is most apparent when we look at our fellow primates, but we can see such proto-moral behavior in a range of species.[34]

The implications of such a realization are far-reaching, for they suggest not only that humankind is fallen but that all of creation is as well. Why would it imply this? In the story of Adam and Eve, the original state is paradise, the subsequent state one of hardship. But the evolutionary framework suggests no such original paradisiacal state. Instead, from life's beginning we see both competition and cooperation at work. While many have overdramatized the notion of nature "red in tooth and claw," the broad outlay of natural history includes plenty of unsavory moments. Many millennia of animal suffering are implied before human beings even arrive on the scene. This is important, but it is not the only issue, not least because of our tendency to anthropomorphize much of plant and animal behavior as well as the evolutionary process itself. Darwin wrestled mightily with the cruelty of digger wasps, but it is unclear whether the wasps or their victims actually experience conscious pain or pleasure. What is most important, at least for our purposes here, is that suffering, competition, and cooperation were already part of the warp and woof of evolution well before humankind arrived on the scene and, moreover, are part of the tale of human origins as well. Humankind does not instantaneously appear on the scene but has its own evolutionary history, one that links us first to the other primates and then to mammals but ultimately to all living things.

The origins of sinfulness, it seems, are rooted not in the act of an original historical couple but in the complicated evolutionary process itself. At first blush, such a claim may seem to be at odds with a genuinely theological account of human nature. Where, after all, is God amid all this suffering? Yet, strictly speaking, such a perspective is not in direct conflict with the theological tradition, and further reflection suggests that there is much to commend it. The apostle Paul himself speaks of the "groaning of creation" (Romans 8:22) and the book of Revelation speaks not simply of human redemption but of a new heaven and a new earth. The real difficulty has been the expressing of such poetry in a way that makes sense. It is only recently that theologians have begun to take up this task.

On the level of theodicy, John Polkinghorne has argued that freedom is not limited to human beings but is in some sense characteristic of the universe as a whole.[35] Whereas traditional arguments have explained the existence of evil as due to human freedom (with natural evil a result of the fall), Polkinghorne has argued that it is the freedom of creation as a whole that is the cause of suffering in the cosmos. On Polkinghorne's account, our fallenness stems from the freedom that God gave the cosmos from the beginning, a freedom that, at least in theory, is worth the price of suffering and pain. The implication for human nature is that, as Augustine and Luther argued in their own ways, we are indeed bound to suffer and even to sin. This necessity is not due to the lust of our parents but to the constraints that evolution itself has placed on human nature. To amplify Polkinghorne's position (which he provides only in sketch), we are who we are because of our biological heritage. That heritage provides us with the ability to compete and to cooperate but inevitably compels us to do so in a way that often falls short of our true potential.

In contrast to Polkinghorne's global approach, Philip Hefner has concentrated more centrally on the question of human nature in the light of our evolutionary ancestry.[36] Hefner understands human nature in terms of the interaction of our genetic and cultural inheritance in the face of the adaptive changes posed by the environment. Original sin is thus due to the influence of our genetic and cultural inheritance toward selfish behavior. Hefner, however, also emphasizes the human capacity for freedom, a capacity that enables us to do both great good and great harm.

Together, Polkinghorne and Hefner have provided insights for a theological account of human nature in the light of evolutionary biology. Original sin is reinterpreted, seen not naively as the result of the actions of an original couple as understood by Augustine, but as a dynamic that emerges out of our evolutionary history. Yet there is more to be said. Our current state can be portrayed in terms of fallenness, and original sin is understood in terms of the biological and social forces that impel us to *hamartia*, to miss the mark. Some, however, object to calling these biological and social forces "sin." Denis Edwards, for instance, limits sin to our voluntary acts.[37] On his view, original sin is the sum history of such voluntary acts that each of us has inherited. Original sin is not truly sin as such, since we have no choice in our heredity. Moreover, original sin does not include our evolutionary and biological heritage, even though it is acknowledged that we are a "fallible symbiosis of genes and culture."[38]

Edwards's position amounts to a terminological distinction. Like Hefner, Edwards acknowledges that the fallible character of our genetic, biological heritage is intrinsic to our being. Also like Hefner, Edwards seems to want some role for human freedom. We are in a sense bound by our past but not determined by it. Edward's limitation of the category of sin to our own volitional actions, however, might be too limiting. Creation as a whole also misses the mark, filled as it is with both beauty and tragedy. Nevertheless, the fallenness of creation, however we may want to characterize it, is not of the same kind as our own fallenness. Liberation theologians, in speaking of the economic and political forces that often overwhelm individual choices, refer to sinful structures. Something similar might be said of natural processes, which have their own limiting influences.

Ultimately, however, this approach to natural history and human nature is incomplete, for it fails to explain why there needs to be a distinction between the fallenness of creation and the fallenness of human beings. Here our nature as cognitive beings once again plays an important role. Rocks neither feel pain nor suffer anguish. The victims of Darwin's digger wasps conceivably suffered pain, although we can perhaps never know whether insects possess conscious experience of anything. Insects certainly do not experience anguish, and one would be surprised to see a preying mantis mourning over the loss of its young. Anguish is something that humans experience and share with only a select group of other mammals, at most. In recognizing this, we begin to recognize more fully the character of human nature, for our increased complexity and increased freedom imply an increased capacity to suffer. When Augustine spoke of the fall, he spoke of it as a once-and-for-all event that occurred at a historical point in time. Such a static view, however, is at odds with the fecundity and creativity present in the evolutionary process. In an evolutionary framework, it might be more accurate to speak not of "the fall" but of *falling*. Irenaeus may prove to be more insightful than Augustine in emphasizing suffering as the result of our immaturity. In an evolutionary context, immaturity is not simply that of our own species but of all conscious life. As each new species and even individual comes to be, we see the advent of something new, full of potential but also impeded by tragic limitations.

Recognizing this, we might not speak simply of falling, but of *falling up*. However we may construe the cause (which will be taken up in the next chapter), the history of life on Earth has been characterized by the continuing appearance of increasingly complex organisms. Increased complexity allows for increased freedom, which in turn allows for greater potential for both good and evil. The emergence of our own species, Homo sapiens, is testimony to this fact. The great plasticity of our behavior allows us to act selfishly, to cooperate, and even to cooperate selfishly. Yet our freedom is not complete, and all too often we find ourselves constrained by both biology and culture, unwilling and sometimes simply unable to do good. As such, falling is in a significant sense a psychological event, both for each of us individually and for our species as a whole. The psychological character of fallenness was first given prominent attention by Søren Kierkegaard, who understood fallenness as a necessary concomitant of human freedom and the anxiety it produces.[39] Falling is not simply what happens to us; it is what we do. It is only because of our considerable sophistication that we do it in the first place, and it is because of our psychological sophistication that such falling seems to be an inevitable consequence of human freedom.

Falling, however, indicates only the negative side of human nature. That we are falling up suggests better the full complexity of human nature. We are indeed capable of truly good and wonderful things.

This complexity of human nature is suggested in John Haught's account of original sin in *God after Darwin*.[40] Haught acknowledges the constraints of our evolutionary heritage but also emphasizes the need for eschatological hope. Rather than lamenting the loss of a paradisiacal past that never existed, we should look forward to the future yet to come. Indeed, it is this ability to envision and even in limited ways to implement realities that have never existed that characterizes the kind of freedom, the kind of nature, that we have.

PART FOUR

MINDING GOD

8

The Mind of God

In 1988 Stephen Hawking concluded his bestselling *A Brief History of Time* with the claim that physicists will eventually be able to produce a complete theory that will account for all of the physical laws that govern the universe. This "theory of everything" would explain both the origins and fate of the universe and, Hawking claimed, consequently reveal to us the mind of God. This theological flourish in the final chapter of an otherwise sober text in modern physics was certainly little more than a poetic allusion, but the phrase is taken seriously by many who have regard for the beauty and order that underlie the cosmos. To say that the laws of the universe reveal the mind of God implies that the universe is not simply a cold, dark, and chaotic place but the result of intention from the beginning, laden with meaning and purpose. From the late medievals onward, many have regarded nature itself as a second book of revelation alongside the Bible and have believed that from nature we can perceive God's thoughts and intentions as surely as we can from any humanly designed artifact.

But what are we claiming when we say that God has a mind? Strange as it may seem, theologians have wrestled with this question over the centuries. The understanding of God as person is central to the great monotheistic traditions of the world but, if God is a person, God is a kind of person significantly different from us. What kind? In what way is it legitimate to speak of the mind and intentions of the divine?

While such questions may not preoccupy the ordinary believer, they are of central importance to the theological tradition. The modern era has witnessed a steady assault on the intellectual viability of belief in a personal God by philosophers, psychologists, and sociologists who often claim that such a belief is so incredible as to be pathological in character and is due to overriding psychological and sociological forces. Conversely, many theists continue to argue that the only means of rationally understanding the origin and nature of the universe is by appeal to the creative intent of an intelligent designer or agent. Once such an appeal is made, however, accounting for the way God subsequently acts in the universe again becomes a problem, and further claims must be made as to what kind of agent God is.

Because all of these issues touch on the nature of persons and minds, both divine and human, scientific models of person and mind become relevant even for speaking of God. This may seem surprising at first. Cognitive scientists, after all, do not study God, but it is a central task of theologians to develop models of God, and inevitably they develop models that rely in various ways on our understandings of human beings. Consequently, the cognitive sciences have some role to play even in these central tasks of theological thinking. They might even shed some light on matters of considerable current debate.

God as Person

In the context of modern thought, belief in a personal God is seemingly incredible. Much of our modern education explains events in terms of impersonal causal forces that sweep human beings along in their wake. Indeed, the founding mythologies of a number of academic disciplines are described in terms of emancipation from a religious worldview that ascribes the causes of events to God or the gods. Thus modern historical writing traces its roots in Herodotus and Thucydides, in part because they were the first to explain the events of history without recourse to the divine. Physicists turn to mythologized tales of Galileo, biologists to Charles Darwin and Thomas Huxley.

For Christianity as for many other faiths, such impersonal descriptions of the cosmos might be useful, but they are ultimately insufficient. A deeper analysis of the situation is required, one that must ultimately appeal to the agency of a personal God whose creative and sustaining acts provide purpose and meaning for the cosmos as a whole. The emphasis on the personal character of God is central to both Jewish and Christian scriptures. The creation of the world is itself an intentional act, and the subsequent history of humankind as unfolded in the Old Testament is the result of the interplay of God's will and human action. God is described as father, mother, and lover, and God's actions are primarily understood in personal terms. God loves, gets angry, guides, and promises much in the way that we expect of human beings.

The emphasis on the personal quality of the divine is thus central to theological tradition, but it has been expressed in quite different ways. Biblical texts themselves seem to reflect an evolution in Hebrew and Christian understandings of God, as the anthropomorphic and jealous God of the Pentateuch gives way to the God of the prophets who calls for justice and rejects any attempt at being represented in bodily form. While God is understood as Father in the New Testament, God's actions tend to be even more abstracted, conveyed primarily through the actions of angels and, most importantly, through the incarnate actions of the Son. The prologue of the Gospel of John, which understands Christ in terms of the eternally existing Logos, continues the trend of abstracting the concept of God. The personal, however, is never given up but changes as the Hebrew faith transforms, responds, and interacts with its environment.

Belief in a personal God has been the prevailing view of many throughout the centuries. In the United States today, 95 percent of Americans believe in God. Any such survey of academics generally and social scientists specifically would, however, result in a much lower percentage. One reason for this is the long disciplinary antagonism that the social sciences in general have displayed toward religion. Such antagonism first found voice in the work of Ludwig Feuerbach, who claimed that our beliefs about God are merely projections of our own desires onto an external and completely fictional entity. Feuerbach's analysis was deepened both by Karl Marx, who understood religion as a means of class oppression ("the opiate of the masses"), and Sigmund Freud, who argued that belief in God is due to unconscious, unresolved neuroses that prevent individuals from emerging into healthy adulthood. For both Marx and Freud, one need not take the grounds of religion seriously. So incredible is religious belief that it requires an explanation based on social or psychological factors rather than the believer's reasons.

Partly because of this legacy, both sociologists and psychologists have treated belief in God specifically and religion generally as a kind of pathology rather than as a normal—let alone necessary—part of healthy functioning. Indeed, Freud's antagonism to religion greatly influenced psychoanalytic thought and therapeutic psychology more generally. For years, the standard manual of mental illness used by therapeutic psychologists, the DSM III, frequently linked religion to mental illness.[1] Behaviorism also had little positive to say about religion (when it said anything at all), and there was in the twentieth century a general perception that psychology necessarily takes a negative stance toward religious belief: religion is not something to be explained but something to be explained away. The result for many psychologists has been that religious belief and practice are treated quite differently from most other forms of belief. While a number of psychologists, from Carl Jung to Abraham Maslow, have viewed religion in a more positive fashion, their views have often been treated as idiosyncratic or unrepresentative of mainstream psychology.

If Marx and Freud are right, belief in a personal God is irrational—either the sign of an unhealthy mind or a mind shaped by social forces beyond its own control that work to its own detriment. If cognitive psychology could confirm their claims, religious belief would be in clear conflict with the results of cognitive science. Moreover, there is good reason to believe that Marx and Freud are at least partially correct. There can be little doubt that religious belief is profoundly shaped by social forces and that religion frequently functions in society as a support for the status quo, however unjust that may be. The religious justification of slavery in the United States and the debates over whether slaves should be converted is but one instance of the role of religion in the maintenance of social institutions. There is also little reason to doubt that personal psychology plays an important and even profound role in the shaping of religious belief, and sometimes in a way that may be fairly described as irrational or even antirational.

Empirical psychological research at least partially supports claims that, for most people, religious belief is not based strictly on rational considerations and conscious decisions. Genetic studies by Lindon Eaves (referred to in chapter 7, above) show a correlation between religious conservatism and genetic relatedness, implying at least that genes play a role in brain development, which in turn influences broad temperaments and attitudes that would include (but presumably not be limited to) religious beliefs. William James first noted the psychological aspects of conversion experiences, and his observation that personal psychology can play an important role in conversion has been born out by later studies. The great majority of conversion experiences, for instance, take place between the ages of fifteen and sixteen, a period of important growth and transformation in the life of the individual.[2]

While these and other studies testify to the influence of social and psychological factors in religious belief, they stop well short of implying that religious belief is pathological or completely irrational. Indeed, there is good evidence to the contrary. Several studies conducted in the 1990s indicated a positive correlation between religious belief and longevity, hardly a sign of oppression or mental dysfunction.[3] Psychologist Donald Campbell, in a then controversial speech, argued that, since religious traditions have often survived for thousands of years, they should be understood as well-winnowed wisdom rather than as perpetrators of mental dysfunction.[4] More recently (as referred to in chapter 5, above), Andrew Newberg and Eugene d'Aquili have insisted that religious experiences should be considered as a part of normal adult functioning.[5]

There is therefore little in cognitive science to support claims that belief in God is somehow necessarily delusional or merely an opiate of the masses. Indeed, it would be surprising if this were the case. That belief in God should be singled out as pathological is as much the result of ideological polemic as of genuine empirical observation. The arguments of Feuerbach, Marx, and Freud are all essentially reductionistic in character, attempting to explain a higher-order phenomenon (belief in God) in terms of lower-level mechanisms (social pressure and unconscious dysfunction). Such reductive arguments can be important, for they are frequently illuminating in their ability to discern hidden motives and unseen costs and benefits. At the same time, they can be equally dangerous because of the ease with which they dismiss what may in fact be genuine, rational considerations. More generally, they threaten to undermine rational discourse altogether, for any set of beliefs and arguments can be shown not to have completely rational social and psychological bases when placed in their historical contexts. Simply to dismiss beliefs and arguments on this basis is to misunderstand the embodied character of human reasoning. It also conflates a hermeneutic of suspicion, which searches for hidden motives and then evaluates their significance, and the genealogical fallacy, which rejects an argument or belief based on its origin rather than on its merits.

Furthermore, psychological reductionism assigns particular negative value to what in fact may be a healthy aspect of religious belief: projection. Especially for Freud, projection was belief in the absence of evidence. Such belief is so irrational, according to Freud, that it could only be the result of neurosis. But what Freud calls projection others might call hope. While many strongly associate religion with certain kinds of beliefs about the past (for example, the creation of the world, the origins of humankind, or the physical resurrection of Jesus), religious belief—particularly Christian belief—is preeminently concerned with the future. Beliefs about the future are not merely shaped by the realities of the past but are significantly open to new possibilities. For human beings, hope shapes the future as much as anything else. Hope is not based simply on what we expect to happen but what we believe should happen. The role and psychology of hope finds voice in the work of Jewish psychoanalyst Victor Frankl, who testified to the power of hope among individuals in Nazi concentration camps.[6] But the psychology of hope is to date little explored, even though it is potentially significant for understanding religious belief.

From Design to Mind

It is one thing to show that belief in a personal God cannot be simply reduced to social or psychological factors and quite another to show that such belief is in fact rational. The motivations for belief in God are many, ranging from the personal and existential to the logical and philosophical, depending upon both rational and empirical considerations. Among the most important arguments for belief in God has been the argument from design, which infers the agency of an intelligent and purposive designer based on the complexity and apparently artifact-like quality of natural objects. Unlike many other reasons given for belief in a personal God, arguments from design make direct claims about the personal, agent-like character of God. The argument depends on the premise that certain kinds of objects bear the telltale signs of a personal, intelligent agent, and that finding such objects can give conclusive evidence to the presence (and sometimes even the character) of a designer.

Design arguments have a long history, including some roots in such biblical books as Psalms and Job, which understand creation as a kind of testimony to God's power and goodness. Design arguments appear as early as Cicero in the first century, B.C.E., were used by early theologians such as Irenaeus and Origen,[7] and had their heyday in the wake of the scientific discoveries of the sixteenth and seventeenth centuries. The discoveries of Newton revealed for the first time both the complexity and orderliness of the physical laws that govern the universe. Then the gradual growth of biological knowledge—due to increased understanding of basic anatomy as well as the exploration of other continents—revealed the vast diversity of plant and animal life. Design arguments were most famously propounded in a series of books known as the Bridgewater treatises, and reached their apex in William Paley's *Natural Theology*, first published in 1802. Paley compared the appearance of complexity in nature to the finding of a watch on a beach. Anyone who found such a watch would immediately infer human agency. Likewise, Paley argued, objects of comparable complexity in nature should be considered to be designed as well, pointing to an intelligent and, in this case, divine designer. The arguments of Paley and like-minded philosophers and scientists were influential, so much so that Paley's text was required reading by Oxford students at the time that Charles Darwin was studying biology there.

Darwin's theory of natural selection led to the demise of design arguments from the latter nineteenth to the twentieth centuries. Natural selection seemed to be a mechanism that could produce design without intelligence. For Darwin, the sublime perfection of the eye was not due to the concerted acts of a supernatural creator but rather to the slow, mechanical winnowing process of natural selection exerting its pressure on generation upon generation of organisms. Indeed, as later generations of biologists discovered, eyes come in many forms, some decidedly more sublime than others. As a result, biologists abandoned the concept of design. Among philosophers, however, design arguments had already fallen out of favor. Already in the eighteenth century David Hume had criticized design arguments on a number of grounds, particularly ridiculing claims about detecting the intention of God from the nature of the world.[8] Since the world is full of evil and suffering, one might legitimately infer a wicked designer. Indeed, no evidence from nature could even tell whether there was one designer or many. By the time of the early nineteenth century, many if not most philosophers had given up on the design argument and had moved to other grounds for believing in the existence of a personal God.

It was only in the late twentieth century that design arguments again began to be taken seriously. One reason for this is what has become known as the anthropic principle. As modern physics progressed, it became clear that there were a number of coincidences in such things as the structure of matter and physical constants that govern the growth and development of the universe, coincidences so improbable they appeared to rule out random variation. More importantly, these coincidences determined the difference between the kind of universe habitable by human beings and one that would be uninhabitable by any known form of life. Thus, if the expansion rate of the universe had been smaller by one part in a hundred thousand million million (100,000,000,000,000,000) in the first second after the Big Bang, it would have recollapsed, and if it was larger by one part in a million, it would have expanded so quickly that matter would never be able to congeal into galaxies, stars, and planets.[9]

On the weak form of the anthropic principle, physicists simply note that, since we exist, it is necessarily the case that the kind of universe we observe is one that is structured to support life. Advocates of the strong version, however, go a step further and argue that not only is the observable universe structured to support life but a life-supporting universe such as our own is the only possibility. While the logic of the strong anthropic principle has little to ground itself on, even the weak form inspired a number of philosophers, theologians, and scientists to reconsider the argument from design. John Polkinghorne, for instance, has claimed that the extreme improbabilities associated with the likelihood of a life-sustaining universe are so great as to suggest the agency of an intelligent designer as the best solution, comparing the situation to a man before a firing squad that misses him completely.[10] In such a case, Polkinghorne observes, the man only has two real options: he can chalk it up to luck or he can assume that there was intelligent agency working in his favor. Given the unlikelihood of the event, Polkinghorne argues that it is more rational to look for intelligent causes to explain the complex orderliness of the cosmos. Likewise, the number of improbable physical coincidences necessary for a life-sustaining universe are too great to be mere random happenstance. Intelligent agency is the best answer.

In recent years, however, the focus of design arguments has returned to biology. Michael Behe has argued that Darwinian approaches have failed to explain many of the complexities of biochemistry.[11] For Behe, certain biological structures such as the flagellum of a bacteria feature what he calls irreducible complexity. Objects that are irreducibly complex are typically composed of a number of interacting parts, of which the removal of any one part causes catastrophic collapse of the system. Because all parts would need to appear all at once, irreducibly complex structures could not have evolved over time. Therefore, the only logical explanation for the sudden appearance of such complexity is intelligent design.

While Behe has received a great deal of press, the theoretically important work has come primarily from William Dembski, who has argued that design arguments should be understood as forms of inference rather than an analogy from human creativity to divine creativity.[12] Dembski has attempted to formalize design arguments into a logical/mathematical structure that is based on probability. In place of irreducible complexity, Dembski speaks of specified complexity. For Dembski, an object displays specified complexity if it is both a low probability event and if it is capable of fitting a preexisting pattern. Objects that display both sufficiently low probability and specified complexity can, according to Dembski, be intelligently designed. Dembski even proposes a kind of design filter. If there are no physical laws that can account for the event, and if the probabilities are too wildly low to be merely a result of chance, then one *must* conclude that intelligent design is involved.

Dembski claims that most traditional critics of the design argument misunderstand it as an argument from analogy, comparing divine design to human design, when it should be properly understood as an inferential argument. Provided that any object demonstrates the appropriate criteria of specified complexity and sufficiently low probability, one should always infer intelligent design. Furthermore, Dembski argues, there are many organisms that demonstrate these criteria, and Dembski cites Behe's example of the bacteria flagella as a case in point.

While Dembski develops a number of important points and insights that merit attention, they are frequently marred by an all too familiar anti-evolutionary polemic that makes it difficult to take intelligent-design theory (as it has come to be called) seriously. The movement as a whole employs many of the rhetorical strategies of earlier creation-science movements and has yet to publish any of the theoretical work or any empirical data in an appropriate peer-reviewed scientific journal.[13]

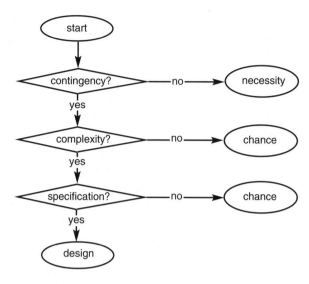

Fig. 8.1. Dembski's design filter. [From William Dembski, *The Design Inference* (1999)]

There certainly are instances where it is appropriate to infer from artifacts the existence of a designer. Human beings frequently do this in what might otherwise be ambiguous situations. As one example, Dembski cites election-fixing schemes in which vote tallies are rigged in a way that excludes the explanation of chance.[14] When this happens, investigations are carried out and sometimes the perpetrators are caught. A more straightforward example, however, would be for someone to walk into a room and find a spilled Scrabble gameboard and pieces strewn about the floor. One might not be surprised to find simple two- or three-word combinations such as "is" or "the" appear by chance on the floor. One would be very surprised, however, to find an entire sentence or phrase, such as "methinks it a weasel."[15] We would be even more surprised, however, if it spelled out the first page of *Hamlet*. If in the course of space exploration we came across an unknown planet that had *Hamlet* (or its extraterrestrial equivalent) carved in large letters on the face of a mountain, we would be similarly justified in inferring intelligent agency rather than natural causes, even if it required inferring the existence of yet unseen extraterrestrials. Chance would not suffice as an explanation.

Dembski contends that the same process of inference should take place when we look at naturally complex objects. His argument is primarily about probability and should be analyzed mainly on those grounds. His design inference, however, seems highly problematic when applied to the biological sciences, not least because his mode of inferential argument has little relation to the actual conduct of biology as a science. Dembski's probability argument assumes a kind of completeness of knowledge that is rarely available in the physical sciences. For intelligent design to work as a biological theory, it would have to provide concrete, coherent, and testable hypotheses that explain the facts in question.

There are good reasons to believe that doing good biology is not what intelligent-design theorists are up to, despite their protests to the contrary. This does not mean, however, that all design arguments are false. Since we regularly and successfully apply design inferences in the human world, it is clearly legitimate to do so. The challenge is to generalize the argument in a clear and intelligible way.

To do this, we need to reflect not only on issues of probability but on the nature of intelligence itself. Unfortunately, the term "intelligence" is an overly broad and much-contested word in the history of psychology. Like its cousins "reason" and "rationality," intelligence denotes something that is both familiar and yet difficult to define. Dembski's definition of intelligence as the ability to select between alternatives is not very helpful. A simple robot can select between two paths (e.g., move toward the light or away from the light), but we might not want to consider it very intelligent or even intelligent at all.[16] It has traditionally been argued that intelligence represents a single, unitary ability. Intelligence is the ability to reason, whether deductively, inductively, or analogically. Intelligence involves learning and memory, and is what you use when you play chess or figure out the quickest route to the grocery score. Intelligence is a kind of general-purpose problem solver. Most contentiously, some claim that intelligence is largely hereditary and is measurably by an IQ test or something similar.

While intelligence often functions in such a unitary way in human beings, there is also good reason to believe that human intelligence has multiple roots. Reference to animal cognition is in many ways enlightening when thinking about the nature of intelligence. Cognitive ethologists Dorothy Cheney and Robert Seyfarth have observed that animals often have a kind of "laser beam" intelligence, capable of tasks of incredible complexity within a narrow, specified domain.[17] Animals as varied as termites, honeybees, and beavers are able to construct complex objects. Social mammals such as chimpanzees and wolves are capable of memorization of complex social relations, inference of social relations, and perhaps even have some level of self-consciousness, but they are incapable of building anything. The complexity and difficulties of AI also testify to this specialized and constructed character of intelligence as well. The symbolic, deductive paradigm of early AI succeeded at developing expert systems within limited domains (such as SHRDLU, described in chapter 6, above) but totally failed in the plethora of tasks we take for granted. The move toward distributed models (either by PDP or the development of robots with a distributed, emergent intelligence) reinforces the notion that intelligence as we usually conceive it is not one thing but many things.

This trend is also in evidence in attempts to understand human intelligence. Cognitive psychologist Howard Gardner has hypothesized that human intelligence can be broken down into seven main faculties (e.g., logical, linguistic, interpersonal).[18] Utilizing data from brain injuries and brain scans, we have an increasingly better picture of the often specialized character of human intelligence, more capable (as described in chapter 7, above) of detecting cheaters than detecting logical fallacies.

More recently, a number of researchers have noted parallels between intelligence and Darwinian processes. A prime characteristic of both is what may be called a ratcheting effect. For evolution to take place, the existence of simple variation and mutation is not enough. Natural selection must also include a means by which some variations survive and spread. These variations, in turn, form the basis of new variations. On a Darwinian account, a new species does not emerge from scratch but as the result of a large number of small, retained steps achieved by the line of species preceding it. Intelligence often works in a similar fashion. It takes some eighteen years for a human being to reach intellectual maturity, and in modern industrialized societies most of those years are spent in school. While we often focus on geniuses like Immanuel Kant or Albert Einstein, we tend to overlook the important social and networked character of intelligence. Einstein could develop his theory of relativity only because of the previous work of others. Less abstractly, philosopher Karl Popper once noted that the advantage of intelligence is that it allows our ideas to die in our stead. Whereas nature selects organisms by allowing organisms to act out possibilities, intelligence allows us to select alternatives before acting on one.

Computer programmers, who have developed genetic algorithms to solve what are otherwise computationally difficult problems, have capitalized on this apparent similarity between intelligence and natural selection. In contrast to traditional modes of programming, in which each step of the program is logically and (largely) sequentially laid out, genetic programs are designed to create mutations of themselves. The mutations are then assessed according to a set of success criteria, and those that are most successful are allowed to survive. Cross-fertilized mutations from these survivors form the next generation, which undergo the same process until an appropriate solution is produced. The success of evolutionary algorithms in limited domains has inspired some to see intelligence as an evolutionary process. The similarity has led some (most notably Daniel Dennett) to understand even natural selection as an algorithmic process, thereby attributing a kind of intelligence to nature itself.[19]

What has this to do with God? Everything, once we begin to construe God as an intelligent designer. According to design argument, there are objects whose nature points unequivocally to the actions of an intelligent agent. To do so, one must have an adequate theory of intelligence. It is therefore striking that a theory of intelligence is one of the central things that modern intelligent-design theory lacks. Contemporary intelligent-design theorists such as Michael Behe and William Dembski have purposefully eschewed any attempt to provide an account of intelligence or (more specifically) of the nature of God, the designer in question. They claim that to do so is to go beyond the bounds of science and into the realm of theology. It is a curious claim on many levels.

Without an account of intelligence, it is unclear why a proposal should be called a theory of *intelligent* design. Such a proposal could be taken simply as a sophisticated statement of our own ignorance about many physical and biological systems. Dembski has argued that evolutionary algorithms are not truly evolutionary, because they have initial parameters that are programmed by human beings. This is a fair criticism, although human beings can also be said to be programmed by genes and environment to a certain extent. And while many have emphasized the modular character of mind, others have tended to emphasize the ultimately unitary character of intelligence in a way that might be more amenable to intelligent-design theory.[20] The problem is that Dembski and Behe lack any such theory altogether. In essence, their refusal to deal with the central theological question of the nature of God as designer significantly weakens the scientific status they allege for their theory. Indeed, the willingness to accept the claim that the discipline of theology is unscientific seems to be a central flaw in the modern intelligent-design movement. Intelligent-design theory fails not simply because it does not take biology seriously but because it does not take theology seriously.

This criticism of intelligent-design theory, however, should not be taken to mean that all design arguments are necessarily doomed to failure. Dembski's insight that design arguments can be understood as an inference rather than as an argument from analogy is an important one. Any successful design argument, however, must be explicitly theological in character. Rather than relegating theology to the realm of the unscientific, design arguments must be clear on what is being implied about the nature of God and, more specifically, in what way it makes sense to attribute intelligence to God. The arguments must also be clear about the kind of empirical data being considered. Proceeding in this fashion would be more in keeping with scientific methods than intelligent-design theory has been so far. One reason why intelligent-design theory has struck many scientists as artificial is that it takes an approach more inspired by mathematics than by the physical and biological sciences. To determine probability accurately, one must have complete knowledge of a physical system, something that is almost never available to the practicing scientist. Science proceeds instead by the development and testing of hypotheses. An inference is made not directly to the "correct" explanation but to the best among several possible explanations, none of which, as far as the scientist is concerned, is absolutely certain.

That God is the best ultimate explanation of the existence and nature of the world is the position of the great monotheistic traditions. The conviction that this is so rests ultimately on broader criteria than those considered by intelligent-design theorists. Both intelligence and design are fairly narrow categories, evoking more the watchmaker God of the Enlightenment than the Lord of creation. Indeed, it is an important tenet of intelligent-design theory that creation itself has no creative power; that creation is an essentially inert lump upon which divine and human intelligence acts. Yet, as we have seen, intelligence comes in many forms, lending credence to the idea that creativity is part of the world and not simply an attribute of God.

Such an insight is more in keeping with the God who emptied God's self into creation than with the watchmaker God implied by a narrow concept of design.

God:World::Mind:Body

Intelligent-design arguments raise the question of how it makes sense to think of God as an intelligent agent. Intelligence is but one of several personal qualities traditionally attributed to God. It is linked to concepts of reason and knowledge, which have been important theologically but need to be complemented by other characteristics, such as God's goodness, love, and power. Perhaps most centrally, God is understood to be purposive, and it is from God's will that the purposes of the universe and even ourselves as individuals are understood.

Nevertheless, the theological tradition has had difficulty in expressing God's personhood. Tradition asserts that we are made in the image of God, a claim that acknowledges both our likeness to God as well as our unlikeness. God is not simply a human writ large, a cosmic king who rules over us like a benign despot, a point that already finds expression in the commandment forbidding the making of graven images and in the prophetic denunciations of idolatry. As a result, God has often been conceived as having many of the mental and spiritual qualities of a person, but not the physical aspects. As Christian theology developed from the second century onward, theologians have utilized philosophical and scientific conceptions of mind to think about the nature and personlike character of God. These conceptions, in turn, inform ideas about how God acts in the world. The result has often been a kind of analogy between the human mind and body, on the one hand, and God and the world, on the other, expressed by a number of current theologians and philosophers of religion as God:world::mind:body. Conceptions of mind are thus used not only to argue for the existence of God but to explain God's very nature.

Platonic conceptions of the mind-body relation have had a historically important role in conceiving God and the God-world relation. Plato's sharp distinction between the rational soul and the material body was taken up by some early Jewish and Christian thinkers to express an understanding of God that avoided anthropomorphism.

Such a model tended to emphasize God's transcendence and power over creation, just as the rational mind was conceived, in the final analysis, to have power over the body. More importantly, while rationality was seen as the central characteristic of the mind, emotions were understood to have their root causes in the body and were often seen as a negative force in the life of the soul. Early Christian theology often had difficulty with those passages of the Bible that attributed emotional states to God. Theologians like Augustine and Origen chose to understand such passages metaphorically, as a shorthand for the unsophisticated. A true understanding of God, so the argument went, involves the conviction that God is *a se*, unaffected and unaffectable by the events of this world. This comparison between the human mind and divine nature was perhaps most obvious in the work of Augustine, who understood the Trinity in psychological terms.[21]

Among contemporary philosophers of religion, Charles Taliaferro has made this form of the God:world::mind:body analogy explicit.[22] Taliaferro argues explicitly that our understanding of the God-world relation is based directly upon our understanding of the human mind-body relation. If there does not exist an immortal soul separate from the body, argues Taliaferro, then there is little reason to believe in an immortal, transcendent God. In short, belief in God requires belief in mind-body dualism. For other thinkers, it is precisely this kind of argument that is the problem, for it provides both an inadequate view of God and an inadequate view of human nature. Feminist theologians have argued that the emphasis on the rationality of God and the rejection of emotional states has privileged the masculine models of God. Theologians in the science-religion dialogue have noted that such a model understands God's power primarily in terms of a kind of miraculous intervention that coheres poorly with contemporary scientific understandings of the natural world. Equally important, such a model, based as it is on a mind-body dualism, is not consistent with what we now know about the human mind.

Consequently, alternative models of God have gained some ascendancy. The most prominent of these is panentheism. While transcendent theism understands God and the world as completely separate entities, and pantheism collapses God and the world into a single, unitary whole, panentheism insists on understanding the world as related, yet distinct realities. While the concept has roots in eighteenth-century German Idealism, panentheism largely owes its current development to process theology.[23] Charles Hartshorne argued that God must be in constant relation with the world and therefore in some sense dependent upon it as well.[24] Consequently, Hartshorne argued, one should understand the world as being in some sense *in* the greater reality of God.

The meaning of the "in" in panentheism has often been elaborated in analogy to a holistic or emergent account of the mind-body relation. Just as the mind is more than the sum of its physical parts—and even more than simply the sum of individual neurons—so too is God more than the individual components of the world. To emphasize the connection between God and the world, both Grace Jantzen and Sallie McFague have argued that it would be fruitful to think of the world as God's body.[25] This points to the value of the natural world during a time of intense ecological devastation. Rather than understanding God's action as a supernatural intervention into the world, God's action can be understood—much as the mind acts on the body—as a form of top-down causation that does not violate the laws of nature. While the mind and body are not completely separate, the mind nevertheless exerts a profound influence on the health, maintenance, and goals of the body.

A somewhat different approach to the panentheistic analogy has been taken by Philip Clayton.[26] Like Jantzen and McFague, Clayton strongly endorses a panentheistic model of the God-world relation and understands this relation in analogy to the human mind-body relationship. Clayton relies on a philosophy of mind that understands the mind and person as being an emergent reality above and beyond its constitutive brain, body, and social environment. All of these, in a sense, constitute and influence the human person, but their influence is not completely determinative. Just as the body and brain influence the mind, so too does the mind influence the body and brain. At the same time, Clayton rejects the claim that the human person can be understood in purely physical categories. To do so, he argues, ultimately entails the reduction of what is distinctive and important about mental and personal qualities.

Clayton's model of God's relation to the world relies heavily on this emergentist account of the mind-body relationship. Just as the mind is present in the body, so too is God present in the world. Just as the mind is affected by the body, so too God is affected by and interacts with the world. In maintaining the analogy with the human person, the understanding of God as a person is intellectually justifiable. The mind-body relationship makes conceivable the God-world relationship. But, Clayton argues, there is an important "disanalogy" as well. While the human mind is understood to arise out of and be dependent on the human body, God cannot be similarly understood to be emergent from and dependent on the world. God as creator is prior to the world.

While much is interesting and important about panentheism, Clayton's acknowledgment of the disanalogy between God/world and mind/body reveals the limitations of basing our understanding of God on models of the human mind. To speak of the world as God's body is a beautiful metaphor, but it also forces us to recognize the "is not" quality of the metaphor as much as the "is." While the human mind is importantly connected to the activities of the brain, there is no such equivalent to the brain in the universe as a whole. Indeed, just as emergence theories provide models for how consciousness can be said to arise out of the brain without ever specifying how, so panentheistic appeals to the mind-body relation provide a useful picture but stop short of becoming a genuine theory. This disanalogy raises the seriousness of the theological question of how to speak of God as person. Our only direct experience of persons is that of our fellow human beings and, at a lower level, the other animals with which we share the planet. One of the things that the cognitive sciences reveal, however, is how much our personhood is constructed out of the many elements of biology and society. Awareness of the sheer specificity of human personhood seems to require that any disanalogy between God's personhood and our own be far greater than any analogy.

The strength of this disanalogy is recognized by some theologians. Although he is a strong advocate of panentheism, Arthur Peacocke acknowledges the difficulties of speaking of God as person. Emphasizing the metaphorical quality of language about God, Peacocke argues that to speak of God as person is the "least misleading" option available.[27] Acknowledging the metaphoric character of personal language in reference to God is perhaps the first step toward appropriately rethinking God's personhood. While many contemporary thinkers have emphasized potential commonalities between God/world and mind/body, it may be that the disanalogies are what should be emphasized. Personal attributes of God are important, but it is equally important to recognize that God is a different kind of person from what we are.

It therefore seems that theology requires us to speak of God's personhood as significantly different from what cognitive science can inform us of. While cognitive science can serve as a kind of metaphorical inspiration, it necessarily remains at a broad and metaphoric level. Indeed, some of the most promising metaphors in speaking of God may have only a tangential relation to cognitive science. Categories of field, chaos, and information have all been used as alternative metaphors for thinking about God's nature. Cognitive science here may function as a reminder of the requirements for personhood while at the same time acknowledging that these requirements may not be appropriate when speaking of the divine.

Indeed, cognitive science may best function as a kind of *via negativa*: by looking at ourselves we also see how unlike us God is. We may come to understand God phenomenologically as a person and yet recognize that God's ultimate nature is ultimately quite different from our own. In doing so we recognize the most radical claim of all, that there is not simply one mode of personhood but many, and to speak of God as person is in fact to reach the boundary of language.

9

The Nature and Destiny of Minds

No mind is an island. Not only do we as individuals exist as part of a broader community but even our communities exist by virtue of their interconnection with and dependence on the natural world. We exist in symbiosis with some organisms, such as the *E. coli* bacteria that live in our stomachs and aid our digestion, and in competition with others. We derive our sustenance from plants and other animals and use a wide range of organic and physical materials, from oil to iron, to provide shelter and livelihood. In turn, these materials are available because of the particular history and make-up of the Earth and the solar system, while our available energy is almost entirely due to the sun. This kind of dependence makes life, including human life, possible. We exist in no small part because we live in a particular corner of the universe that is friendly to our existence.

This friendliness obtains not only in the present but back through the eons of time. It is estimated that the Earth was formed 4.5 to 5 billion years ago and that life has existed for 3.5 to 4 billion of those years. Some 400 million years ago or so, life emerged from the seas and stretched across the continents and into the air. It is only a comparatively recent 5 million years ago that the line of hominids broke off from other primates and a mere 200,000 years ago that we see signs of the first Homo sapiens. If we take the art of such places as Chauvet cave in France as the first evidence of modern human beings, we jump to a comparatively short 30,000 to 40,000 years ago. We, the most mindful of Earth's species, are comparative youngsters, inheritors of a long and winding evolutionary process.

This observing of our evolutionary dependence has provoked what up until recent centuries have been considered purely theological questions. Why are we here at all? Where are we going? What is our destiny? While the questions are inherently theological, they are not merely so, and it is becoming increasingly clear that any answers must include scientific perspectives. While related, the scientific questions and answers are also slightly different from the purely theological ones, for scientists ask not simply why we (Homo sapiens) are here but why there should be any intelligent life—any minds—at all. Moreover, are we the apex of evolution or should we expect greater things ahead?

The answers that scientists give these questions are important to theologians, partly because they inform the theological options available and partly because scientists unwittingly cross the border into theology, mixing facts and values without fully considering the implications. When considering questions of human destiny, science easily slips into soteriology, and the boundary between the two must be observed carefully.

The Crown of Creation?

Doctrines informing the nature and destiny of humankind are among the most important for the Christian faith. The importance of theology as a discipline is not simply that it speaks of God but that God-talk is vitally important in understanding the human situation. Theology tells us who we are and where we are going. The theological tradition has understood humankind as the apex and culmination of creation. Humans are the last and—presumably—best of God's creation, and this special status has been enshrined in an understanding of the image of God that separates us from the rest of creation. The notion that we are the apex of creation, however, goes beyond claims of human uniqueness. It is often taken to mean not simply that we are the highest point but also the ultimate purpose of creation. God did not simply create the world; God created the world *for us*.

That humankind is the apex of creation should be understood not simply ontologically but also in a historical framework. Salvation histories derived from the Bible typically begin with the creation and fall, then move through the patriarchs and Hebrew kingdoms up to God's ultimate act in the human incarnation of Christ. In many Old Testament narratives, especially the Deuteronomistic history found in 1 Samuel—2 Kings), the fate of nations depends on their relationship to God and God's ordinances. The Hebrew nations were judged according to their faithfulness to the covenant, and lack of faithfulness led to their downfall. The unfaithfulness of other nations was also punished and, occasionally (as in the book of Jonah), their return to faithfulness was rewarded as well.

Salvation history is reflected also, albeit in more complex form, in the theological tradition. The complexity comes from the varied understandings of eschatology. Especially during times of adversity, laypersons and theologians alike have looked forward to Christ's return and a final consummation of the historical process, which would ultimately be replaced by the new heaven and Earth described in the closing passages of the book of Revelation. In *The City of God*, Augustine understood the history of humankind as unalterably tainted by sin; for him this explained not only the demise of the Roman Empire, which he witnessed, but the ultimate demise of all human kingdoms and ambitions. Other theologians and eras, however, have emphasized a realized eschatology. Drawing on Jesus' proclamation of the coming and present kingdom of God and Christ's promise of the Holy Spirit in the Gospel of John, advocates of realized eschatology look not to decline but to the dawn of a new era in relationship with the Spirit. This expectation of a new era was in part behind the modern idea of progress, often accompanied by ethical exhortation, which reached its apex in the nineteenth century. Even here, however, some sense of the tragedy of life remains, and the hope of a final resurrection endures.

The Christian vision of human nature and destiny, often symbolic in character, is expansive, encompassing our creation, cultural history, and final fate. Since the time of Charles Darwin, it has also had to acknowledge scientific claims about a range of issues related to these themes. Some of this research has focused on the human species itself and especially the question of human origins. More broadly, however, scientists have asked not only about human origins but also about the likelihood of the genesis of intelligent life and its possible evolutionary options. Such research ultimately impinges on claims about the nature and destiny of humanity and the centrality of humankind in the cosmic drama.

The Place of Mind in the Universe

Science fiction is replete with tales of contacts with extraterrestrial species. Ever since Johannes Kepler wrote *Somnium*, a story about a civilization that lived on the surface of the moon, we have been fascinated and sometimes repelled by the possibility of extraterrestrial life.[1] At root is our insecurity about our place in the universe. Because people in the past believed the universe was much smaller than we now know it to be, it was easier in earlier times than it is now to believe that we are somehow central to the nature of the universe. While the Ptolemaic universe was certainly vast, it encompassed only the solar system and an outer shell that contained the stars. It was only with the discoveries of Galileo that we began to realize that the universe was staggeringly larger than previously thought and that other stars might also contain planets and therefore other civilizations. To ask about the possibility of extraterrestrial life is to ask about human uniqueness, but it is also to ask whether we are meant to be here in the first place. If the laws of nature favor the formation of life, then one should be able to find many extraterrestrial civilizations. If they do not, why are we here at all?

From the perspective of evolutionary biology, there is no absolute reason for human beings to be here. Evolution takes many paths, and there is no scientific evidence to support the notion that life on Earth was set up explicitly for the arrival of Homo sapiens. But whether the laws of the universe and of evolution are fashioned to make intelligent life not only possible but inevitable is another, more complex question that is intensely debated. At heart is the question whether, from a physical and biological perspective, we should consider ourselves mere flukes of nature or an inevitable outcome.

The study of physical cosmology has shown that the laws that govern the nature and evolution of the universe can take a number of different values and that only an increasingly small set of these provide for the conditions that allow the development of life as we know it. These sets of cosmic coincidences together form the anthropic principle (see chapter 8, above). For some physicists and theologians, like John Polkinghorne, the anthropic principle is testimony to a universe designed for life. The point is contentious, however, and some have argued for alternative cosmologies that do not invoke the divine. Of these, the most popular is a cosmology that postulates the development of multiple universes. In such a framework, most universes would be uninhabitable, but probability would suggest that some would have the conditions for life.[2] As Polkinghorne points out, such theories are highly speculative and in the end no more certain of truth than is the postulating of a designer. Furthermore, it simply pushes back the argument a step, for it can still be asked why life is one possibility among others, however low the probability for it may be. What can be said is that our own universe in many subtle ways appears to be fine-tuned for life in a way that seems, on the face of it, unusual and surprising.

There is a significant difference, however, between a universe fine-tuned for the mere possibility of life and a universe in which life necessarily or even probably arises. Evidence from biochemistry is ambiguous at best. Since Harold Urey and Stanley Miller created amino acids by administering electric current (purportedly simulating lightning) to a test-tube soup of chemicals, scientists have been aware that a number of organic compounds can exist naturally, some of which may even be found on meteorites.[3] But the step from these simple compounds to life is immense. Several biochemists have argued that we have enough evidence to think that, given the kind of planet we live on, it was almost inevitable that life should arise.[4] Most will acknowledge, however, that much of the empirical evidence for this is lacking, and the truth has been hidden by more than 3 billion years of history.

If life on Earth were probable or inevitable, one would reasonably expect to find it elsewhere in the universe. There are an estimated 125 billion galaxies in the universe, with any individual galaxy containing billions of stars. By virtue of numbers alone, it seems almost impossible for life not to exist elsewhere in the universe. While scientific advances, especially the discovery of extrasolar planets, might one day confirm that there is life elsewhere, it is now uncertain. Moreover, there is a significant distinction between life and intelligent life; the former may be probable and the latter not. Frank Drake, one of the founding figures of SETI (Search for Extra-Terrestrial Intelligence) formulated the probability of being able to discover an extraterrestrial civilization; this is now known as the Drake equation.[5] The likelihood of extraterrestrial intelligent life in our galaxy depends on the number of stars in our galaxy, the percentage of stars that have planets, the percentage of planets on which life evolves, and the percentage of life-bearing planets that actually produce intelligent life. While we can roughly estimate the number of stars in our galaxy (around 100 billion), the other parts of the equation remain speculative. The ongoing discovery of extrasolar planets suggests that there are many stars with planetary systems, although all of the planets discovered so far are almost certainly uninhabitable. Despite this, there are a number of reasons to suppose that, even if life exists elsewhere, it is comparatively rare, and intelligent life even rarer. Features of our solar system may be unique and there is good reason to believe that two critical, life-supporting features of Earth—its magnetic field and large moon, which serves to deflect large meteoric impacts—are the result of a highly unlikely chance collision with a rogue planet early in its history.[6]

Rare, however, does not mean unique. Given the sheer number of stars throughout the vast number of galaxies, it seems almost certain that life has come into being elsewhere. But since ours is the only life-bearing planet we know of, we have only one model to go by. That life appears to have begun quite early on our planet has suggested to a number of scientists that, once the conditions are right, life would almost inevitably arise. The path from life to intelligent life, however, is a long and tortuous one, interrupted by several mass extinctions. This has led some to conclude that, while the evolution of some life may be a probability on a planet like ours, the evolution of intelligent life is so increasingly improbable that we should consider ourselves a fluke of nature. Paleontologist Stephen Jay Gould, in particular, has argued that there are no upward trends in evolution. Beguiled by the myth of progress, he argues, we read into evolution our desire to declare ourselves the crown of creation. In this vein, Gould has criticized many popular portrayals of evolution as a ladder leading upward.[7] Gould argues that evolution often proceeds by chance events, and that other forces besides a linear process of natural selection are at work. While more complex life-forms inevitably follow simple ones, this does not mean that there is an evolutionary impulse toward complexity but only that there is room for complexity. Evolution begins in a simple way because it has to. Complexity emerges later because it develops from simpler forms. But, notes Gould, this does not constitute a trend. Less complex life-forms continue to evolve even after more complex forms appear on the scene. On most scores of biological success, Gould argues, we have lived and always will live in the age of bacteria.

Humankind, however, is noteworthy only as the last branch of an otherwise dead tree.[8]

Gould's opinions are by no means universal. Holmes Rolston III counters Gould's claims, noting that evolutionary history shows a steady increase in complexity and diversity, even after events of mass extinction.[9] Robert Wright puts this argument more strongly by contending that cooperation is the central feature of biological and cultural evolution.[10] Wright's thesis is based on the principle of nonzero-sum cooperation, derived largely from game theory. While competition typically occurs in what are called zero-sum situations (if I win, everybody else loses), cooperation can often produce situations where the benefit of working together exceeds the benefit of working individually. Thus, Paleolithic hunter-gatherers may have the choice between hunting antelope individually or hunting mastodons together. To hunt antelope individually may result in a zero-sum situation, as my gain potentially means your loss. To hunt mastodon together, however, creates a nonzero-sum situation. No hunter alone could successfully hunt a mastodon. If hunters cooperate, however, not only could they successfully hunt the mastodon but the result of their efforts would far exceed the amount of meat they would have received from individually hunting several antelope.

Wright sees this form of nonzero-sum cooperation as not only central to cultural evolution but to biological evolution as well. The great achievements of evolution, argues Wright, are the result of such forms of nonzero-sum cooperation. While neo-Darwinian biologist Richard Dawkins emphasizes the notion of selfish genes, Wright is impressed by how much genes must work together by being part of the same genome. Various forms of this type of cooperation are found throughout the scale of nature, from the level of genes and cells all the way up to ourselves.

For Wright, the trend toward complexity in evolution is built into the laws of nature and ultimately leads to the emergence of intelligent beings like ourselves. Wright cites Moore's law, a principle originally applied to computer-chip innovation, as a general principle that underlies all evolutionary and cultural development. Gordon Moore, cofounder of Intel, first predicted in 1965 that the processing speed of computer chips would double approximately every eighteen months. Amazingly, Moore's law has proved true up to the present, and a number of thinkers have come to see it as a general principle of technological innovation. Wright argues that this exponential growth can be found in the evolutionary process itself. Exponential growth begins exceedingly slowly but, as the rate of doubling increases, it gradually begins to skyrocket. Wright notes that this general pattern applies to evolutionary history, which begins quite slowly, with nothing but bacteria for the first three billion years. With the advent of multicellular organisms, however, the rate of evolutionary innovation increases. For Wright, it is no accident that mammals have larger brains than reptiles, as they genuinely represent the next stage in evolution. While Homo sapiens in particular may not have been inevitable, Wright argues that something like us was. Gould's mistake, according to Wright, is not in observing the continuing evolution and diversity of simpler forms but in failing to notice that there is no intrinsic limit to the evolution of complexity. While evolution must inevitably start against a "left wall" of complexity, there is no intrinsic right wall that limits its development. And, Wright observes, when evolutionary trends are left to themselves, increased complexity seems to be a natural result.

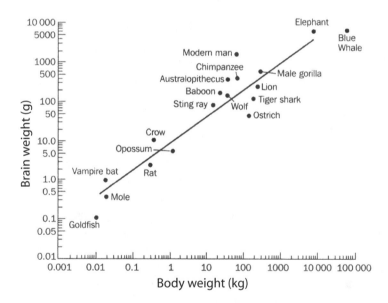

Fig. 9.1. Logarithmic plot of brain size against body size. Primates are distinctive in the unusual size of brain in comparison to body. [From John Cartwright, *Evolution and Human Behavior* (2000). Used with permission from MIT Press.]

Some aspects of Wright's arguments, such as the appeal to Moore's law, may be dubious, but he is certainly correct that there has been a gradual and quickening pace of complexity in evolution. Whether this is a trend in a statistical sense has yet to be fully verified empirically; the issue is complicated by the vicissitudes of the paleontological record. Nevertheless, as Wright observed, life on Earth has certainly not reached any right wall of complexity.

When we look at the specifics of human evolution, the story is equally complicated. Paleontologist Harry Jerison and others have noted that relative brain size has increased over evolutionary time, showing a sudden leap in the evolutionary trajectory that leads to human beings.[11] Evolution generally exhibits a gradual trend toward increased intelligence, although the cause of this is not altogether clear. While the intelligence enabled by large brains has obvious benefits, there are important costs as well. Brains are metabolically expensive, requiring a disproportionate amount of energy to operate. A human brain uses about twenty percent of the body's energy but represents only two percent of its mass.[12] One obvious advantage of intelligence is the flexibility of behavior that it provides. Mammals generally possess a larger behavioral repertoire than reptiles, a fact most obvious among social mammals. Only mammals go through a play stage when they are young, probably because play is an important part of early learning. Intelligence also pays off in the simple act of finding and remembering the locations of food and water.

It is not altogether clear what factors played a role in the dramatic growth of the human brain. Our species' relative brain size is about twice that of chimpanzees and well above the expected brain size for a mammal of our body weight. Most of this larger bulk is in the neocortex, the area most responsible for language and reasoning skills. Early researchers tended to emphasize the role of both toolmaking and hunting. The ability to manipulate tools allowed the manufacture of better weapons (spears) which in turn allowed the killing of larger game. Having plenty of meat made it possible to satisfy the metabolic requirements of the brain. Besides the latent sexism behind these "man the hunter" scenarios, many paleoanthropologists regard the fairly limited tool kit of early hominids as insufficient to explain the radical growth in brain size. A number of scientists therefore favor the theory of social intelligence as the driving force in human evolution. Among mammals, primates are unique in their sociality, and human beings are the most social of all mammals. Sociality provides protection against competitors and increases the prospects of finding and gathering resources. At the same time, sociality requires the development of a Machiavellian intelligence (see chapter 7, above) that is sensitive to shifting dominance hierarchies, cooperation, cheaters, and possible deception. According to this hypothesis, the need to detect cheaters and maintain social alliances drove the increase in the size of the neocortex, which in turn allowed the formation of larger groups. Larger groups provided additional benefits but also required extra vigilance as well. Data collected by Robin Dunbar indicated a correlation between brain size and group size, and similar studies have provided other positive evidence for this hypothesis.[13]

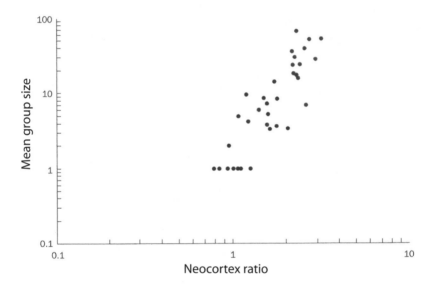

Fig. 9.2. Plot of group size in relation to neocortex volume for various species of primates. [From John Cartwright, *Evolution and Human Behavior* (2000). Used with permission from MIT Press.]

The centrality of social intelligence fits well with Robert Wright's thesis that nonzero-sum cooperation is the key to the evolution of complexity. Even so, there were likely a number of other factors involved as well. While sociality may have played a prime role in evolution, intelligence has other important benefits. In addition, the growth of the human brain is so great and so rapid (by evolutionary standards) that it calls into question the claim that a species like us was eventually destined to come into being. Why did such growth occur only along our distinct line of primates? Paleontologists point to the shrinking forests and widening plains of East Africa, caused by a shift in ocean currents, caused in turn by rising ocean levels that flooded modern-day Panama, creating a link between the Pacific and Atlantic Oceans and consequently altering global climate. While such an explanation is partial (there have been other forests that have given way to plains), it does highlight the apparently chance factors involved: if no global warming approximately 5 million years ago, then no rising ocean levels; if no flooding of Panama, no climate change. No climate change, then no savanna in East Africa; if no savanna, then no social, bipedal primates. If progress-oriented thinkers such as Wright are correct, then some other mammal somewhere (and sometime) else might have developed in similar fashion. But their story would likely have been very different.

The scientific understanding of the place of mind in the universe, therefore, is complicated and in significant ways incomplete. There is enough evidence to suggest that the universe is set up not only to allow the appearance of rational beings like ourselves but perhaps even so that it would be likely. At the same time, any individual story, including our own, is bound to be filled with many contingencies. Our ascent, if one may call it that, is far from linear and full of mishaps. Furthermore, the conclusion that we are the apex of creation is scarcely endorsed in this broader scientific picture. We may, in fact, be one of many intelligent life-forms that populate the universe, and it would be presumptuous to claim that God cares only for human beings. Likewise, it is anything but clear that the roughly 4.5 billion years of Earth's natural history were destined to culminate in our own species. We must conclude either that God's intent through the intervening millennia is inscrutable or that the "us" that God intended was much broader than we have traditionally thought.

Theologians have tended to focus on the twin roles of chance and necessity in the evolutionary story, with some preferring one and some the other. The suggestion that the universe was set up for the arrival of human beings or a species like us is certainly coherent with broader claims of divine purpose. Physicist and theologian Howard Van Till, for instance, has spoken of creation as being fully gifted, meaning that

God has designed creation with the built-in capacity for creativity and the natural propensity to develop in ways friendly to life.[14] Jesuit theologian and paleontologist Teilhard de Chardin understood evolution as a directional process moving toward ever greater levels of complexity. Evolution could thus be understood within the broader context of divine purpose, culminating in a process of divinization for human beings as we ourselves evolved higher levels of complexity and cooperation.[15] While Teilhard's language is often poetic in character and dates to a period before the strength of neo-Darwinism was fully felt, his influence has touched many. Developing Teilhard's insights, John Haught sees in the evolutionary trend toward complexity room to speak of divine purpose. Unlike Teilhard, however, Haught is keenly sensitive to the tragic aspects of evolution, which, he argues, calls for a kenotic understanding of Christ's love.[16]

Emphasizing necessity and the completeness of creation can present a problem for theology, because a creation that is utterly complete may seem to support deism and exclude the need for God. This perception seems partly to underlie the aims of intelligent-design theorists such as William Dembski and Michael Behe, who see room for God's agency primarily in events of such low probability that natural law and the directions of evolution are insufficient to account for them. From a different perspective, Harvard theologian Gordon Kaufman is more impressed by the role of chance in human evolution as a point in which the divine purpose can be spoken of. For Kaufman, God's action is best understood in terms of the serendipitous creativity of the evolutionary process that has culminated in us.

Arthur Peacocke, however, has written most extensively on issues of evolution and divine purpose.[17] Peacocke argues that both chance and necessity are key ingredients in the evolutionary process. Divine purpose can be seen both in the friendliness of the universe toward life and in the trend of evolution toward greater complexity. Although chance is at play, the dice are loaded. It is through this interplay of chance and necessity that Peacocke understands God's action in the natural world. For Peacocke, God's action is not coercive but operates in a form of top-down causation through creation's hierarchical levels. Peacocke compares the history of evolution to a kind of cosmic dance, or an orchestra with God as conductor. In Peacocke's view, the universe is significantly free and open, but the divine hand is nevertheless present.

At the end, one may still ask, Why are we here? To say that the universe is designed for life, even intelligent life, is quite different from saying that it is designed specifically for human beings. At the very least, the broader vision of the cosmos and the possibility of intelligent life in it suggests a more humble perspective. We may be *an* apex of creation, but we are not necessarily *the* apex. To the extent that we can speak of divine purpose, we will need to do so in a much broader context than we are used to.

Techno-Sapiens: The Future of Human Minds

To be the apex of creation implies that we are the end point, that all things lead to us. It also is usually taken to imply that we are essentially in our finished form. While the former statement is now widely seen to be problematic, the latter statement is still often tacitly held. We have grown to accept our evolutionary past and to see ourselves as part of a lineage that links us to other hominids and primates. Yet we often think of ourselves as the end result of this lineage, with little expectation for continued change in our species. Evolution, however, does not work that way. Biologists do speak of adapting to a particular niche, and there are individual species and genera (such as the coelacanth, turtles, and alligators) that have undergone very little change over the millennia. But there is no guarantee of this. Evolution is characterized more by change than by constancy, and shifts in an organism's environment can often spur a shift in adaptation. Typically, such changes take place over geological time spans of 10,000—100,000 years, so that any potential evolutionary changes for our own species are, in practical terms, so unimaginably distant as to be not worth pondering. Still, the possibility of change has intrigued some and, given our current and growing knowledge of science and technology, provoked speculation that we can control our own evolution. Are we the end of our own evolution or merely at the halfway point?

A number of biologists and anthropologists have observed that, with the advent of culture, human beings entered a phase of evolution that is unprecedented in Earth's history. To a certain extent, Darwinian evolution must always start over with each succeeding generation. A bird whose slightly larger wingspan enables it more readily to escape speedy predators will be able to pass on this benefit to its offspring. A bird that learns to eat the seeds in Mrs. McGill's yard between three and five o'clock, when her cat is away, will not be able automatically to pass on this useful trait. Any offspring she has will have to learn it after birth. More to the point, a bird that realizes it might be useful to have a larger beak cannot simply chose to grow one. Every organism is stuck with the body it receives in the genetic raffle.

The advent of culture, however, begins to change the situation. Whereas biology is Darwinian, culture is Lamarckian. In the early nineteenth century, Jean-Baptiste Lamarck proposed that the behavior of an organism could be inherited in the next generation. Lamarck was primarily wrong about biological evolution but right about cultural evolution.[18] The advent of culture allows us to learn directly from one another. Such learning can be transmitted not only among contemporaries but also down the generations, where it can provide the basis for new insights. Because of this, cultural evolution can occur at a much more rapid pace than biological evolution. Moreover, there is good reason to believe that cultural evolution can dramatically influence our own biological evolution. Once we have the ability to manipulate symbols and communicate with one another, cultural evolution starts to exert its force, creating a feedback loop that gives an advantage to individuals talented in the use of symbols.

So great is the force of cultural evolution that, in the eyes of many, it has completely overtaken biological evolution, a point conceded even by die-hard neo-Darwinist Richard Dawkins, who sees cultural evolution operating on the same principles as biological evolution. For Dawkins and his followers, cultural evolution is also a process of competition and selection, with the genes of biology now replaced by "memes."[19] Ideas compete with one another, grow and develop, with the fittest ideas (those that confer survival benefits) reproducing themselves through communities and down the generations. Biological evolution has essentially stopped, and cultural evolution is the driving force of the human species.

Some, however, still argue that biological evolution is beginning once again. The enormous growth of scientific knowledge in the twentieth century has for the first time led to the possibility that we may be able to modify ourselves as organisms. With the sequencing of the human genome and the beginning of research on gene therapies, we now have the potential artificially to alter ourselves as a species. Some have even argued that the continuing growth of computer technology will also allow artificial modifications, as we gradually (and literally) graft our technology into ourselves. For the first time we now have to grapple with the possibility of such changes and the extent to which they may irrevocably alter our nature as a species.

Many of our fears regarding genetic engineering revolve around the possibility of altering personality and intelligence traits, thereby creating a potential superrace and possibly new divisions of class and race. Such fears are reasonable, particularly given the association of eugenics programs with racist and totalitarian regimes. At this point, however, the extent to which such programs would be successful, let alone desirable, is unclear. In the coming decades we can reasonably expect to see gene therapies that prevent specific diseases that may be caused by a single gene or a small complex of genes, such as Parkinson's or multiple sclerosis. These therapies are not intended to improve the human species as much as to remove obvious debilitating conditions. Eugenic programs, by contrast, seek to improve what is already there. Although there seems to be current widespread disapproval of eugenics, it is unclear whether individuals seeking eugenic enhancement (possibly for themselves, but more likely for their children) can be adequately controlled or monitored. The United States Olympic commission is already starting discussions on the possibility of genetically enhanced athletes and the extent to which such modifications can be detected. Moreover, what may be seen as a debilitating condition to one person may seem a lifestyle choice to another. If gene therapy can be provided for obesity, will such therapy be sought for health reasons or for the obvious social benefits of being thin?

The extent to which intelligence or personality can be changed at this point in evolutionary history is much more speculative. Studies of identical twins reared apart indicate that up to 69 percent of mental ability and 50 percent of personality traits (as measured by IQ tests and personality surveys) are due to inheritance.[20] Intelligence, however, is not the product of any one gene, and it is significantly affected by the environment. The genetic history of intelligence is undoubtedly complicated, and any attempt to modify intelligence artificially is likely to have unpredictable results. Intelligence is no doubt linked to other personality traits, which are similarly complicated. Even more, such enhancement of human intelligence would have to depend on an ethically unacceptable trial-and-error process. This does not mean that such genetic enhancement could never occur but that it remains in the realm of science fiction.

Few modern scholars speculate on the possibility of eugenics, in large part due to the social taboos on the subject. This is far less true with regard to the possibility of technological enhancement. In 1999, researchers at the Wilmer Eye Institute at Johns Hopkins University successfully implanted a microchip in the human retina that enabled sight sufficient to read large print. Ongoing research also aims at providing prosthetic limbs connected to the nervous system and perhaps even use computational technology to cure paralysis. Even such comparatively modest changes stand to alter how we think of ourselves. Culture critic Donna Haraway has argued that we need to understand ourselves as cyborgs, a combination of nature and technology.[21] Indeed, we have always been so. Human beings are tool users, and modern human beings are tool users par excellence. So familiar has our technology become that it is often invisible to us. But any individual who wears glasses or contacts is in a sense a cyborg. So too is anyone who has an artificial hip. Even the act of taking medicine merges us in the most intimate way with our technology, as our bodies absorb chemicals that may never have existed in nature.

Haraway is cognizant of the many dangers of technology. Others, however, paint a more optimistic picture. Both Ray Kurzweil and Hans Moravec envision a future in which we are intimately tied to computational technology. Like Robert Wright, Kurzweil and Moravec are inspired by Moore's law, which predicts a doubling of computing speed every eighteen months.[22] Projecting into the future, Kurzweil anticipates computing power 1000 times that of the human brain by the year 2029 and the gradual interfacing of human minds with computers. Human beings will increasingly abandon bodies altogether (except when they need them) and live in virtual communities connected by enormous networks. Humans in this state will be able to live effectively forever. For those who participate in this cyber-utopia, death, pain, and disease will be vanquished as our cyber-descendants are able to contemplate questions and pleasures beyond our reckoning.

Such projections are based far more on faith than on science. The proposal that Moore's law is an inviolable law of nature is intriguing, but there is no guarantee that the future of computation will be like the past. Furthermore, as we have occasionally seen elsewhere, such proposals are based on the confidence that the human mind can be explained wholly by a computational-functionalist approach. While there are important reasons to consider such a possibility, it is by no means certain. Indeed Kurzweil's proposal provokes basic questions about the computational approach. Is a downloaded version of me the same me? If a backup (on an enormously large hard drive!) is provided for my personality and the original me is lost in an accident, is my backup me or simply my identical twin? Equally important, Kurzweil's version of the human person too neatly divides mind from body. We have become increasingly aware that the mind is intimately connected to physical states. We are not simply disembodied reasoning machines but persons in a bodily and communal context.

These visions of the future have a broadly theological concern. Kurzweil, Moravec, and other technological futurists are not simply projecting into the future but also attempting to chart a path that they perceive as desirable. In the future, they claim, our hopes for immortality and personal transformation can be answered by our growing knowledge of biology, cognition, and information systems. For those of us who live past 2029, hope remains. In projecting such a future, the difficulties and dystopian features of this Earthly paradise are given little consideration. As George Orwell observed, some are more equal than others, and the history of technological innovation reveals that new achievements inevitably bring new problems.

It is therefore tempting to dismiss such biological and technological optimists as both wishful thinkers and opposed to a genuinely theological understanding of the future, replacing the eschatological hopes of the Christian faith with a naturalized eschatology of the near future. Indeed, many religious thinkers, sensitive to the perils of both biological and information technology, prefer to take a reactionary route. To change human nature is to violate the order of things—to play God.

To do so completely, however, is a denial of our nature and our place in creation. Ted Peters has argued that to engage in the use of genetic technology is not to play God but to play human.[23] Playing human is both a wonderful and a dangerous thing. As a species we have been playing human for at least tens of thousands of years. We have in many ways changed dramatically through that time but in many ways have stayed the same. As we begin the twenty-first century, the stakes of playing human have become much higher, and we must be appropriately wary of eugenics and similar agendas in our foreseeable future.

A truly Christian view of the future is not simply individualistic but communal, and it is difficult to see how such technologies will be used both fairly and equitably. At the same time, it is important to keep in mind how open the future is. Both optimists and pessimists presume to be able to predict the outcomes of technology and science, but that rarely happens. As the future unfolds, it is this freedom, this creativeness for good and for ill, that will likely be our central, defining trait, and it will nullify any claims to certainty.

Such a point is made by Philip Hefner, encapsulated in his understanding of human beings as created co-creators.[24] As a species, we are a seamless blend of nature and culture, of the organic and the technological. We are not simply creators of artifacts but also creators of ourselves. From this creativity has come both our highest and our darkest moments. But we are also created, and in acknowledging our createdness we acknowledge our finitude. The immortality promised by the likes of Kurzweil and Dyson remains a very limited one and falls far short of the Christian hope and expectation of redemption. Happiness derived from a virtual reality cheats fate rather than conquers it. Any physical immortality is truly such, for it can always end. Since it can always end, it will always be subject to the familiar doubt, uncertainty, and insecurity that plague the human condition. Even if we do achieve immortality, we will still need to hope, to long for something greater than we can now even imagine.

Conclusion: The Ultimate Future of Minds

For some, however, the idea of techno-sapiens does not go far enough. Even if we could prolong life indefinitely here on Earth, it is still limited by the lifespan of the planet and solar system, as the sun gradually grows larger and larger until it becomes too unbearably hot and eventually swallows up the inner planets, including Earth. To be truly immortal, humankind must explore and emigrate out to the stars, where we will hopefully find other planets to colonize. Yet, even this will not be ultimately sufficient. Beginning in the 1980s and 1990s, theoretical physicists began looking far into the future of the universe, extrapolating from what we now know about the physical laws that govern its development. Such extrapolated futures look very bleak from a human perspective, as they suggested that the universe will eventually cease to be hospitable to any form of organic life. The universe is currently expanding, and in the future it may continue to expand (which current evidence supports), reach an equilibrium state, or eventually contract, resulting in a "big crunch" that ends it all. The future does not look promising, even for techno-sapiens.

Some have suggested, however, that this need not be the end, that it is possible for minds to survive in these bleak conditions. In a highly controversial work, Frank Tipler proposed that a big crunch is, contrary to intuition, the ideal condition for physical immortality.[25] Tipler envisions humankind gradually populating the whole of the universe. Humankind will eventually develop itself into a robotic/computational form of intelligence that will work to actually engineer the big crunch in such a way as to harness energy and information to resurrect all previously existing human beings, something Tipler sees as possible because he understands human beings to be nothing more than matrixes of information. While the universe is finite in a big crunch, subjective experience will be infinite, thanks to the time-dilation provided by Einstein's theory of relativity. Paradoxically, our experience will never end, although the universe will.

Tipler gave his theory the veneer of science, but it has not stood the test of time well. Current evidence suggests that the universe will continue to expand indefinitely regardless of human action, rendering his theory moot. According to the model most widely accepted, matter will become increasingly scattered in the universe. Stars will wink out one by one, and the cosmos will become too chilly to support life. Freeman Dyson has proposed that, while no organic life as we now know it could survive in such a future, our descendants may be able to transform themselves into a kind of being that can survive in such a situation.[26] Like Kurzweil, Dyson sees what may be called a robotic future, as we construct intelligent beings who will be, in essence, our descendants to survive in pockets in the long dark ahead. Such beings could perhaps survive in such a very cold and dark universe.

Again, such projections are science bordering on science-fiction, or perhaps the reverse, and they share the same sort of weaknesses of Kurzweil's and Moravec's envisioning of immortality, presuming that minds are like computers and then extravagantly extrapolating on this assumption. Such a future is a distinctly disembodied one. In the end, it also falls short of the hope of resurrection expressed within the theological tradition. For Christians, resurrection is not merely prolongation, but the hope of an existence that is lived in the presence of God and that transcends the travails of our current existence. Here, we find an important tension between the theological tradition and what current science and even science speculation can offer us. The universe itself does not point toward its own transcendence. On the contrary, its future looks rather bleak. Even if Dyson's projection of futuristic beings came true, they too would eventually die. As time rolls inexorably on, even matter itself will begin to decay, and all possibility of mind will cease. What, then, of the new Jerusalem?

One alternative is to argue that our knowledge of the cosmos is incomplete, that there are physical principles of which we are unaware that will make such transformation possible. Another is to put faith in the claim that God will make such transformation possible. Yet another is to suggest that the physical reality we experience is but a shadow of a greater reality, which we yet fail to comprehend. In all of these cases, the sciences fail us as guides, except as a source of metaphor. The cognitive sciences cannot tell us of existence in alternative realities. The logic of eschatology, ultimately, is a logic of hope that transcends current knowledge. While that hope is grounded in part on scripture and tradition (not least on the story of Jesus), it is also grounded on our awareness of the call to live a just life in the face of what so often appears to be an unjust universe. Such a hope suggests that suffering and even death in defiance of evil is not futile in the end, but has some ultimate purpose and meaning. Such a hope turns, inevitably, to metaphor, so that even scripture can only speak of the future in terms of the limited knowledge of the present, a heavenly Jerusalem, with streets of gold and life-giving water.

This might suggest that here theology and the sciences, including the cognitive sciences, are in conflict; the former asserting what the latter cannot support. This would be a mistake. Rather, it is the prerogative here to suggest that the sciences are incomplete, that there are things of which we are deeply unaware. We have confidence and hope of these things not because of the scientific evidence, but because they fit with our experiences and needs as spiritual and moral beings. It is to put faith in not merely a God of minds, but a God who minds, both for our future, and for us now.

Glossary

artificial intelligence (AI). As a field of research, AI focuses on creating computers, programs, and robots able to perform or simulate intelligent behavior. While early AI often focused on modeling distinctly human capabilities such as reasoning and language, modern AI includes developing computers, programs, and robots with a wide range of abilities and behaviors. While weak AI is concerned mainly with modeling and achieving practical ends, strong AI aims ultimately to create a computer or robot of human-like intelligence and capability.

altruism. An altruist is one who engages in selfless aid to others. In the biological sciences, altruism specifically refers to one who helps others at some sacrifice to oneself. Biologists use the term kin altruism (kin selection) in cases where aid is given to a genetic relative. Reciprocal altruism refers to aid given with the expectation that aid will be returned at some later time (encapsulated in the saying, "If you scratch my back, I'll scratch yours").

amygdala. Part of the limbic system of the brain, it plays a pivotal role in the fear response.

anosognosia. A condition that results in loss of awareness and denial of the left half of the body and visual field. It is normally caused by a stroke that affects the right parietal lobe of the brain.

cognitive ethology. The study of animal cognitive behavior. Animal psychology is sometimes used as a related term.

corpus callosum. A structure in the brain that connects the left and right cerebral hemispheres.

dualism. Philosophical position that makes a distinction between the mental and the physical. Supernatural dualism claims that mental properties should be attributed to a separate, supernatural soul. Property dualism claims that mental properties are fully natural, but can be said to exist at a different level than the physical.

emergence. Philosophers speak of emergence to explain the nature and existence of higher-order properties. Emergence is often understood to express the character of the whole in contradistinction to the individual parts. Thus, it may be said that the cell is a functional (emergent) whole that is made up (but not simply reducible to) its constituent molecules. Likewise, the mind can be understood as an emergent property of the brain and body.

functionalism. A position that understands mental properties, including consciousness, in terms of information processing in analogy with modern computers. Functionalism is often (but not always) taken to imply a property dualism between mind and body, much like the distinction between hardware and software in a computer.

glossolalia. Also known as "speaking in tongues," a phenomenon associated primarily with Pentecostal and charismatic forms of Christianity, where it is claimed that the spirit speaks through individuals, resulting in unusual verbal expressions.

hippocampus. Area of the brain involved in the formation of declarative memories.

intelligent design. Also known as the intelligent design argument or the argument from design, which claims that the existence of God can be inferred from the complexity (design) of the world. The argument has had a tumultuous history, but has been revived by new developments in cosmology and (especially) by the development of intelligent design theory. Often labeled as a new creationism, intelligent design theorists claim that a science of intelligent design can be developed that shows that biological structures in particular must have been designed and could not have developed by chance.

module. A term used by cognitive scientists to indicate that the mind and brain can be broken down into specific functions or modules that are designed to perform specific tasks, such as language or vision. Psychological modules are understood primarily in terms of their function. An attempt is often made to correlate these with neurological models to show that the function in question (for example, language) is carried out by a specific brain region (Broca's area in the left hemisphere).

natural selection. The theory that evolution occurs by the development of mutations that result in traits that turn out to be advantageous in the organism's environment. Because of these advantageous traits, the organism is more likely to survive and reproduce, passing on its genes to the next generation. Because of Darwin's influence in promoting the theory, the terms "Darwinism" and "natural selection" are often used interchangeably.

panentheism. Literally "all-in-God," panentheists understand God to be in inextricable relationship to the world in such a way that the two cannot be separated. Panentheism is usually contrasted with pantheism, which identifies God with the world, and classical or transcendent theism, which emphasizes God's separateness from the world.

panpsychism. The view that there every component of reality, including inanimate objects, possess some kind of experience or subjectivity. Panpsychism is most identified with process theology and the thought of Alfred North Whitehead.

prosopagnosia. A medical condition caused by damage to the brain that results in the inability to recognize faces.

soteriology. Literally, the study of salvation. A soteriological worldview is one that emphasizes the role or possibility of salvation, either personally or collectively.

supervenience. A concept complementary to emergence, supervenience theories seek to explain the relationship between higher level and lower level phenomena, with most of the research concerned with the mind-body relationship. Central to supervenience debates is the question of what causal role higher order states (for example, the mind) can be said to have on lower level states (for example, the brain or body).

theory of mind. An organism is said to have a theory of mind if it can think about the thoughts of other organisms. Whether animals (particularly primates) might have a theory of mind is the topic of considerable research and debate in cognitive ethology.

Notes

1. What Does Silicon Valley Have to Do with Jerusalem?

1. Tertullian, *On the Prescription of Heretics*, 7.19.
2. For a description, see Barbour 1997, chapter 4.
3. Kurzweil 1999; Moravec 1990.
4. Goleman 1997; Gardner 1993.
5. E.g., Peacocke 1993; Polkinghorne 1996.
6. MacKay 1980; Ashbrook and Albright 1997.
7. Cf. Barbour 1997.
8. Kaufman 1993.
9. Torrance 1969; Burhoe 1981.
10. Pannenberg 1976.
11. Murphy 1990.
12. Barbour 1997.
13. Gould 1999.
14. Pinker 1997.
15. Blackmore 2000.
16. Donald 1991.
17. Ashbrook and Albright 1997; d'Aquili and Newberg 1999.
18. Brown, Murphy, and Maloney 1998 is but one recent example of the modern reemphasis of this doctrine.

2. How the Mind Works: A Cognitive Science Perspective

1. Chomsky 1966.
2. Turing 1950.
3. Kuhn 1962.
4. Chomsky 1959.
5. Searle 1984; Dreyfus 1979.
6. Lakoff and Johnson 1999.
7. Gardner 1985.

8. Flanagan 1992.
9. MacLean, 1970.
10. P. S. Churchland 1986, 159–60.
11. Ibid., 201-4.
12. Damasio 1994.
13. La Mettrie 1748/1912.
14. James 1890/1950.
15. Ryle 1949.
16. Cf. Gardner 1985.
17. Dreyfus 1979; Weizenbaum 1976.
18. Fodor 1980.
19. Rumelhart and McClelland 1986.
20. Edelman 1992, especially chapter 19 and the postscript.
21. Penrose 1989, 1996.
22. Gardner 1984, 323–39.
23. Von Eckardt 1993.
24. Ashbrook and Albright 1997.
25. Anderson 1998.
26. Edelman 1987.
27. Cf. Pinker 1994, chapter 9.
28. Giedd, et al. 1999; Spear 2000.
29. Clark 1997, 66–67.

3. Fitting Square Pegs into Round Wholes: The Problem of Consciousness

1. Hume 1748/1955.
2. James 1890/1950, 488.
3. Ryle 1949.
4. Chalmers 1997.
5. Crick 1994.
6. Jaynes 1976.
7. Damasio 1999; Edelman 1992.
8. Edelman 1992, 123.
9. Putnam 1960.
10. Chomsky 1966, 1983.
11. Hofstadter 1980.
12. Churchland 1995.
13. Nagel 1974.
14. Jackson 1982.
15. Searle 1982.
16. Churchland 1995, 195–208.
17. Searle 1992.
18. Dennett 1991.
19. Stich 1983; Churchland 1981; Churchland 1986.
20. Callebaut 1993.

21. Crick 1994, 3.

22. Broad 1929.

23. Peacocke 1976, 1986.

24. See, respectively, Campbell 1974; Wimsat 1976; Hofstadter 1980; Dennett 1995.

25. For downward flow of information, see Peacocke 1993. For structuring cause, see Dretske 1997.

26. Dennett 1995; Dawkins 1996.

27. Kim 1993.

28. For an overview, see Kim 1993; Bielfeldt 2000.

29. Baars 1989.

30. Kurzweil, 1999.

31. Hofstadter 1982.

32. McGinn 199.

33. Chalmers 1997.

34. Whitehead 1929/1985.

35. Griffin 1998; Barbour 1997.

36. Wheeler 1982.

37. Penrose 1989.

38. Popper and Eccles 1977.

39. Swinburne 1997.

40. Cullmann, 1958.

41. Green 1999.

4. Do Split Brains Listen to Prozac?

1. Both treatises, by Luther and by Erasmus, can be found in Rupp, Watson, and McNeil 1995.

2. Of course, Augustine's later works increasingly emphasize that the good we do is only by means of God's grace.

3. Antonio Damasio (1999) uses the terms "core" and "extended consciousness." Gerald Edelman (1992) distinguishes between primary and extended consciousness, but the meanings are essentially the same.

4. W. B. Scoville and B. Milner 1957. H. M.'s case has been extensively studied and analyzed in the psychological and neuroscientific literature. Cf. Ledoux 1996.

5. This research has been reviewed in numerous places. See, e.g., Gazzaniga and Ledoux 1978; Churchland 1986, 172–93.

6. Levy, Travarthen, and Sperry, 1972.

7. Gazzaniga 1988.

8. Dennett 1991, 423–26.

9. Churchland 1996, 182.

10. Popper and Eccles 1977.

11. Weiskrantz 1986.

12. Described in Ramachandran and Blakeslee 1998, 143.

13. Ramachandran and Blakeslee 1998, chapters 6 and 7.

14. Pinker 1997, chapter 6.

15. James 1884.

16. E.g., Schacter and Singer 1962. For a review, see Ledoux 1996.

17. Pinker 1997. Although, as most veteran hikers know, running from an angry bear or any other fast carnivore usually seals your fate. Running is a good option only if you are with someone slower!

18. MacLean 1970.

19. Ekman 1980, 84.

20. Ledoux 1996.

21. Antonio Damasio 1994; Hanna Damasio et al. 1994.

22. Kramer 1993.

23. Flanagan 1992; Libet 1985.

24. Baron-Cohen, Tooby, and Cosmides 1997.

5. *Mysterium Tremendum*

1. Cf. Hood et al. 1996, 246–48, for an analysis.

2. Alston 1991; Murphy 1990; Van Huysstein 1999.

3. Proudfoot 1985.

4. Stanley and Singer 1962.

5. Damasio 1999; Gardner, et al. 1983.

6. James 1902, 14–15.

7. Hood et al. 1996, 407.

8. Masters and Houston 1966; Leary 1964.

9. Hood and Morris 1981.

10. For a summary and evaluation of this research, see Hood et al. 1996, 196–98; Austin 1998, 20–22.

11. M. Kasamatsu and T. Hirai 1969.

12. Ramachandran and Blakeslee 1998; Persinger 1987.

13. Albright 2000; Wildman and Brothers 1999.

14. d'Aquili and Newberg 1999.

15. Lévi-Strauss 1963.

16. Newberg et al., 1997.

17. Newberg, d'Aquili, and Rause 2001.

18. Ibid.

19. Alston 1991.

20. Murphy 1990.

21. Peacocke 1999.

22. Ramachandran and Blakeslee 1998, 174.

6. Alone in the Universe?

1. Aristotle, *Nicomachean Ethics* 1.7

2. See Peterson 1996, chapter 2.

3. See, e.g., Irenaeus, *Against Heresies* 4.37.6; Thomas Aquinas, *Summa Theologiae* I.93.6.

4. Schleiermacher 1822/1986; Brunner 1935/46.

5. Descartes 1968.

6. Peterson 1996, chapter 2.

7. Singer 1975.

8. See Allen and Bekoff 1997, chapter 4.

9. Dennett 1989.

10. Damasio 1999.

11. E.g., Griffin 1998; Barbour 1997.

12. Griffin 1992, chapter 1.

13. Cheney and Seyfarth 1990.

14. Premack 1976.

15. Pepperberg 2000.

16. Cf. Griffin 1992; Hauser 2000.

17. Chomsky 1957.

18. Gardner and Gardner 1969, 1980.

19. Fouts 1989.

20. Patterson 1978.

21. Terrace 1981.

22. Savage-Rumbaugh et al., 1986; Savage-Rumbaugh and Lewin, 1994.

23. Savage-Rumbaugh et al., 1993.

24. Deacon 1997. Savage-Rumbaugh et al. (1996) have argued that there is at least one instance of symbolic communication among bonobos in the wild, some of whom apparently use sticks as directional markers for trails.

25. Gallup 1977.

26. See Dennett 1987, chapter 7; Cheney and Seyfarth 1990.

27. Premack and Woodruff 1978.

28. de Waal 1996.

29. Byrne 1995; Cheney and Seyfarth 1990.

30. de Waal 1996, 76.

31. Hare, Call, and Tomasello 2001.

32. Cf. Bekoff 2000.

33. Povinelli, Bering, and Giambrone 2000.

34. Allen and Bekoff 1997.

35. Barbour 1993, 168.

36. Rosenfield 1968.

37. Turing 1950.

38. Ryle 1949.

39. Cf. Gardner 1985.

40. Winograd 1972.

41. Rumelhart and McClelland 1987; Churchland 1995.

42. Brooks 1999.

43. Breazeal 2002.

44. Turing 1950.

45. Ibid.

46. Searle 1982.

47. Clark 1997.

48. Searle 1992.

49. Moravec 1990.

50. Penrose 1989.

51. Crowe 1997.

52. Sittler 1961; Cobb 1972; McFague 1993.
53. Linzey 1995.
54. Adams 1990.
55. Teilhard de Chardin 1976.
56. E.g. , Haught 2001.
57. Foerst 1996.
58. Foerst 1998.
59. Cf. Peterson 1996.
60. Gilkey 1993; see also Peterson 1999.
61. Rolston 1991.

7. Whence Original Sin?

1. Romans 7:15.
2. *Confessions*, book 2, chapter 4.
3. Wilson and Ruse 1985, 52.
4. Darwin 1887, 105.
5. Cartwright 2000, 36–37.
6. Dawkins 1976/1989.
7. Hamilton 1964; Cartwright 2000.
8. Cartwright 2000, 76.
9. Hoogland 1983.
10. Trivers 1971.
11. See Cartwright 2000, 293–97.
12. Wilkinson 1984.
13. Boesch and Boesch 1989.
14. Margulis 2000.
15. Sober and Wilson 1998.
16. Tooby and Cosmides 1992.
17. Pinker 1994.
18. Cosmides and Tooby 1992.
19. Barkow, Cosmides, and Tooby 1992.
20. Buss 1992; Cartwright 2000.
21. Cartwright 2000, 276–77.
22. Byrne and Whiten 1988.
23. de Waal 1996.
24. de Waal 2000.
25. Sober and Wilson 1998.
26. Jolly 1999.
27. See Cartwright 2000.
28. Deacon 1997.
29. See Cartwright 2000.
30. Brunner et al., 1993; Anderson 1998.
31. Eaves 1997.
32. Edelman 1987.
33. Ayala 1998.

34. Peterson 2000.

35. Polkinghorne 1996.

36. Hefner 1993.

37. Edwards 1999.

38. Ibid., 65.

39. Kierkegaard 1844/1981.

40. Haught 2001.

8. The Mind of God

1. Hood et al., 1996, chapter 12.

2. Ibid., chapter 8.

3. E.g., Oman and Reed 1998.

4. Campbell 1976.

5. Newberg, d'Aquili, and Rause 2001.

6. Frankl 1959/2000.

7. Cicero, *De Natura Deorum*, 2.12–14; Irenaeus, *Against the Heresies*; Origen, *On First Principles.*

8. Hume 1779/1989.

9. Barbour 1997; Hawking 1988.

10. Polkinghorne 1995, 5. Polkinghorne attributes the original inspiration of the metaphor of the firing squad to philosopher John Leslie of the University of Guelph.

11. Behe 1998.

12. Dembski 1998, 1999.

13. Cf. Peterson 2002.

14. Dembski 1998.

15. An example used first by Richard Dawkins and commented on extensively by intelligent design theory proponents.

16. Dembski argues that the robot is not truly intelligent, as its behavior is programmed by another intelligence, a human being. This however confuses origins with ability. Since Dembski would argue that human beings are created by God, it would seem to follow that human beings are not intelligent either—not a helpful argument.

17. Cheney and Seyfarth, 1990, 17.

18. Gardner 1983.

19. Dennett 1995.

20. E.g., Deacon 1997.

21. Augustine, *On the Trinity.*

22. Taliaferro 1994.

23. Peterson 2001.

24. Hartshorne 1948.

25. Jantzen 1984; McFague 1993.

26. Clayton 1997.

27. Peacocke 1993.

9. The Nature and Destiny of Minds

1. For a brief history, see Crowe 1997.
2. Smolin 1999.
3. See Davies 1996.
4. de Duve 1995; Kauffman 1996.
5. Discussed in Drake and Sobel 1992.
6. Halliday and Drake 1999.
7. Gould 1989.
8. Gould 1996.
9. Rolston 1999.
10. Wright 1999.
11. Jerison 1973; Cartwright 2000.
12. Cartwright 2000, 169.
13. Dunbar 1993; Byrne 1995; Cartwright 2000.
14. Van Till 1986.
15. Teilhard de Chardin 1976.
16. Haught 2000.
17. Peacocke 1986, 1993.
18. Modern evolutionary theory does include Lamarckian elements, notably the Baldwin effect and the discovery of transposons by Barbara McClintock.
19. Dawkins 1976/1989.
20. Anderson 1998.
21. Haraway 1991.
22. Moravec 1990; Kurzweil 1999.
23. Peters 1997.
24. Hefner 1993.
25. Tipler 1995.
26. Dyson 1988.

Bibliography

Adams, Carol J. 1990. *The Sexual Politics of Meat: A Feminist-Vegetarian Critical Theory.* New York: Continuum.

Alexander, Richard. 1987. *The Biology of Moral Systems.* New York: Aldine de Gruyter.

Allen, Colin, and Marc Bekoff. 1997. *Species of Mind: The Philosophy and Biology of Cognitive Ethology.* Cambridge, Mass.: MIT Press.

Alston, William P. 1991. *Perceiving God: The Epistemology of Religious Experience.* Ithaca, N.Y.: Cornell University Press.

Anderson, V. Elving. 1998. "A Genetic View of Human Nature." In *Whatever Happened to the Soul? Scientific and Theological Portraits of Human Nature,* ed. Warren S. Brown, Nancey C. Murphy, and H. Newton Malony. Theology and the Sciences. Minneapolis: Fortress Press.

Ashbrook, James B., and Carol Rausch Albright. 1997. *The Humanizing Brain: Where Religion and Neuroscience Meet.* Cleveland: Pilgrim.

Austin, James H. 1998. *Zen and the Brain: Toward an Understanding of Meditation and Consciousness.* Cambridge, Mass.: MIT Press.

Axelrod, Robert. 1984. *The Evolution of Co-operation.* New York: Basic.

Ayala, Francisco. 1998. "Human Nature: One Evolutionist's View." In *Whatever Happened to the Soul? Scientific and Theological Portraits of Human Nature,* ed. Warren S. Brown, Nancey C. Murphy, and H. Newton Malony. Theology and the Sciences. Minneapolis: Fortress Press.

Baars, Bernard. 1989. *A Cognitive Theory of Consciousness.* Cambridge: Cambridge University Press.

Barbour, Ian. 1993. *Ethics in an Age of Technology.* San Francisco: HarperSanFrancisco.

————. 1997. *Religion and Science: Historical and Contemporary Issues.* San Francisco: Harper Collins.

Barkow, Jerome H., Leda Cosmides, and John Tooby. 1992. *The Adapted Mind: Evolutionary Psychology and the Generation of Culture.* New York: Oxford University Press.

Baron-Cohen, Simon, John Tooby, and Leda Cosmides. 1997. *Mindblindness.* Cambridge, Mass.: MIT Press.

Behe, Michael. 1998. *Darwin's Black Box: The Biochemical Challenge to Evolution.* New York: Touchstone.

Bekoff, Marc, ed. 2000. *The Smile of a Dolphin: Remarkable Accounts of Animal Emotions.* New York: Discovery.

Bielfeldt, Dennis. 2000. "The Peril and Promise of Supervenience for the Science-Theology Discussion." In *The Human Person in Science and Theology,* ed. Niels Gregerson, Willem Drees, and Ulf Görman. Grand Rapids, Mich.: Eerdmans.

Blackmore, Susan. 2000. *The Meme Machine.* New York: Oxford University Press.

Boesch, C., and H. Boesch. 1989. "Hunting Behavior of Wild Chimpanzees in the Taï National Park." *American Journal of Physical Anthropology* 78: 547–73.

Breazeal, Cynthia. 2002. *Designing Sociable Robots.* Cambridge Mass.: MIT Press.

Broad, C. D. 1929. *The Mind and Its Place in Nature.* New York: Harcourt, Brace.

Brooks, Rodney. 1999. *Cambrian Intelligence.* Cambridge Mass.: MIT Press.

Brown, Warren S., Nancey C. Murphy, and H. Newton Malony, eds. 1998. *Whatever Happened to the Soul? Scientific and Theological Portraits of Human Nature.* Theology and the Sciences. Minneapolis: Fortress Press.

Brunner, Emil. 1935/1946. "Nature and Grace." In *Natural Theology,* trans. Peter Fraenkel. Edinburgh: J. & J. Gray.

Brunner, H. G., M. R. Nelen, P. van Zandvoort, et al. 1993. "X-Linked Borderline Mental Retardation with Prominent Behavioral Disturbance: Phenotype, Genetic Localization, and Evidence for Disturbed Monoamine Metabolism." *American Journal of Human Genetics* 52: 1032–39.

Burhoe, Ralph Wendell. 1981. *Towards a Scientific Theology.* Belfast: Christian Journals.

Buss, David M. 1992. "Mate Preference Mechanisms: Consequences for Partner Choice and Intrasexual Competition." In *The Adapted Mind: Evolutionary Psychology and the Generation of Culture,* ed. Jerome H. Barkow, Leda Cosmides, and John Tooby. New York: Oxford University Press.

Byrne, Richard W. 1995. *The Thinking Ape.* Oxford: Oxford University Press.

Byrne, Richard W., and Andrew Whiten. 1988. *Machiavellian Intelligence: Social Expertise and the Evolution of Intellect in Monkeys, Apes, and Humans.* Oxford: Clarendon Press.

Callebaut, Werner. 1993. *Taking the Naturalistic Turn or How Real Philosophy of Science Is Done.* Chicago: University of Chicago Press.

Campbell, Donald T. 1974. "'Downward Causation' in Hierarchically Organised Biological Systems." In *Studies in the Philosophy of Biology: Reductionism and Related Problems,* ed. Francisco Jose Ayala and Theodosius Dobzhansky. Berkeley: University of California Press.

Cartwright, John. 2000. *Evolution and Human Behavior.* Cambridge Mass.: MIT Press.

Chalmers, David. 1997. *The Conscious Mind: In Search of a Fundamental Theory.* New York: Oxford University Press.

Cheney, Dorothy L., and Robert M. Seyfarth. 1990. *How Monkeys See the World: Inside the Mind of Another Species.* Chicago: University of Chicago Press.

Chomsky, Noam. 1957. *Syntactic Structures.* The Hague: Mouton.

———. 1959. "A Review of B. F. Skinner's Verbal Behavior." *Language* 35: 26–58.

———. 1966. *Cartesian Linguistics.* New York: Harper & Row.

Chomsky, Noam, and R. W. Reiber. 1983. "Noam Chomsky's Views on the Psychology of Language and Thought." In *Dialogues on the Psychology of Language and Thought: Conversations with Noam Chomsky, Charles Osgood, Jean Piaget, Ulric Neisser and Marcel Kinsbourne,* ed. Robert W. Rieber. New York: Plenum.

Churchland, Paul M. 1981. "Eliminative Materialism and the Propositional Attitudes." *Journal of Philosophy* 78: 67–90.

———. 1995. *The Engine of Reason, the Seat of the Soul: A Philosophical Journey into the Brain.* Cambridge, Mass.: MIT Press.

Churchland, Patricia Smith. 1986. *Neurophilosophy: Toward a Unified Science of the Mind/Brain.* Cambridge, Mass.: MIT Press.

Clark, Andy. 1997. *Being There: Putting Brain, Body, and World Together Again.* Cambridge, Mass.: MIT Press.

Clayton, Philip. 1997. *God and Contemporary Science.* Grand Rapids, Mich.: Eerdmans.

———. 2000. "Neuroscience, the Person, and God: An Emergentist Account." *Zygon* 35: 613–52.

Cobb, John Jr. 1972. *Is It Too Late? A Theology of Ecology.* Beverly Hills, Calif.: Bruce.

Cosmides, Leda, and John Tooby. 1992. "Cognitive Adaptations for Social Exchange." In *The Adapted Mind: Evolutionary Psychology and the Generation of Culture,* ed. Jerome H. Barkow, Leda Cosmides, and John Tooby. New York: Oxford University Press.

Crick, Francis. 1994. *The Astonishing Hypothesis: The Scientific Search for the Soul.* New York: Scribner.

Crowe, Michael J. 1997. "A History of the Extraterrestrial Life Debate." *Zygon* 32: 147–62

Cullmann, Oscar. 1958. *Immortality of the Soul or Resurrection of the Dead?* New York: Macmillan.

Damasio, Antonio. 1994. *Descartes' Error: Emotion, Reason, and the Human Brain.* New York: Avon.

———. 1999. *The Feeling of What Happens: Body and Emotion in the Making of Consciousness.* New York: Harvest.

Damasio, Hanna, T. Grabowski, R. Frank , A. M. Galaburda, and A. R. Damasio. 1994. "The Return of Phineas Gage: The Skull of a Famous Patient Yields Clues about the Brain." *Science* 264: 1102–5.

d'Aquili, Eugene G., and Andrew B. Newberg. 1999. *The Mystical Mind: Probing the Biology of Religious Experience.* Theology and the Sciences. Minneapolis: Fortress Press.

Darwin, Charles. 1887. "Letter to Asa Gray, May 22, 1860." In *The Life and Letters of Charles Darwin,* vol. 2, ed. F. Darwin. Appleton, New York.

Dawkins, Richard. 1976/1989. *The Selfish Gene,* 2d edition. New York: Oxford University Press.

———. 1996. *The Blind Watchmaker: Why the Evidence of Evolution Reveals a Universe without Design.* New York: Norton.

Davies, Paul. 1996. *Are We Alone? Philosophical Implications of the Discovery of Extraterrestrial Life.* New York: Basic.

Deacon, Terence W. 1997. *The Symbolic Species: The Co-evolution of Language and the Brain.* New York: Norton.

de Duve, Christian. 1995. *Vital Dust: The Origin and Evolution of Life on Earth.* New York: Basic.

Dembski, William. 1998. *The Design Inference: Eliminating Chance through Small Probabilities.* New York: Cambridge University Press.

———. 1999. *Intelligent Design: The Bridge between Science and Theology.* Downer's Grove, Ill.: Intervarsity Press.

Dennett, Daniel. 1987. *The Intentional Stance.* Cambridge, Mass.: MIT Press.

———. 1989. "Cognitive Ethology: Hunting for Bargains or a Wild Goose Chase?" In *Goals, No-Goals and Own Goals: A Debate on Goal-Directed and Intentional Behavior*, ed. Alan Montefiore and Denis Noble. London: Unwin Hyman.

———. 1990. "The Interpretation of Texts, People and Other Artifacts." *Philosophy and Phenomenological Research* 50: 177–94.

———. 1991. "Real Patterns." *Journal of Philosophy* 88: 27–51.

———. 1991. *Consciousness Explained.* Boston: Little, Brown.

———. 1995. *Darwin's Dangerous Idea: Evolution and the Meanings of Life.* New York: Touchstone.

Descartes, René. 1968. *Discourse on Method and the Meditations*, trans. F. E. Sutcliffe. New York: Penguin.

de Waal, Frans. 1996. *Good Natured: The Origins of Right and Wrong in Humans and Other Animals.* Harvard University Press.

———. 2000. *Chimpanzee Politics: Power and Sex among Apes.* Baltimore, Md.: Johns Hopkins University Press.

Donald, Merlin. 1991. *Origins of the Modern Mind: Three Stages in the Evolution of Culture and Cognition.* Cambridge Mass.: Harvard University Press.

Drake, Frank, and Dava Sobel. 1992. *Is Anyone Out There? The Scientific Search for Extraterrestrial Intelligence.* New York: Delacorte.

Dretske, Fred. 1997. *Naturalizing the Mind.* Cambridge, Mass.: MIT Press.

Dreyfus, Hubert L. 1979. *What Computers Can't Do: The Limits of Artificial Intelligence.* New York: Harper & Row.

Dunbar, Robin. 1993. "Coevolution of Neocortical Size, Group Size and Language in Humans." *Behavioral and Brain Sciences* 16: 681–735.

Dyson, Freeman. 1988. *Infinite in All Directions.* New York: Harper & Row.

Eaves, Lindon. 1997. "Behavioral Genetics, or What's Missing from Theological Anthropology?" In *Beginning with the End: God, Science, and Wolfhart Pannenberg*, ed. Carol Rausch Albright and Joel Haugen. Chicago: Open Court.

Edelman, Gerald M. 1987. *Neural Darwinism: The Theory of Neuronal Group Selection.* New York: Basic.

———. 1992. *Bright Air, Brilliant Fire: On the Matter of the Mind.* New York: Basic.

Edwards, Denis. 1999. *The God of Evolution: A Trinitarian Theology.* New York: Paulist.

Ekman, Paul. 1980. "Biological and Cultural Contributions to Body and Facial Movement in the Expression of Emotions." In *Explaining Emotions*, ed. A. O. Rorty. Berkeley: University of California Press.

———. 1984. "Expression and Nature of Emotion." In *Approaches to Emotion*, ed. K. Scherer and P. Eckman. Hillsdale, N.J.: Erlbaum.

Flanagan, Owen. 1992. *Consciousness Reconsidered.* Cambridge, Mass.: MIT Press.

Fodor, Jerry. 1980. *Language of Thought.* Cambridge, Mass.: Harvard University Press.

Foerst, Anna. 1998. "Cog, A Humanoid Robot, and the Question of the Image of God." *Zygon* 33: 91–111.

———. 1996. "Artificial Intelligence: Walking the Boundary." *Zygon* 31: 681–93.

Fouts, D. H. 1989. "Signing Interactions between Mother and Infant Chimpanzees." In *Understanding Chimpanzees*, ed. P. G. Heltne and L. A. Marquardt. Cambridge, Mass.: Harvard University Press.

Frankl, Victor. 1959/2000. *Man's Search for Meaning.* New York: Beacon Press.

Gallup, G. G., Jr. 1977. "Self-Recognition in Primates: A Comparative Approach to the Bidirectional Properties of Consciousness." *American Psychologist* 32: 329–38.

Gardner, B. T., and R. A. Gardner. 1969. "Teaching Sign Language to a Chimpanzee." *Science* 165: 664–72.

———. 1980. "Two Comparative Psychologists Look at Language Acquisition." In *Children's Language*, vol. 2, ed. Keith E. Nelson. New York: Gardner.

Gardner, Howard. 1983. *Frames of Mind: The Theory of Multiple Intelligences*. New York: Basic.

———. 1985. *The Mind's New Science: A History of the Cognitive Revolution*. New York: Basic.

Gardner, H., H. Brownell, W. Wapner, and D. Michelow. 1983. "Missing the Point: The Role of the Right Hemisphere in the Processing of Complex, Linguistic Materials. In *Cognitive Processes in the Right Hemisphere*, ed. E. Perecman. New York: Academic Press.

Gazzaniga, Michael S. 1988. "Brain Modularity: Towards a Philosophy of Conscious Experience." In *Consciousness in Contemporary Science*, ed. A. J. Marcel and E. Bisiach. Oxford: Clarendon.

Gazzaniga, Michael S., and Joseph Ledoux. 1978. *The Integrated Mind*. New York: Plenum.

Giedd, J. N., J. Blumenthal, N. O. Jeffries, F. X. Castellanos, H. Lui, A. Aijdenbos, T. Paus, A. C. Evans, and J. L. Rapoport. 1999. "Brain Development during Childhood and Adolescence: A Longitudinal MRI Study." *Nature Neuroscience* 2: 861–63.

Gilkey, Langdon. 1993. *Nature, Reality, and the Sacred: The Nexus of Science and Religion*. Theology and the Sciences. Minneapolis: Fortress Press.

Goleman, Daniel. 1997. *Emotional Intelligence*. New York: Bantam.

Gould, Stephen Jay. 1981. *The Mismeasure of Man*. New York: Penguin.

———. 1989. *Wonderful Life: The Burgess Shale and the Nature of History*. New York: Norton.

———. 1996. *Full House: The Spread of Excellence from Plato to Darwin*. New York: Three Rivers Press.

———. 1999. *Rocks of Ages: Science and Religion in the Fullness of Life*. New York: Ballentine.

Gould, Stephen Jay, and Richard Lewontin. 1979. "The Spandrels of San Marco and the Panglossian Paradigm: A Critique of the Adaptionist Programme." *Proceedings of the Royal Society of London* 205: 581-98.

Green, Joel. 1999. "Restoring the Human Person: New Testament Voices for a Wholistic and Social Anthropology." In *Neuroscience and the Person: Scientific Perspectives on Divine Action*, ed. Robert J. Russell et al. Notre Dame, Ind.: University of Notre Dame Press.

Griffin, David Ray. 1998. *Unsnarling the World-Knot: Consciousness, Freedom, and the Mind-Body Problem*. Berkeley: University of California Press.

Griffin, Donald. 1992. *Animal Minds*. Chicago: University of Chicago Press.

Halliday, Alex N., and Michael J. Drake. 1999. "Origin of Earth and Moon: Colliding Theories." *Science* 283: 1861–63.

Hamilton, W. D. 1964. "The Genetical Evolution of Social Behavior, I and II." *Journal of Theoretical Biology* 7: 1–52.

Haraway, Donna. 1991. *Simians, Cyborgs, and Women: The Reinvention of Nature*. New York: Routledge.

Hare, B., J. Call, and M. Tomasello. 2001. "Do Chimpanzees Know What Conspecifics Know?" *Animal Behavior* 61: 139–51.

Hartshorne, Charles. 1948. *The Divine Relativity: A Social Concept of God.* New Haven: Yale University Press.

Haught, John. 2001. *God after Darwin: A Theology of Evolution.* Boulder: Westview.

Hauser, Marc D. 2000. *Wild Minds.* New York: Holt.

Hawking, Stephen. 1988. *A Brief History of Time: From the Big Bang to Black Holes.* New York: Bantam.

Hefner, Philip. 1993. *The Human Factor: Evolution, Culture and Religion.* Theology and the Sciences. Minneapolis: Fortress Press.

Hick, John. 1999. *The Fifth Dimension.* Oxford: Oneworld Publications.

Hofstadter, Douglas. 1982. "A Conversation with Einstein's Brain." In *The Mind's I: Fantasies and Reflections on Self and Soul*, Douglas Hofstadter and Daniel Dennett. New York: Bantam.

———. 1980. *Gödel, Escher, Bach: An Eternal Golden Braid.* New York: Vintage Books.

Hofstadter, Douglas R., and Daniel Dennett C. 1982. *The Mind's I: Fantasies and Reflections on Self and Soul.* New York: Bantam.

Hood, R. W., Jr., and R. J. Morris. 1981. "Sensory Isolation and the Differential Elicitation of Religious Imagery in Intrinsic and Extrinsic Persons. *Journal for the Scientific Study of Religion* 20: 261–73.

Hood, Ralph W., Jr., Bernard Spilka, Bruce Hunsberger, and Richard Gorsuch. 1996. *The Psychology of Religion: An Empirical Approach.* 2d edition. New York: Guilford.

Hoogland, J. L. 1983. "Nepotism and Alarm Calls in the Black-Tailed Prairie Dog (Cynomys Indovicianus)." *Animal Behavior* 21: 472–79.

Hume, David. 1748/1955. *Inquiry concerning Human Understanding.* Indianapolis: Bobbs-Merrill.

Hume, David. 1779/1989. *Dialogues concerning Natural Religion.* Buffalo: Prometheus.

Jackson, Frank. 1982. "Epiphenomenal Qualia." *Philosophical Quarterly* 32: 127–36.

James, William. 1884. "What Is an Emotion?" *Mind* 9: 188–205.

———. 1890/1950. *The Principles of Psychology.* New York: Dover.

———. 1902. *The Varieties of Religious Experience.* New York: Modern Library.

Jantzen, Grace. 1984. *God's World, God's Body.* Philadelphia: Westminster.

Jaynes, Julian. 1976. *The Origin of Consciousness in the Breakdown of the Bicameral Mind.* Boston: Houghton Mifflin.

Jerison, H. J. 1973. *Evolution of the Brain and Intelligence.* New York: Academic Press.

Jolly, Alison. 1999. *Lucy's Legacy: Sex and Intelligence in Human Evolution.* Cambridge, Mass.: Harvard University Press.

Karmiloff-Smith, Annette, and Patricia Kitcher. 1995. *Beyond Modularity: A Developmental Perspective on Cognitive Science.* New York: Bradford.

Kasamatsu, M., and T. Hirai. 1969. "An Electroencephalographic Study on the Zen Meditation (*zazen*)." In *Altered States of Consciousness*, ed. C. Tart. New York: Wiley.

Katz, Stephen T. 1992. *Mysticism and Language.* New York: Oxford University Press.

Kauffman, Stuart. 1996. *At Home in the Universe: The Search for Laws of Self-Organization and Complexity.* New York: Oxford University Press.

Kaufman, Gordon. 1993. *In the Face of Mystery: A Constructive Theology.* Cambridge, Mass.: Harvard University Press.

Kierkegaard, Søren. 1844/1981. *The Concept of Anxiety*, trans. Reidar Thomte and Albert B. Anderson. Princeton: Princeton University Press.

Kim, Jaegwon. 1993. *Supervenience and Mind: Selected Philosophical Essays*. Cambridge: Cambridge University Press.

Kramer, Peter D. 1993. *Listening to Prozac*. New York: Penguin.

Kuhn, Thomas. 1962. *The Structure of Scientific Revolutions*. Chicago: University of Chicago Press.

Kurzweil, Ray. 1999. *The Age of Spiritual Machines: When Computers Exceed Human Intelligence*. New York: Viking.

Lakoff, George, and Mark Johnson. 1999. *Philosophy in the Flesh: The Embodied Mind and Its Challenge to Western Thought*. New York: Basic.

La Mettrie, J. O. 1748/1912. *Man, a Machine*, trans. Gertrude Bussey. Chicago: Open Court.

Leary, Timothy. 1964. "Religious Experience: Its Production and Interpretation." *Psychedelic Review* 1: 324–46.

LeDoux, Joseph. 1996. *The Emotional Brain: The Mysterious Underpinnings of Emotional Life*. New York: Touchstone.

Lévi-Strauss, Claude. 1963. *Structural Anthropology*. New York: Anchor.

Levy, J., C. Trevarthen, and R. Sperry. 1972. "Perception of Bilateral Chimeric Figures following Hemisphere Disconnection." *Brain* 95: 61–78.

Libet, Benjamin. 1985. "Unconscious Cerebral Initiative and the Role of Conscious Will in Voluntary Action." *Behavioral and Brain Sciences* 8: 529–66.

Lindbeck, George. 1984. *The Nature of Doctrine: Religion and Theology in a Postliberal Age*. Louisville: Westminster.

Linzey, Andrew. 1995. *Animal Theology*. Chicago: University of Illinois Press.

MacKay, Donald M. 1980. *Brains, Machines and Persons*. Grand Rapids: Eerdmans.

MacLean, Paul. 1970. "The Triune Brain, Emotion, and Scientific Bias." In *The Neurosciences: The Second Study Program*, ed. F. O. Schmitt. New York: Rockefeller University Press.

Margulis, Lynn. 2000. *Symbiotic Planet: A New Look at Evolution*. New York: Perseus.

Masters, R. E. L., and J. Houston. 1966. *The Varieties of Psychedelic Experience*. New York: Delta.

McFague, Sallie. 1982. *Metaphorical Theology: Models of God in Religious Language*. Minneapolis: Fortress Press.

———. 1993. *The Body of God: An Ecological Theology*. Minneapolis: Fortress Press.

McGinn, Colin. 1991. *The Problem of Consciousness*. Oxford: Blackwell.

Miller, George A. 1956. "The Magical Number Seven, Plus or Minus Two: Some Limits on Our Processing of Information." *Psychological Review* 63: 81–97.

Moravec, Hans. 1990. *Mind Children: The Future of Robot and Human Intelligence*. Cambridge, Mass.: Harvard University Press.

Murphy, Nancey. 1990. *Theology in the Age of Scientific Reasoning*. Ithaca, N.Y.: Cornell University Press.

Murphy, Nancey, and George F. R. Ellis. 1996. *On the Moral Nature of the Universe: Theology, Cosmology, and Ethics*. Theology and the Sciences. Minneapolis: Fortress Press.

Nagel, Thomas. 1974. "What Is It Like to Be a Bat?" *Philosophical Review* 83: 435–50.

Newberg, A. B., A. Alavi, M. Baime, P. D. Mozley, and E. G. d'Aquili. 1997. "The Measurement of Cerebral Blood Flow during the Complex Cognitive Task of Meditation Using HMPAO-SPECT Imaging." *Journal of Nuclear Medicine* 38: 95.

Newberg, A. B., Eugene d'Aquili, and Vince Rause. 2001. *Why God Won't Go Away: Brain Science and the Biology of Belief.* New York: Ballentine.

Nowak, M., and K. Sigmund. 1998. "Evolution of Indirect Reciprocity by Image Scoring." *Nature* 393: 490.

Oman, D., and D. Reed. 1998. "Religion and Mortality among the Community-Dwelling Elderly." *American Journal of Public Health* 88: 1469–75.

Pannenberg, Wolfhart. 1976. *Theology and the Philosophy of Science.* Philadelphia: Westminster Press.

Patterson, Francine G. 1978. "The Gestures of a Gorilla: Language Acquisition in Another Pongid." *Brain and Language* 5: 72–97.

Peacocke, Arthur. 1976. "Reductionism: A Review of the Epistemological Issues and Their Relevance to Biology and the Problem of Consciousness." *Zygon* 11: 307–36.

———. 1986. *God and the New Biology.* London: J. M. Dent.

———. 1993. *Theology for a Scientific Age: Being and Becoming—Natural, Divine, and Human.* Enlarged edition. Theology and the Sciences. Minneapolis: Fortress Press.

———. 1999. "The Sound of Sheer Silence." In *Neuroscience and the Person: Scientific Perspectives on Divine Action,* ed. Robert J. Russell et al. Notre Dame, Ind: University of Notre Dame Press.

Penrose, Roger. 1989. *The Emperor's New Mind: Concerning Computers, Minds, and the Laws of Physics.* New York: Penguin.

———. 1996. *Shadows of the Mind: A Search for the Missing Science of Consciousness.* New York: Oxford University Press.

Pepperberg, Irene. 2000. *The Alex Studies: Cognitive and Communicative Abilities of Grey Parrots.* Cambridge, Mass.: Harvard University Press.

Persinger, Michael A. 1987. *Neuropsychological Bases of God Beliefs.* New York: Praeger.

Peters, Ted. 1997. *Playing God: Genetic Determinism and Human Freedom.* New York: Routledge.

Peterson, Gregory. 1996. "Are We Unique? The *Locus Humanus,* Animal Cognition, and the Theology of Nature." Ph. D. Diss. University of Denver and Iliff School of Theology.

———. 1999. "The Evolution of Consciousness and the Theology of Nature." *Zygon* 34: 283–306.

———. 2000. "God, Genes, and Cognizing Agents." *Zygon* 35: 469–80.

———. 2001. "Whither Panentheism?" *Zygon* 36: 395–405.

———. 2002. "The Intelligent Design Movement: Science or Ideology?" *Zygon* 37: 7–23.

Pinker, Steven. 1994. *The Language Instinct.* New York: Penguin.

———. 1997. *How the Mind Works.* New York: Norton.

Polkinghorne, John. 1995. *Serious Talk: Science and Religion in Dialogue.* Valley Forge, Pa.: Trinity Press International.

———. 1996. *The Faith of a Physicist: Reflections of a Bottom-Up Thinker.* Theology and the Sciences. Minneapolis: Fortress Press.

Popper, Karl R., and John C. Eccles. 1977. *The Self and Its Brain: An Argument for Interactionism.* New York: Springer International.

Povinelli, D. J., J. M. Bering, and S. Giambrone. 2000. "Toward a Science of Other Minds: Escaping the Argument by Analogy." *Cognitive Science* 24: 509–541.

Premack, David. 1976. *Intelligence in Ape and Man.* Hillsdale, N.J.: Erlbaum.

Premack, David, and Guy Woodruff. 1978. "Does the Chimpanzee Have a Theory of Mind?" *The Behavioral and Brain Sciences* 4: 515–26.

Proudfoot, Wayne. 1985. *Religious Experience.* Berkeley: University of California Press.

Putnam, Hilary. 1960. "Minds and Machines." In *Dimensions of Mind,* ed. S. Hook. New York: New York University Press.

Pylyshyn, Zenon. 1984. *Computation and Cognition: Toward a Foundation for Cognitive Science.* Cambridge, Mass.: MIT Press.

Ramachandran, V. S., and Sandra Blakeslee. 1998. *Phantoms in the Brain: Probing the Mysteries of the Human Mind.* New York: Morrow.

Rolston, Holmes, III. 1991. "Does Nature Need to be Redeemed?" *Zygon* 29: 205–29.

———. 1999. *Genes, Genesis, and God: Values and Their Origins in Natural and Human History.* New York: Cambridge University Press.

Rosenfield, Leonora. 1968. *From Beast-Machine to Man-Machine: Animal Soul in French Letters from Descartes to La Mettrie.* New York: Columbia.

Rumelhart, David, and James McClelland. 1987. *Parallel Distributed Processing.* Volume 1. Cambridge Mass.: MIT Press.

Rupp, E. Gordon, Philip S. Watson, and John T. McNeil, eds. and trans. 1995. *Luther and Erasmus: Free Will and Salvation.* Louisville: Westminster Press.

Russell, Robert J. et al., eds. 1999. *Neuroscience and the Person: Scientific Perspectives on Divine Action.* Notre Dame, Ind.: University of Notre Dame Press.

Ryle, Gilbert. 1949. *The Concept of Mind.* London: Hutchinson.

Savage-Rumbaugh, E. Sue, and Roger Lewin. 1994. *Kanzi: The Ape at the Brink of the Human Mind.* New York: Wiley.

Savage-Rumbaugh, E. Sue, et al. 1986. "Spontaneous Symbol Acquisition and Communicative Use by Pygmy Chimpanzees (*Pan paniscus*)." *Journal of Experimental Psychology: General* 115: 211–35.

Savage-Rumbaugh, E. Sue, et al. eds. 1993. *Language Comprehension in Ape and Child.* Chicago: University of Chicago Press.

Savage-Rumbaugh, E. Sue, et al. 1996. "Language Perceived: Paniscus branches out. In *Great Ape Societies,* ed. W. McGrew et al. Cambridge: Cambridge University Press.

Schachter, Stanley, and Jerome Singer. 1962. "Cognitive, Social, and Psychological Determinants of Emotional States." *Psychological Review* 69: 379–99.

Schleiermacher, Friedrich. 1822/1986. *The Christian Faith,* trans. H. R. MacIntosh and J. S. Stewart. Edinburgh: T. & T. Clark.

Scoville, W. B., and B. Milner. 1957. "Loss of Recent Memory after Bilateral Hippocampal Lesions." *Journal of Neurology and Psychiatry* 20: 11–21.

Searle, John R. 1982. "Minds, Brains, and Programs." In *The Mind's I: Fantasies and Reflections on Self and Soul,* ed. Douglas R. Hofstadter and Daniel C. Dennett. New York: Bantam.

———. 1984. *Minds, Brains and Science.* Cambridge, Mass.: Harvard University Press.

———. 1992. *The Rediscovery of Mind.* Cambridge, Mass.: MIT Press.

Singer, Peter. 1975. *Animal Liberation: A New Ethics for Our Treatment of Animals.* New York: Random House.

Sittler, Joseph. 1961. "Called to Unity." *The Ecumenical Review* 14:177–87.

Smolin, Lee. 1999. *The Life of the Cosmos.* New York: Oxford University Press.

Smuts, Barbara. 1985. *Sex and Friendship in Baboons.* New York: Aldine.

Sober, Elliott, and David Sloan Wilson. 1998. *Unto Others: The Evolution and Psychology of Unselfish Behavior.* Cambridge Mass.: Harvard University Press.

Spear, Linda Patia. 2000. "Neurobehavioral Changes in Adolescence." *Current Directions in Psychological Science* 9: 111–14.

Stich, Stephen. 1983. *From Folk Psychology to Cognitive Science: The Case against Belief.* Cambridge, Mass.: MIT Press.

Swinburne, Richard. 1997. *The Evolution of the Soul.* New York: Oxford University Press.

Taliaferro, Charles. 1994. *Consciousness and the Mind of God.* Cambridge: Cambridge University Press.

Teilhard de Chardin, Pierre. 1976. *The Phenomenon of Man.* New York: Harper.

Terrace, H. S. 1979. *Nim.* New York: Knopf.

Tipler, Frank. 1995. *The Physics of Immortality: Modern Cosmology, God, and the Resurrection of the Dead.* New York: Anchor Books.

Tooby, John, and Leda Cosmides. 1992. "The Psychological Foundations of Culture." In *The Adapted Mind: Evolutionary Psychology and the Generation of Culture,* ed. Jerome H. Barkow, Leda Cosmides, and John Tooby. New York: Oxford University Press.

Torrance, Thomas. 1969. *Theological Science.* Oxford: Oxford University Press.

Trivers, Robert. 1971. "The Evolution of Reciprocal Altruism." *Quarterly Review of Biology* 46: 35–57.

Turing, Alan. 1950. "Computing Machinery and Intelligence." *Mind* 49: 433–60.

Van Huyssteen, J. Wentzel. 1999. *The Shaping of Rationality: Towards Interdisciplinarity in Theology and Science.* Grand Rapids: Eerdmans.

Van Till, Howard. 1986. *The Fourth Day: What the Bible and the Heavens Are Telling Us about the Creation.* Grand Rapids: Eerdmans.

Von Eckardt, Barbara. 1993. *What Is Cognitive Science?* Cambridge, Mass.: MIT Press.

Weiskrantz, Lawrence. 1986. *Blindsight: A Case Study and Implications.* Oxford: Oxford University Press.

Weizenbaum, Joseph. 1976. *Computer Power and Human Reason: From Judgment to Calculation.* San Francisco: W. H. Freeman.

Wheeler, John. 1982. "Bohr, Einstein, and the Strange Lessons of Quantum Mechanics." In *Mind and Nature,* ed. Richard Elvee. San Francisco: Harper & Row.

Whitehead, Alfred North. 1929/1985. *Process and Reality.* New York: Free Press.

Wildman, Wesley, and Leslie Brothers. 1999. "A Neuropsychological-Semiotic Model of Religious Experiences." In *Neuroscience and the Person: Scientific Perspectives on Divine Action,* ed. Robert J. Russell, et al. Notre Dame, Ind.: University of Notre Dame Press.

Wilkinson, G. S. 1984. "Reciprocal Food Sharing in Vampire Bats." *Nature* 308: 181–84.

Wilson, E. O. 1975. *Sociobiology: The New Synthesis.* Cambridge Mass.: Harvard University Press.

———. 1978. *On Human Nature.* Cambridge Mass.: Harvard University Press.

Wilson, E. O., and Michael Ruse. 1985. "The Evolution of Ethics." *New Scientist* (October 17): 50–52.

Wimsat, William C. 1976. "Reductionism, Levels of Organization, and the Mind-Body Problem." In *Consciousness and the Brain: A Scientific and Philosophical Inquiry*, ed. Gordon G. Globus, Grover Maxwell, and Irwin Savodink. New York: Plenum.

Winograd, Terry. 1972. *Understanding Natural Language*. New York: Academic Press.

Wisdom, John. 1968. "Gods." In *Religious Language the Problem of Religious Knowledge*, ed. Ronald Santoni. Bloomington, Ind.: Indiana University Press.

Wrangham, Richard, and Dale Peterson. 1997. *Demonic Males: Apes and the Origins of Human Violence*. New York: Houghton Mifflin.

Wright, Robert. 2000. *Nonzero: The Logic of Human Destiny*. New York: Pantheon.

Young, J. Z. 1981. *The Life of Vertebrates*. New York: Oxford University Press.

Index